Using SideKick®:

The Desktop Organizer

Using SideKick®:
The Desktop Organizer

Phillip R. Robinson

BORLAND·OSBORNE/McGRAW·HILL
B U S I N E S S   S E R I E S

Osborne **McGraw-Hill**
2600 Tenth Street
Berkeley, California 94710
U.S.A.

For information on translations and book distributors outside of the U.S.A., write to Osborne **McGraw-Hill** at the above address.

A complete list of trademarks appears on page 387.

Using SideKick ®: The Desktop Organizer

1234567890 DODO 8987

ISBN 0-07-881296-8

Contents

Foreword   xi

Introduction   xiii

Part I   SideKick and Its Companion Programs

1   **SideKick and the Computing Environment**   1
        Multitasking Dreams   2
        SideKick's Resume   4
        TSR: Terminate and Stay Resident   6

2   **Loading and Starting SideKick**   11
        Quick Start   12
        System Requirements   17
        Disk Backups   20
        SideKick's Files and README   24
        Registering Your Copy of SideKick   25
        Versions of SideKick   28
        Getting Underway   28
        The Main Menu   31

The Utility Windows   **32**

Help   **36**

Limited SideKicks   **37**

Removing SideKick   **39**

TSR Controllers   **39**

Installation for Customization   **40**

Setup   **45**

Summary   **46**

3   The Notepad: Opening and Setup   **47**

Opening the Notepad   **48**

Notepad Window Anatomy   **52**

Moving and Resizing Windows   **53**

Choosing and Loading a File   **60**

Saving a File   **66**

Changing the Notepad with the Installation
Program   **67**

Editing Modes   **74**

Time and Date Stamping   **77**

4   The Notepad: Editing Commands   **79**

WordStar-Style Commands   **80**

Opening and Exiting the Notepad   **81**

Loading a File   **81**

Editing Help   **82**

Adding Blank Lines   **82**

Adding Text   **83**

The Insert Mode   **83**

The Overwrite Mode   **86**

Deleting Text   **87**

Moving the Cursor   **88**

Block Operations   **92**

Pasting a Block   **95**

Importing Data   **100**

Sorting a Block   **103**

Searching Operations: Find and Find and
Replace   **105**

Find   **106**

Find and Replace   **112**

Resuming Work After Find or Find and Replace   **115**
Printing a File   **116**
Turbo Lightning   **117**

5   **The Calculator**   **133**
Loading and Activating SideKick   **135**
Choosing the Calculator   **135**
The Calculator Window on Top of Another
    SideKick Window   **136**
Moving the Calculator Window   **137**
Fundamental Calculator Commands   **137**
Four-Function Arithmetic   **139**
Clearing the Display or the Calculator   **142**
Modes: Hexadecimal and Binary   **143**
Memory   **145**
Pasting Numbers   **149**
Using the Calculator with the AT   **151**

6   **The Calendar**   **153**
Opening the Calendar   **154**
Monthly Calendar Anatomy   **156**
Opening a Daily Schedule   **160**
Appointment Files   **162**
Daily Schedule Commands   **165**
Printing Schedules   **170**
Traveling SideKick   **171**

7   **The Dialer and Phone Directory**   **173**
The Dialer Requires Immediate Installation   **175**
Opening the Dialer Window   **180**
Picking and Dialing a Number from Another
    Program   **181**
Telephone Directory Window   **183**
Traveling SideKick   **194**

8   **The ASCII Table**   **197**
Standard and Extended ASCII   **198**
Control Characters   **199**
Opening the ASCII Table   **199**

Opening the ASCII Table on Top of Another
    SideKick Utility   **201**
Moving the ASCII Table Window   **202**
ASCII Table Anatomy   **202**
ASCII Table Commands   **204**
Touring the Characters   **204**
Using the Characters   **207**

9   The Setup Utility   209
Opening the Setup Window   **210**
Opening the Setup Window on Top of Another
    SideKick Utility   **211**
Moving the Setup Window   **212**
The Setup Window's Anatomy   **213**

Part II   SideKick in a Team

10   Traveling SideKick   221
Meeting the Traveler   **222**
First Things First: Make Backups   **223**
The README File   **223**
Installation   **224**
Starting Traveling SideKick   **225**
Menu Commands   **226**
Addresses   **228**
Engagements   **242**
Setup Menu   **252**

11   SuperKey   257
Hardware Requirements   **258**
Making a Backup   **259**
Installation   **259**
The README File   **261**
Loading SuperKey into Memory   **261**
Activating SuperKey   **264**
Getting Help   **264**
Keyboard Type-Ahead Buffer   **265**
DOS Command Stack   **266**
Keyboard Lock and Unlock   **268**
Screen Off and On   **268**

Screen Protect 269
Running Options Automatically 269
Cut and Paste 270
Changing the Keyboard Layout 271
Encryption 274
Macros 279
Using SuperKey with SideKick 288

12   DOS 289
SideKick's Notepad 290
SuperKey's Command Stack 295
SuperKey's Macros 297
SuperKey's Layout Program 300

13   Using SideKick with Lotus 1-2-3 and Other Spreadsheet Packages 301
The Notepad 302
The Calculator 307
Turbo Lightning 307
SuperKey 308

14   Using SideKick with WordStar and Other Word Processors 313
Turbo Lightning 314
Notepad 314
Calculator 318
SuperKey 319
Macros 319
SuperKey's Layout Program 325
SuperKey's Encryption Routines 328

15   Using SideKick with dBASE III PLUS and Other Database Managers 329
Notepad 330
Calculator 334
Dialer 334
Traveling SideKick 335
Turbo Lightning 335
SuperKey 335

**16   Using SideKick with Crosstalk
and Other Communications Programs**   **341**
  SideKick's Notepad   **342**
  SuperKey's Macro   **349**
  Encryption   **353**

**17   Using SideKick with Turbo Pascal
and Other Programming Languages**   **355**
  ASCII Table   **356**
  Calculator   **356**
  Notepad   **360**
  SuperKey   **363**

***Appendix A   Patches to Fix or Enhance SideKick
and SuperKey***   **367**
  DEBUG's Place   **368**
  Getting Help   **368**
  Choosing a Patch   **368**
  Starting and Using DEBUG   **369**
  SideKick Patches   **369**
  SuperKey Patching   **376**

***Appendix B   Incompatibility Problems
and Solutions***   **383**
  Lotus 1-2-3   **384**
  Lotus Symphony   **384**
  Microsoft Windows   **385**
  Microsoft Word   **385**
  Smartcom   **385**
  XYWrite   **385**
  TSR Programs   **386**

Index   **389**

Foreword

Borland International, Inc. introduced SideKick: The DeskTop Organizer in 1984 to help you apply the power of your personal computer to your daily business activities. With SideKick you can jot down thoughts or messages, make quick calculations, plan and schedule appointments, check calendar days and dates, find phone numbers, dial calls automatically, and look up ASCII codes. Best of all, because SideKick is memory-resident, you can access its handy tools at any time —without exiting from other applications.

Now Phil Robinson introduces *Using SideKick: The DeskTop Organizer,* explaining SideKick in a way that makes it easier than ever to use. First, he gets the user up and running by presenting the computing environment and instructions for starting SideKick. Then, he moves on to the SideKick utilities, discussing the features and use of each of these powerful desktop tools.

Once the user is comfortable with each utility, Robinson delves into details for the advanced user. Finally, he devotes the last chapters of the book to techniques for using SideKick with other applications including WordStar, 1-2-3, Crosstalk, dBASE III PLUS, and Turbo Pascal, as well as DOS. He includes basic and advanced tips for using SuperKey and Traveling SideKick, two other Borland applications that are packaged with SideKick.

Robinson has been an avid SideKick user since the application first appeared. He once wrote an entire book manuscript with the Notepad utility. Robinson is a former West Coast editor of *BYTE* and his articles have appeared in many computer publications. He is a regular columnist for a West Coast newspaper and has written several computer books.

In *Using SideKick*, Robinson applies his expertise and easy writing style to bring the power of SideKick to novice and veteran users alike.

Philippe Kahn
President
Borland International, Inc.

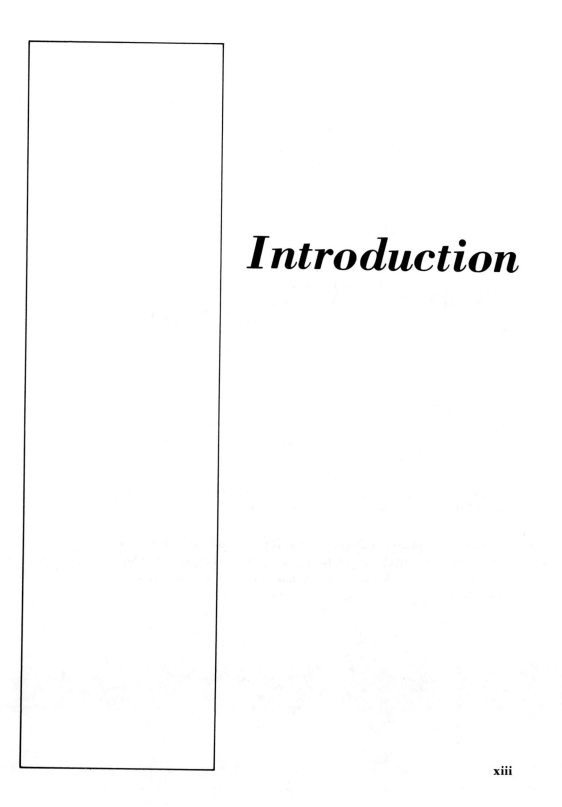

Introduction

SideKick is a set of small, handy programs that you can use on an IBM PC or compatible alongside any application program. They can be so addictive that you wonder why all computers don't come with such tools. That question has certainly occurred to many of the million people who have bought SideKick and helped to make it one of the best-selling programs of all time.

Although SideKick is relatively easy to use, it offers much more power than even some of its most ardent fans realize. Many learn just the basics of the Notepad and the Calculator and then never delve any deeper to discover features and options that are sitting dormant, waiting to make computing tasks faster and easier. This book is dedicated to explaining SideKick from first startup to advanced use. Along the way, we'll also discuss some other programs that combine well with SideKick, and make the program even more enticing and powerful.

The first half of the book begins with installing and starting SideKick, and then walks through the commands and uses of each major SideKick tool: the Notepad, Calculator, Calendar, Dialer, ASCII Table, and Setup window. The last two chapters of Part I introduce two companion programs for SideKick: Traveling SideKick and SuperKey. Part II explores the possibilities and advantages of teaming SideKick with other popular applications. Each chapter in this section focuses on a major category of application, combining information with specific examples from widely used programs: DOS for operating systems, WordStar for word processors, Lotus 1-2-3 for spreadsheets, dBASE III PLUS for database managers, Crosstalk for telecommunications, and Turbo Pascal for programming languages. If you already know SideKick and want to start with the applications, go directly to Part II. But if you want to learn about features and commands you might have missed, or if you're new to SideKick, start with Part I and read the chapters in order.

I

SideKick and Its Companion Programs

1

SideKick and the Computing Environment

Remember punch cards? A program that now runs in seconds on any desktop microcomputer once had to be punched onto special cards and delivered to a computer center for processing, which would rarely be accomplished before the next day. As much as we've progressed, today's computers have their own limitations that will likely cause amazement to future computer users.

In retrospect, the greatest drawback of today's microcomputers will probably be their single-mindedness. People will wonder why we bothered to work on computers that could run only one program at a time. Right now, for instance, if you're writing — or "word processing" — with a microcomputer, that's about all you can do. If you discover in the middle of a paragraph that you need to make a phone call to get some information, don't look to your computer. To access your database of phone numbers you'll have to save your file, leave the word processor, start a database management program, load the phone number file into it, and so on and so on. It's not as primitive as punch cards, but in a few years it may seem nearly that unwieldy. The obvious solution to this problem is multitasking.

Multitasking Dreams

Multitasking is the ability to run more than one program at a time. Multitasking doesn't require a new kind of computer hardware or a special, new component for your old computer hardware. Rather, it is a different way of running that old computer hardware. It is a facet of the operating system — the main software that animates a computer. Hardware can be tailored to make multitasking easier, but it is the operating system that really makes multitasking work.

Even with the right operating system, today's computers can't really run several programs at exactly the same time. They just aren't built to do anything but sequential operations, putting one instruction after the other in a straight, single-file line. But a powerful computer can mimic real multitasking by switching back and forth between programs so quickly that the result looks like programs marching abreast. Microcomputers have used this scheme for years to provide multitasking and multiuser (more than one person hooked up to the same computer) systems. The operating system tells the computer to spend a little time on the first program, then to move to the second program and spend a little time on it, then to move to the next program, and eventually to return to the first program. That "eventually" can be a fraction of a second, because the elementary actions of computers are so swift.

Unfortunately, the IBM PC line (from the original PC through the AT and all the compatibles) is not good at multitasking. These machines don't have enough RAM to hold several large programs at once, aren't suited to constant switching between programs, and lack the sheer processor speed to handle all the overhead of switching back and forth between programs. The most popular PC operating system —DOS (also know as PC-DOS or MS-DOS) —makes no provision for multitasking.

There are some competing operating systems and special extensions for DOS that offer forms of multitasking on the PC line. Many of these let you load multiple programs into extended or expanded memory beyond the PC-DOS 640K RAM limit. But in most cases, the applications programs you can use with these other systems don't really run simultaneously, even in the switching method just described. Instead, they are simply loaded into memory and left to await a call from you. With a few keystrokes you can jump from one program to another and then back again. Each time you leave a program, it goes into a sort of suspended animation. You can come back in a second, a minute, or an hour, and the program will think you never left. But other operating systems often forfeit the advantage of compatibility with the colossal library of DOS applications. DOS extensions often require a lot of processor power and memory. (Even the new operating system recently announced by IBM and Microsoft —OS/2—only hints at full multitasking capability. And that operating system won't be available in its final form for several years.)

Thus, if you want even limited multitasking capability, you are forced to trade away speed or compatibility or both —and that's too bad. After all, while we wait for computers and operating systems with full-fledged multitasking capability, we don't really need to cripple our systems by keeping multiple, conventional application programs in memory. The writer who needs a phone number doesn't have to employ the services of a top-of-the-line database manager. All he needs is a little directory program. The accountant deep into a spreadsheet who suddenly remembers she needs to write a quick note doesn't need a sophisticated word processor. She just needs a basic note writing program. It would be nice to have more power at hand, and future systems will undoubtedly deliver those goods. But meanwhile, a practical personal microcomputer system cries out for the limited multitasking capability of having some elemental programs always at hand, programs that are always available, no matter what other software the computer is running.

That's the definition of SideKick in a nutshell.

SideKick's Résumé

SideKick isn't new: It has been around since 1984. It was the second major product from Borland International, a company that made its name with the inexpensive and fast Turbo Pascal compiler. The sale of a half-million copies of Turbo Pascal around the world make it a monumental best-seller. SideKick, in less time, has sold nearly a million copies and so is one of the best-selling programs of all time, for any computer. Even a limited list of active users would include perhaps one quarter of all DOS users.

Those numbers should come as no surprise considering the importance of multitasking. SideKick adds features to a PC that every computer ought to come with. Here are some of SideKick's most useful tools:

The Notepad	A simple word processor for creating and editing files up to 25 pages long.
The Dialer	A routine for dialing phone numbers through a modem. This is not a telecommunications program, but a means to automate number dialing for standard telephone use. The autodialer can work with numbers from a built-in Directory *address file* or from almost any other program.
The Calendar	An appointment calendar that lets you enter and save appointments for any day from now to the year 2099. The Calendar can also be used simply to check the current date.
The Calculator	The equivalent of a hand calculator that appears on the screen. Besides standard arithmetic functions, the Calculator contains a variety of functions useful for computer programming.

The ASCII Table   A list of the ASCII codes and their equivalents. This table is useful for programming as well as for controlling printing tasks.

There's an advantage to getting these features as software instead of as another chip in the hardware: flexibility. You can load only the SideKick tools that you need and avoid using precious RAM for programs you never touch. What's more, Borland issues updates of SideKick that fix bugs or add features to the program. Also, the SideKick tools create files that contain information, such as notes, schedules, and phone numbers, that you'll want to carry with you; providing the programs on a floppy disk instead of in hardware lets you do so.

You can call up any of SideKick's programs while you're using a spreadsheet, a database, a compiler, or any other application (as you'll see in Section II). You can even call up SideKick programs while other SideKick programs are already on the screen. When you leave SideKick, your main application will be waiting right where you left it.

Beyond Coexistence

SideKick is not content simply to coexist peacefully with conventional applications; it can cooperate with them. Thus, don't view SideKick as simply a collection of utilities that won't bother your main application. The SideKick desktop utilities will leave other programs alone if that's how you want to work, but they can also be used to move information between programs, to keep track of the steps you've taken in the other programs, to capture displays, and even to dial phone numbers listed in other programs.

Traveling SideKick

Another Borland program that complements SideKick is Traveling SideKick. It is really a set of programs that extends the scope and utility of SideKick's Calendar and Dialer tools. Where SideKick lets you build only small calendars or directories and view them mainly on screen, Traveling SideKick lets you create large calendars and address files, modify them in many different ways, and then choose from a variety of printed formats to view them as hard copy. Some of the options Traveling SideKick offers are described on the next page.

Address database   Traveling SideKick lets you add, find, change, and remove addresses from files that can be converted to be completely compatible with SideKick. You can create new address databases, work on databases you created with SideKick, and later use either type of database with SideKick. You can also read address listings created with some other programs and convert them into SideKick format. Traveling SideKick lets you sort the addresses and then print them as lists or labels.

Appointments database   Traveling SideKick lets you add, find, change, and remove appointments (what it terms *engagements*) from files that are completely compatible with SideKick. You can create new appointment databases, work on databases you created with SideKick, and later use either type of database with SideKick. Traveling SideKick also lets you print these addresses as daily, weekly, monthly, or yearly calendars.

Binder   Traveling SideKick comes with a small, three-ring binder that contains a calculator, room for all your printed SideKick address and appointment lists and your Traveling SideKick disk, and a wealth of informative charts, including maps, calendars, area-code lists, currency notes, metric-to-English conversions, and command summaries of Borland's major DOS software products (SideKick, SuperKey, Turbo Pascal, Reflex, and Turbo Lightning). This binder is designed to replace other daily organizer binders.

   If you are very busy in personal or professional life, Traveling SideKick lets you build big schedules and phone books and then move right back into SideKick itself and immediately employ the information you sifted in Traveling SideKick. With Traveling SideKick, you can access large databases that would gobble up more RAM than most PC users can afford.

TSR: Terminate and Stay Resident

Although *TSR* stands for "terminate and stay resident," what it really means is "around when you need it." Another phrase sometimes used to describe this quality is *RAM-resident*, but it doesn't really describe the same thing. Almost all programs run from the computer's RAM. Some large programs cannot entirely fit within RAM and so are called *disk based*. But even these run from RAM by swapping parts from disk to RAM, the parts that are active working from RAM.

The difference in a TSR program is that it, or some part of it, remains in RAM after you quit. Other programs give up whatever RAM space they occupied so new programs or data can use the space. A TSR program stays in RAM and so can be called up again at any time, with the proper commands, without your having to wait for the program's instructions to be loaded from the disk. You can be using another program while a loaded TSR program is in the background, basically somnolent but constantly checking the keyboard for the special key-press combination that signals it to put the main program into limbo and come to the foreground itself. When a TSR program is activated, it typically shows its menu or window on the screen, obscuring some or most of the previous display, but not necessarily clearing all of the previous program's display from the screen.

SideKick wasn't the first TSR program, but its success has encouraged the development of scores of other such programs. (Another factor is that PCs have much more RAM than they used to, and more RAM means more room for TSR programs.) A few programs compete directly with SideKick's "basic handy tools" scheme, and others range across the map of software from database managers to outline programs to graphics packages. But SideKick is without question the most popular TSR program in any category. (It runs on almost all DOS-driven computers and requires only 128K of RAM and a single floppy disk drive.)

The second most popular category of TSR software may well be the keyboard-macro program. Borland offers one of these, called *SuperKey*.

SuperKey

Keyboard macro programs are able to capture, store on disk, and replay long sequences of keystrokes. For instance, if you were writing an article about the Middle East, you might tire of typing the phrase *Middle East* over and over again. If you had a keyboard macro program, you could capture the phrase and later play it back with a shorter and simpler keystroke combination, such as ALT-M. Whenever you typed ALT-M, the entire phrase *Middle East* would appear on your screen as if you had just typed it letter by letter.

But macros don't stop at the phrase level. You can store literally thousands of keystrokes with some macro programs. That length would allow you to store entire paragraphs or even pages and then recall them with one or two keystrokes. You could save different sets of macros for different situations, in effect customizing your word processor or other tool to the particular task.

The real power of macros appears when you realize that computer commands are also keystrokes. Not only can you store strings of characters, but you can store commands within a macro. These commands can be relevant to whatever application you're using. For instance, you might make a word processor macro that automatically moves to the beginning of a file, double-spaces all of the paragraphs, and then saves the file. You might make a spreadsheet macro that adds a new column and then calculates totals for all of its rows. Or you could create a macro for a telecommunications program that would automatically log on to a service, request the most recent quotes on your stocks, record the results, and then log off. In essence, a keyboard macro program is an extra feature for every program you have.

SuperKey does all of this and more. It also includes a data encrypter for protecting your files from unwanted readers and a keyboard lock that will stop others from using your PC, as well as other features. Here is a list of SuperKey's main features:

Macros	SuperKey can record, modify, save on disk, load from disk, and replay long sequences of keystrokes. These can represent text, numbers, cursor moves, program commands, or even DOS commands and are available while running other applications programs.
Command stack	SuperKey remembers your most recent commands to DOS and saves them in a stack. If you want to reuse a command or just see what it was you commanded, you can recall these commands with a single keystroke.
Cut and paste	SuperKey lets you cut data from one program and paste it into another. It holds the data within itself as you change programs.

Data encryption	SuperKey can encode files so that only a person with the password for that file can later decrypt and read the file.
Keyboard lock	SuperKey can freeze your keyboard so that it does not respond to any typing until the proper password is typed. You choose the password and you lock the keyboard with a single keystroke.
Screen secrecy	SuperKey can blank out your screen display at any time with just a single keystroke.
Screen blanking	SuperKey can also be set to blank out your screen display after a certain amount of time (that you specify) passes without any activity on the keyboard. This can save power in portable computers or can save screen wear in desktop computers.
SideKick partnership	SuperKey's macros can work with SideKick, and you can jump from SuperKey to SideKick with a single keystroke.

When used in conjunction, SideKick and SuperKey achieve synergy, producing more than the sum of the two programs. Chapter 8 in Section I describes the fundamentals of SuperKey and each chapter in Section II includes some examples of how SuperKey can work with applications and with SideKick. SuperKey merits an entire book of useful macros, but this book mainly discusses how it works with SideKick. Once you've finished reading about SuperKey, you may well agree that it should be considered an essential part of SideKick.

Turbo Lightning

Another Borland TSR program to use in concert with SideKick is Turbo Lightning. Although not directly related to SideKick, this program extends the TSR concept in a practical and fascinating way. Not only does it constantly check the keys you press to see if you want it to "wake up," it also checks your spelling and provides an on-line thesaurus. The major features of Lightning are summarized here.

Dictionary   Turbo Lightning can check your spelling as you type, beeping if you type a word that it cannot find in its 83,000-word dictionary (from Random House). It can perform this chore no matter what program you are using, or even if you are just typing commands to DOS. Once you hear the beep, you can open the Turbo Lightning window and see suggested spelling corrections for the misspelled word.

Custom dictionary   Turbo Lightning lets you add your own words to the spelling checker list. That means you don't always have to tell it to ignore so-called mistakes, words it beeps at just because they aren't in the Random House dictionary. Most people add names, addresses, unusual capitalizations, and special technical words to this part of the dictionary.

Thesaurus   Whenever you want to look for a synonym for a word, you can place the cursor on the word and then open a Turbo Lightning window to have the computer search the Random House Thesaurus for synonyms. If you find a synonym you want to use, you can select it and press ENTER , and it will replace the word that you looked up.

Many of today's word processors offer these functions, but if you use Lightning, you'll have the dictionary and thesaurus online, no matter which word processor you use and, indeed, no matter what application you're running. Chapter 4 and the applications chapters (Chapters 12-17) briefly describe how to use Turbo Lightning.

Other TSR Programs

As mentioned previously, there are now many TSR programs in the microcomputing world. Even some of the public-domain (free) software available from users' groups work as TSR programs. In most cases you can comfortably use these alongside SideKick, though some compatibility problems may occur. A memory problem may also occur if you use too many TSR programs at once. Whereas standard programs are like nomads who occupy memory and then go home when they are done, TSR programs come to stay and may eat up so much memory that your main application cannot run. Chapter 2 discusses compatibility and memory crowding problems in depth.

2

Loading and Starting SideKick

It is easy to get started with SideKick if you just want to use its fundamentals: to start a simple calendar, make a quick note, or add a few numbers on the calculator. But SideKick offers a lot more power if you learn more about it. You don't have to use this power, but it is there waiting for you. Nor do you have to learn to use it all at once. Within a utility, you can learn a few commands at a time, absorbing them into your vocabulary as you use them. Also, each of the utilities is independent, so you can learn about them one at a time, as your work requires.

This chapter provides detailed information about setting up and loading SideKick. It addresses all the problems you might encounter, suggests various precautions, and shows you how to tailor SideKick to your hardware. Before you tackle the fine points, however, you might enjoy a chance to get a feel for the program. The first section describes in brief how to load SideKick and start a utility. There are numerous on-screen menus and help screens that should allow you to flex a few of SideKick's muscles before you read any further. If you have trouble getting started, or when you're ready to dig deeper into SideKick and mold the program to your specific needs, proceed with the section called "System Requirements."

Quick Start

SideKick loads a set of programs on a single disk. If you run the main program —SK.COM—it will load the SideKick utilities into RAM so that they can be called upon at any time.

Loading SideKick

To load SideKick, follow these steps:

1. Turn on your computer.

2. Answer the DOS questions about time and date or just press RETURN to accept the default answers. The DOS prompt will be a drive symbol such as A> or C>.

3. Make drive A the active disk drive. The DOS prompt tells you which drive is active. If, for example, your screen shows C>, C is the active drive. Type **A:** and press RETURN to change the active drive to A. Note that the colon is important in this command and must be typed.

4. Place the SideKick disk in drive A, type **sk**, and then press RETURN. Notice that you don't need to type capital letters for these commands.

You should now see a display similar to that shown in Figure 2-1. (Notice that the figures in this text were created using a hard disk, and so show a C> where the A> would otherwise appear.) If you don't see this display, check whether you have the right disk in the right drive and that you have typed the right command. If none of these factors are in error, type **dir**, for "directory," to see whether the file SK.COM is on your SideKick disk. If it isn't, or if you try the preceding four steps again and still don't see a display similar to Figure 2-1, contact your dealer or

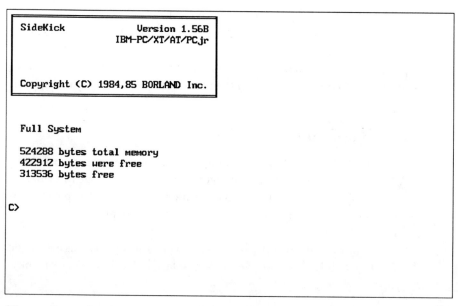

Figure 2-1.   Display after loading SideKick from disk into RAM

Borland for technical support. (Details of how to contact Borland are provided later in this chapter.)

The display in Figure 2-1 shows how much memory you had, how much was free before you loaded SideKick, how much SideKick is occupying, and how much is left. Knowing how much memory is left is sometimes important in determining what programs you can run with SideKick. In the rare circumstance in which you don't have enough memory to run your chosen application program, there are ways you can customize SideKick to use less memory. These are mentioned later in this chapter (see "Limited SideKicks" and "Notefile Size").

Your loading display may not be exactly the same as that in Figure 2-1, because the numbers in the display depend on the amount of memory in your system and how much is used by DOS and other utilities.

Getting the Main Menu

Once SideKick is loaded into RAM, you can call up its main menu to access the SideKick utilities. You do this by using either of two commands: (1) You can press the CTRL and ALT keys at the same time (this is often written as ALT-CTRL); or (2) you can press the two SHIFT keys at the same time (this is written as SHIFT-SHIFT and means simultaneously pressing the right-side SHIFT key and the left-side SHIFT key). Use either of these key combinations, and the main menu (Figure 2-2) will appear.

Choosing a Utility

SideKick's utilities are the programs you actually use to get work done. Although the utilities work well together and can exchange information in a variety of ways, each is also a separate program that appears in its own window on the screen. To use a utility, first you must call its window onto the display.

Getting a window is the same as choosing a utility. This is easy to do once the SideKick main menu is displayed. Use any one of these methods:

- Press the function key that corresponds to your chosen utility.

- Press the key of the highlighted letter in the name of your chosen utility.

- Press the key of the highlighted letter in the name of your chosen utility and at the same time press the ALT key. (When you work with multiple open windows later, you'll need to press the ALT key along with the utility's name key.)

- Use the arrow keys to move the highlight in the main menu to the name of your chosen utility and then press RETURN.

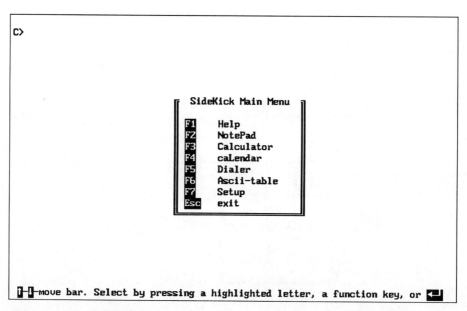

Figure 2-2.   SideKick's main menu

Using Utilities:
Menus and Help Screens

Once you have a utility window open, you can use that utility's commands by following the window menu and using the help key. Figure 2-3
shows an example window; in this case, the Calendar utility is being
used. At the bottom of the screen is a command line that contains a
menu. Here you'll find a list of keys and the operations they perform. The
list is different for each window and even for each state a window is in.
These lists aren't always complete, but they include the most important
commands.

A command that you'll find on every list is F1, Help. At any time you
can press the F1 key to get on-line information about the task at hand.
This help applies directly to the utility you're using and to the commands
presently available within that utility.

If you're having problems or if you now have a feel for the basics of
SideKick and are ready for more in-depth information, go on with this
chapter. Once you've finished it, you can turn directly to the chapter
covering the utility you want to learn first.

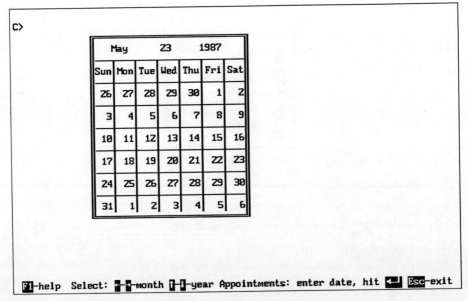

Figure 2-3.   Example of a SideKick utility window: the Calendar

System Requirements

First and most important, make sure you have a system that can run SideKick. The hardware and software required to run SideKick are summarized in the box "Hardware and Software Needed to Run Side-Kick" and are described in detail in the following paragraphs.

PCs and Compatibles

SideKick works on the IBM PC, XT, and AT and on systems compatible with those computers. It also works on the IBM PCjr. The compatibility must be "true" according to Borland, but in practice SideKick works on almost any computer that runs MS-DOS or PC-DOS and is advertised as

---

Hardware and Software Needed to Run SideKick

Required

System: IBM PC, XT, AT, PCjr, or compatibles

Memory: 128K RAM minimum

Disk drives: One floppy disk drive minimum (will work on a hard disk)

Operating system: PC-DOS or MS-DOS 2.0 or a more recent version (2.1, 3.0, 3.1, 3.2, and so on)

Monitor and display adapter: Monochrome or color; works best with IBM MDA or CGA and compatibles as well as Hercules; works on EGA but does not support high-resolution mode.

Suggested peripherals

Modem: Needs a Hayes or Hayes compatible, IBM PCjr internal, or AT&T modem to use the Dialer.

Printer: Works with a wide variety of printers

PC compatible. The PCjr will not work with the copy-protected version of SideKick; it can use only the non-copy-protected version (more about these versions in a minute).

Memory

Your system must have at least 128K of RAM to use SideKick. Today almost any IBM PC or compatible is equipped with that much RAM, and most have 512K or 640K. This requirement is easy to meet; RAM will only be a problem if you want to run a number of TSR programs like SideKick simultaneously, and also use an application that needs a lot of memory. Because you load SideKick before you load your main application, you'll always have enough space for SideKick (and other TSR programs), but a system with a small amount of RAM may then not have enough space for your application. You can use the initial SideKick display, shown in Figure 2-1, to analyze your memory capacity:

- *524288 bytes total memory*   This indicates that your computer has a RAM capacity of 512K. Each K represents 1024 bytes; 512 $\times$ 1024 = 524288. For 256K, 384K, 640K, and other amounts, the calculation works the same way.

- *422912 bytes free*   This indicates how much RAM remains in your computer when SideKick begins to load. The difference between this number (which probably won't be the 422912 shown here) and the total memory is consumed by DOS routines and other TSR programs that were loaded before SideKick.

- *313536 bytes free*   This indicates the RAM you have left for your application program. This number varies depending on your system, your SideKick installation choices (described later in this chapter), and the other TSR programs you use. In this case, 313536 translates into a little over 300K of free RAM. Any program that requires 256K will run fine in this system.

If your application won't start because you've run out of RAM, many solutions exist. For instance, you can check the manual to see if the application can be modified to run with less memory. The SideKick initial display will tell you how much RAM you have initially. Compare this figure to the requirements of your application. If you want to see this display again, reboot your system and reload SideKick from disk. You can also remove SideKick from memory and then see if the application will run. (You won't want to work this way for long, of course.) The procedure for removing SideKick from RAM, without turning off the computer or rebooting, is presented later in this chapter. A third possibility is to start over using fewer TSR programs. Reboot the computer and load only SideKick before trying to run your application. If that works, try loading one other TSR program and SideKick before running the application. Finally, you can use a version of SideKick that takes up less memory. You can use a limited version of SideKick (explained later in this chapter), which doesn't include all of the SideKick utilities, or you can install a smaller Notepad (explained in this chapter and again in Chapter 3).

Disk Drives

SideKick can run on a system with only a single disk drive, but it works better with two floppy disk drives or a hard disk.

Printer

Naturally, it's nice to see some permanent output from programs. The SideKick Notepad utility can drive a printer, and the various printing facilities of Traveling SideKick demand a printer, but the basic uses of SideKick don't call for any printing.

Modem

The SideKick Dialer utility only works if you have one of the following: a Hayes modem, a Hayes-compatible modem, an AT&T Modem 4000, a VOAD keyboard phone, or in the case of the PCjr, an IBM PCjr internal modem.

Disk Backups

Once you have established that your computer can run SideKick, the next step is to make backup copies of your SideKick disk. If anything happens to your original disk, you can return it to Borland for replacement, but that won't restore the data you may have stored in the directory, calendar, and notepad files. It's better to have a backup copy at hand.

The method you should use to make a backup copy of your Side-Kick disk depends on the disk's copy-protection status.

Copy Protection

SideKick is available in two forms: a non-copy-protected version and a less expensive copy-protected version. Borland was one of the first major software firms to remove copy protection from its products, and its license agreement (most software is technically *licensed*, not sold) allows you to make as many copies as you want for your own use. It does ask that you use the program as you would a book, employing and lending it as you wish but not copying it to allow two people to use it in two different locations at the same time.

Copy-protected disks have special codes on them that prevent them from being duplicated exactly. This frustrates people who want to make illegal copies, but it also makes backup procedures more troublesome. If you have a choice, get the non-copy-protected version of SideKick. You can tell whether SideKick is copy protected by looking at the disk label, just beneath the SideKick banner and the copyright notice. There it will say either "Copy Protected" or "Not Copy Protected."

SideKick's copy protection works so that you cannot make a backup disk that can do everything the original disk can do. You must always have the original SideKick disk in the disk drive when you first load SideKick into RAM. After that, you can put the original disk away and replace it with a copy. When the copy-protected SideKick is loading, it looks for special information on the original disk that cannot be copied to a backup disk. It is still worth making backup copies because you can at least save your data files from possible loss. These files can then be used with a replacement disk you get from Borland.

**Making a Floppy Disk
Backup Copy**

You should make a floppy disk backup copy of your SideKick floppy disk
no matter what sort of system you have. In fact, you should make two
backup copies: the first to be your working SideKick disk and the
second to be your backup copy. The original disk can then be stored
safely. Even if you are going to load SideKick onto a hard disk and use it
from there, it's a good idea to have copies of your original disk. To make
backup copies, just follow the instructions presented here twice: once to
make a working copy and then to make a backup of the working copy.

Making a floppy disk backup copy is basically the same whether you
have a single- or double-floppy disk system or a hard-disk system. The
commands differ a bit depending on the copy-protection status of your
disk, but not much. The steps for making a backup copy are as follows:

1. *Prepare the backup disk.* If necessary, format a blank disk
    with the **format b:** command. If you want a bootable disk, type
    the **format b:/s** command and then use **copy command.com
    b:** to copy the command.com file to the new disk.

2. a. *Back up your copy-protected program.* Put the formatted
    disk into drive B and the original SideKick disk into drive A and
    use the **copy a:*.* b:** command. If you have a single-floppy
    drive, first put the original SideKick disk into it, use the same
    command, and then swap disks as the screen instructions
    indicate.

    b. *Back up your non-copy-protected program.* Put the DOS
    disk into drive A (or access DOS from the C drive's directory)
    and use the **diskcopy a: b:** command; then follow the screen
    instructions. If you have a single-floppy drive, first put the
    original SideKick disk into it, use the same command, and then
    swap disks as the screen instructions indicate.

3. *Back up your files on a hard-disk system.* Put the backup
    floppy disks into drive A, call up the SideKick directory (typi-
    cally named sk) on the hard disk, and use the **copy *.* a:**
    command.

Formatting a Backup Disk   The first time you back up any program, you'll be copying the entire original disk onto a blank disk. New disks may be blank, but they aren't formatted —they aren't ready to hold files. The computer can't store information on them until they are provided with a map that shows where information can be put and how to find it again later. Putting that map onto the disk is called *formatting*.

The diskcopy command (sometimes called the *backup* command or something similar on non-IBM systems) available in many DOS systems automatically formats the destination disk and then copies all of the original disk's files to the backup disk in one operation. But diskcopy can't be used with a copy-protected disk. With a copy-protected disk, you have to use the copy command, for which you need a formatted disk.

To format a disk, find the format program on your DOS disk. With that disk in drive A (or using the DOS directory if you're using a hard disk), type **format b:** and press RETURN. The format program will ask you to make sure the right disk is in drive B. Check to make sure the disk in drive B is the disk you want to erase and format as your SideKick backup copy. Make sure it isn't your original SideKick disk. (If you have a hard-disk or a single-floppy system, the format program will use your floppy disk drive as both drive A and drive B. It will periodically ask you to press a key to signal that you have inserted the disk that should be in one or the other of those drives. Just follow the instructions on the screen.)

When you assure the format program that the right disk is in the drive, it begins the formatting operation. This can take anywhere from several seconds to several minutes, depending on your system. The program alerts you when formatting is complete and asks you if you want to format another disk. Answer **N** for no.

Formatting a Bootable Disk   If you format a disk with the format b: command, that disk will be good only for holding files, just as the original SideKick disk is. If you want to make a disk that you can use to boot or start your computer, you need to use a slightly different command and then copy a particular DOS file onto the new disk.

To format a bootable disk, follow all of the preceding instructions, except substitute the **format b:/s** command for the format b: command. Then, when the formatting is complete, copy the command.com file from the DOS disk to your new, formatted disk. Type **copy command.com b:** and press RETURN.

Backing Up Copy-Protected SideKick the First Time   Once
you have a formatted disk, to back up a copy-protected version of
SideKick, put the SideKick disk into drive A and the formatted disk into
B drive, type **copy a:*.* b:**, and press RETURN. Then follow the instructions displayed on the screen. (Again, if you have a single-floppy disk
drive, the computer will periodically ask you to swap disks in that drive
and then to press a key showing that you have done so.)

Backing Up Non-Copy-Protected SideKick the First Time
Once you have a formatted disk, to back up a non-copy-protected version
of SideKick, call up the diskcopy command (either make sure that you
have the diskcopy.com file on your DOS disk or find the hard-disk
directory that contains it). Some systems call this command *backup*. If
that doesn't work, use the preceding procedure for backing up copy-
protected versions of SideKick; this also works for non-copy-protected
versions of SideKick, though it is a bit slower than diskcopy.

Execute the diskcopy command by typing **diskcopy a: b:** and then
pressing RETURN. Follow the instructions on the screen and put the
SideKick disk into drive A and the formatted disk into drive B; then press
any key. (If you have a single-floppy disk drive, the computer will
periodically ask you to swap disks in that drive and then to press a key
showing that you have done so.)

Making Regular Backups   Even if you already have both a working and a backup copy of SideKick, you should go through the backup
process periodically to ensure that your data files will never fall victim to
the failure of a single disk. To make regular backup copies of SideKick,
follow the preceding procedures, but use the working copy in place of the
original SideKick disk and the backup copy disk in place of the new,
formatted disk.

Special Notes for Hard-Disk Systems   If your system has a hard
disk, you'll probably want to run SideKick from that disk. You still
should make a floppy disk backup copy when you first get SideKick, but
you should make regular backup copies from your hard-disk SideKick
directory (explained later in this chapter) onto a floppy disk to save your
data files. To do this, change to drive C (type **c:** and press RETURN) and
then change to the SideKick directory (typically named sk, so type **cd sk**
and press RETURN). Put the SideKick backup disk into drive A, type
copy *.* a:, and press RETURN.

SideKick's Files and README

The following list contains descriptions of the files on the SideKick disk. You don't need all of these files to use SideKick, but you should be aware that they exist:

SK.COM — This is the central SideKick file. This program loads the complete version of SideKick from disk into RAM.

SKN.COM — This file contains one of the limited forms of SideKick made to use less memory by leaving out the Calendar tool. This program also loads Side-Kick from disk to RAM and can be used as a direct replacement for SK.COM.

SKC.COM — This file contains another of the limited forms of SideKick made to use less memory by leaving out the Notepad tool. This program also loads Side-Kick from disk to RAM and can be used as a direct replacement for SK.COM.

SKM.COM — This file contains the final and most limited form of SideKick. It uses the least memory because it drops all of the tools except the Calculator and the ASCII chart. This program also loads Side-Kick from disk to RAM and can be used as a direct replacement for SK.COM.

SK.HLP — This file contains the help information that is always available from within SideKick.

SKINST.COM — This separate program lets you choose a number of SideKick parameters, such as screen colors, notepad size, and monitor type. It then installs your choices into the main SideKick programs. Your choices, however, won't affect SideKick until you remove SideKick from memory and use a newly installed version of one of the SideKick main programs to reload SideKick into memory.

SKINST.MSG   This file contains the program messages for the
                  SKINST.COM program.

NOTES   This sample Notepad file or notefile automati-
                  cally appears on the Notepad window when you
                  activate the Notepad tool.

PHONE.DIR   This sample phone directory file automatically
                  appears with the Dialer tool when you start the
                  directory utility.

README   This text file contains recent information about
                  new features and bugs in SideKick. This is an
                  extension of the owner's handbook and can be
                  read most easily by using the README.COM
                  program.

README.COM   This program is designed to make reading or
                  printing the up-to-the-minute information in the
                  README file easier.

The first file you should pay particular attention to is the README
file, which is a text file containing information about program bugs and
features —information that was too new to make it into the owner's
handbook or that corrects mistakes in that handbook. To read it, just
type **readme** and press RETURN. This starts the README.COM program, which presents the README text file to you in a special window
(shown in Figure 2- 4) along with a menu of scrolling commands that let
you move slowly or quickly through the file. To print the README file,
you can use the printing feature built into README.COM; check the
menu at the bottom of the README window.

Registering Your Copy of SideKick

It's a good idea to fill out and mail the registration form included with
SideKick because this qualifies you to receive technical support over the
phone. You may never need the support, but if you do you'll be glad you
registered. Calling isn't the only way you can find out more about
SideKick. If you have trouble, there are a number of resources.

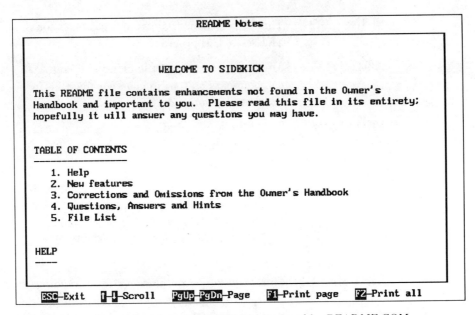

```
                          README Notes
 ┌──────────────────────────────────────────────────────────────┐
 │                                                                │
 │                                                                │
 │                     WELCOME TO SIDEKICK                        │
 │                                                                │
 │  This README file contains enhancements not found in the Owner's │
 │  Handbook and important to you.  Please read this file in its entirety; │
 │  hopefully it will answer any questions you may have.          │
 │                                                                │
 │                                                                │
 │  TABLE OF CONTENTS                                             │
 │  ─────────────────                                            │
 │      1. Help                                                   │
 │      2. New features                                           │
 │      3. Corrections and Omissions from the Owner's Handbook   │
 │      4. Questions, Answers and Hints                           │
 │      5. File List                                              │
 │                                                                │
 │                                                                │
 │  HELP                                                          │
 │  ────                                                         │
 │                                                                │
 └──────────────────────────────────────────────────────────────┘
   ESC-Exit    [↑↓]-Scroll   PgUp-PgDn-Page   F1-Print page   F2-Print all
```

Figure 2-4.   Beginning of the README file displayed by README.COM

- *Users' groups*   Often the fastest way to get help is to ask a friend or office mate who may have encountered the same trouble and found a way to fix it. This mode of communication is most fruitful in the microcomputing community. If you don't know anyone who might know about your software or hardware, visit or join a users' group. Local computer publications and computer dealers probably will know where and when such groups meet.

- *Dealers*   If you bought SideKick from a dealer, turn to the dealer for help.

- *Write to Borland*   Writing is a slow way to get information in the electronic age, but it is sometimes worth doing. If you want to write to Borland, or if you need to send your disk back for any reason, the address is

  Borland International
  SideKick Technical Support
  4585 Scotts Valley Drive
  Scotts Valley, CA 95066

- *Call Borland* Phoning can be a lot faster than writing, but sometimes there is heavy traffic on the phone lines. If you don't need the answer this second, consider using the on-line support services first. The Borland number is (408) 438-8400. Call between 9 A.M. and 5 P.M. Pacific Coast time and ask for SideKick technical support.

- *On-line services* On-line services are large mainframe computers or minicomputers that allow many people to call in (using a computer and a modem) and exchange information. Two such services offer direct access to Borland technical support: Compuserve and BIX (Byte Information Exchange). For either of these, you have to register and pay a fee to the service to get a password. After that, you can call the service at any time, day or night, and pay only an hourly rate (typically $6 to $12) plus the cost of your phone call. That call will probably be local since most major services can be accessed through a packet network such as Tymnet. (The ins and outs of using an on-line service are too much to recount here, but there are a number of good books on the subject you can consult.)

  Once you are online, you can contact Borland and type your question. Borland representatives call in to get questions, then go to find answers, and finally, get back online again to type an answer. A response can take from five minutes to about three days, depending on how busy the support area is.

  BIX, the BYTE Information Exchange, is linked directly to BYTE Magazine. To get information about signing onto its service, call (603) 924-9281. You may be able to get a special rate if you're a BYTE subscriber.

  Compuserve is a much larger on-line service than BIX and is the granddaddy of technical support groups. Borland has been answering questions on Compuserve for several years, and the complaints from Compuserve callers about copy protection were a major part of Borland's reason for introducing a non-copy-protected version of SideKick. Borland periodically bundles special Compuserve sign-up deals with its products. The phone number for Compuserve technical information is (800) 848-8199, or, in Ohio, (614) 457-0802. Once you log onto Compuserve, use the command **GO BOR 100** to contact Borland technical support.

Versions of SideKick

To find answers to questions about SideKick by looking through the manual, asking a dealer, or making a quick call to Borland, you will need to know what version of SideKick you're using. Look at your SideKick disk and see what it says on the lower part of the label, beneath the banner and the copyright notice. Is it copy protected or non-copy protected? What's the serial number? What is the version number? Software developers generally improve and debug their programs over time, and each time they significantly change a program, it is given a new version number. SideKick started with version 1.0 and has now reached version 1.56B. To find out which version you have, you can start SideKick as described at the beginning of this chapter and check the initial loading display (see Figure 2-1). If you already have loaded SideKick, another way to find out the version number is to call up the SideKick Setup window. Within the border of that window you'll find the program's version number.

Getting Underway

Now that you've made backup copies and have checked the README file, it's time to load SideKick into memory.

Loading SideKick from a Floppy Disk

If you are working with a floppy-disk system, use the procedure for loading SideKick discussed at the beginning of this chapter. If you are loading other TSR programs with SideKick, load SideKick last. You'll see the initial loading display shown in Figure 2-1.

Loading SideKick from
a Hard Disk

If you have a hard disk, your program will run faster if you copy your SideKick files onto that hard disk and then load SideKick into RAM. When copying to the hard disk, you can either put all the programs into the main directory or you can put them into a directory of their own. (It is probably best to put them into their own directory so that the main listing doesn't get too long and jumbled.) To make a new directory on the hard disk, call up the main directory by typing (at the C> for the hard disk) the command **cd** \ and pressing RETURN. ("cd" stands for *change directory*, the backslash indicates the main or root directory.) Then type **md sk** and press RETURN. This *make directory* command creates a new directory on the disk with the name "sk." Call up that new directory by typing in the **cd sidekick** command and pressing RETURN. Type **dir** and press RETURN to make sure that this directory is empty.

Now you're ready to copy files. Put the working copy (the one you made using the backup procedures) of the SideKick floppy disk into drive A, type **copy a:*.***, and press RETURN. Since you're already in drive C, you don't need to specify that as your destination. Also, because you're already in the "sk" directory, that's where all the files will be copied. Once the copying is complete, you can put away the working SideKick disk. However, if you have a copy-protected version, keep it close at hand; when you try to load SideKick into RAM from the files in the new directory, SideKick will check to see if the original disk is in the floppy disk drive. If it isn't, SideKick won't load.

With your new SideKick directory on the hard disk, type **sk** and press RETURN. SideKick will load into RAM, and you'll see the display in Figure 2-1.

Special Note for
DOS Experts

Make sure that the SideKick Help file (SK.HLP) is in the start-up directory. This directory is called the *current domain* of SideKick. If the Help file isn't there, then later when you press F1 for immediate help information, SideKick may not be able to find that information. If you're a DOS pro, you may think that by using the *path* command (which lets

DOS know how to find files even if you are in a different directory) you will solve this problem — it isn't true. All SideKick files that end in the .COM and .HLP extensions should be in the start-up directory, or you won't be able to use help or to save new setups (a procedure explained later in this chapter and in the individual utility chapters).

Batch Files and Automatic Startup

DOS offers a special kind of file called a *batch* file that lets you combine a number of commands under a single name. A batch file can be recognized by its .BAT extension. When you type the main file name of a batch file — you don't need to type the extension — and press RETURN , DOS will execute the commands contained within that file.

An especially important batch file is the AUTOEXEC.BAT file, which your computer automatically reads and executes whenever you turn on the power or when you reboot the system. When booting, the computer searches for this file and executes it.

You can instruct your computer to load SideKick automatically by including the proper commands within the AUTOEXEC file. This is sometimes practical in floppy-disk based systems where you can make a bootable SideKick disk or squeeze the SideKick files you need onto your DOS disk along with the AUTOEXEC file and the other necessary DOS routines. It is especially practical on hard-disk systems where there is plenty of space for SideKick and other TSR programs to be stored and automatically loaded when you begin to work.

There are two things to watch out for when loading automatically. First, SideKick should always be loaded last of all TSR programs. Otherwise, it may run into compatibility problems with those programs and possibly freeze your system or lose data later on. This means that the **sk** command must be at the end of the AUTOEXEC file's string of commands. Second, as mentioned previously, you need to make sure you are in the directory with all of the SideKick help files and that you start SideKick from there if you want to use the help function. These directory changes also can be implemented in the AUTOEXEC file.

Creating and modifying the AUTOEXEC file are DOS functions that require the use of an editor program such as Notepad. These functions are discussed in Chapter 12. For now, when using SideKick by itself, understanding the AUTOEXEC file isn't that important. But once you're using SideKick regularly, you'll probably want a variety of batch files that can load it and other programs such as SuperKey in the right combinations to use with your various main application programs.

Activating SideKick

Once SideKick is in RAM, the program can be called by either of two commands: (1) ALT-CTRL (pressing the CTRL and ALT keys simultaneously) and (2) SHIFT-SHIFT (pressing the right-hand SHIFT and the left-hand SHIFT simultaneously). If you don't like using either of these commands, you can change them to your preference with the SideKick Installation program discussed in the section on "Screen Type," near the end of this chapter. You'll know SideKick is activated for the first time when you see the main menu on the screen (as shown in Figure 2-2).

To deactivate SideKick, which clears the main menu from the screen, press either the ALT-CTRL or SHIFT-SHIFT combination, or press ESC. SideKick is still in RAM but is not processing. In this state, you can run any other program and either ignore SideKick or call it up for use later.

The Main Menu

Once SideKick is loaded into memory with the sk command, it constantly monitors your keystrokes. When it senses the ALT-CTRL or SHIFT-SHIFT key combinations, it suspends the application presently running (if any), and returns you to the main menu display screen. (These combinations can also bypass the main menu and call up the most recently used utility. This feature is discussed later in this chapter.) SideKick also displays a menu bar across the bottom of the screen that tells you what you can do within the active SideKick window. There are a few occasions when SideKick cannot immediately be activated, such as when a file is being read from or saved to disk. There are also a few application programs that don't work smoothly with TSR programs such as SideKick. These are mentioned in Appendix B.

The Utility Windows

The main menu window is your gateway to SideKick's individual utilities, each of which appears within a window of its own. As mentioned in Chapter 1, SideKick's utilities include the Notepad, Calculator, Calendar, Dialer, and ASCII table.

Notepad   The Notepad is a simple word processor that was originally intended for jotting down short memos, letters, and notes. However, because it can work with files as large as 45,000 characters, it can be used for a wide variety of writing tasks including papers, book chapters, articles, and the like. Most of its commands are similar to those of WordStar.

Calculator   The Calculator is a screen-display version of a pocket calculator. It has the basic arithmetic functions but no advanced mathematical or trigonometric functions. It is of interest to computer programmers because it includes operations for hexadecimal and octal calculations.

Calendar   The Calendar is useful for calculating specific dates or the current date. It is also extremely handy for keeping an appointments schedule.

Dialer   The dialer is not a telecommunications program; it cannot put your computer in contact with other computers via a modem. What it can do is send out the tones to dial numbers on your regular phone, saving you the trouble of dialing. It can send tones for numbers found in other programs or in its own directory database.

ASCII table   The ASCII table is mainly of interest to programmers, although it can sometimes help if you're struggling to figure out how to make a printer work. The ASCII (American Standard Code for Information Interchange) code establishes a direct one-for-one relationship between the numbers from 1 to 255 and the most commonly used characters. The PC works with ASCII codes internally and then translates them into standard characters for output.

Specifying a SideKick Utility

From the main menu, there are four ways to specify a particular utility or desk accessory.

First, you can press the programmable function key associated with that utility. These are the numbered "F" keys typically found either on the left-hand side of the PC keyboard or in a row across the top of the keyboard. Each line of the main menu shows both a utility (with a capital letter) and the function key for calling that utility.

Second, you can use the up- and down-arrow cursor keys to move the highlight within the main menu. This highlight illuminates one utility at a time. Once you have highlighted the utility you want, press RETURN.

Third, you can press the single letter key associated with the utility you want. For seven of the menu choices this key is the first letter in the utility's name. The exception: Calendar uses an uppercase "L."

Finally, you also can press the letter and the ALT key together. This method is used for opening multiple utilities, which is explained further in the section "Multiple Tools."

When you select a utility, the window for that utility appears, and the menu bar across the bottom of the display shows new instructions and options that refer to the newly activated utility window. Once you have a utility window on the display, you can use commands to move and in some cases resize the window, or you can deactivate the window with either the ESC or ALT-CTRL keys.

Differences Between ESC and
ALT-CTRL or SHIFT-SHIFT

If you use the ALT-CTRL or SHIFT-SHIFT key combination to deactivate a utility, the next time you press ALT-CTRL or SHIFT-SHIFT to return to SideKick, you'll move directly into that same utility window, bypassing the main menu. If, on the other hand, you use ESC to deactivate a utility, the next time you call up SideKick you'll return to the main menu.

Moving Windows

All of SideKick's tools appear as windows that pop up in front of other displays. You can manipulate these windows in several ways. Some, including the Notepad, can be made larger or smaller, which is described in Chapter 3. But all of the windows, including the main menu window, can be moved.

Recall Figure 2-2, the main menu. Across the bottom of the display is a bar of instructions on how to use that menu. If you press the SCROLL LOCK key (often situated at the top right of the keyboard), you'll see a "Scroll Lock" sign appear at the bottom right of the SideKick display. (A similar sign appears when the NUM LOCK key is active.) When this signal is present, you can move the window by pressing the arrow cursor keys. Experiment with this method to move the menu around the display. Figure 2-5 shows how the main menu can be moved to the bottom left corner of the display, out of the way of most DOS directory listing displays and of the important corner cells of most spreadsheets. This feature allows you to see part of a previous display, which might otherwise be covered by a SideKick window. Also note that if you move the window to the edge of the display area, it won't go any further.

Try moving the window and then using ESC or the key combinations —such as ALT-CTRL— to deactivate the main menu window. If you then reactivate the main menu window, it will appear in the new position.

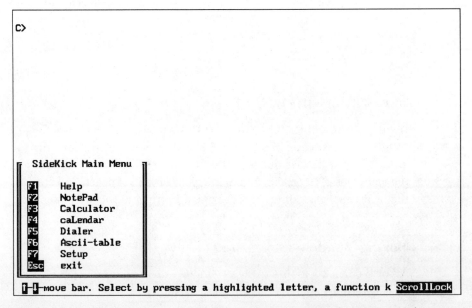

Figure 2-5. Main menu repositioned using SCROLL LOCK and cursor arrow keys

This effect occurs throughout SideKick: The Notepad cursor remains where you left it; the Calculator shows the last number you worked with; and so on. The tools are thus suspended until you return to them or shut off the computer.

To retain the new position of a window even after you turn off your system, you can save the changed position using the Setup option. Then when you reactivate that utility's window, it appears where you left it.

Multiple Tools

As previously mentioned, you can select a utility from the main menu in a number of ways, including pressing ALT and the letter key associated with the desired utility. This combination allows you to call up more than one SideKick utility at a time. Not only can SideKick be activated in the middle of other applications, but SideKick utilities can be activated on top of other SideKick utilities (and in turn, all of them can be activated on top of an application program).

For example, see Figure 2-6. If you press **n** from the main menu, the

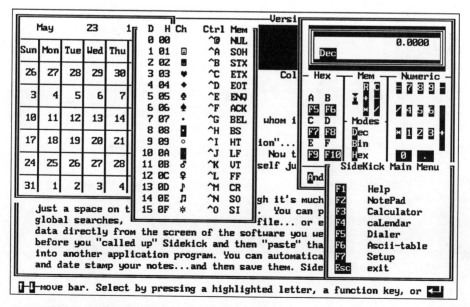

Figure 2-6. Multiple SideKick utility windows

Notepad window appears, replacing the main menu. And if you want to use the Calculator without losing the Notepad (perhaps there are some numbers that you want to add together), press the ALT-C combination (C for Calculator) to activate the Calculator window on top of the Notepad. You also could choose to put the Calendar on top of both of these windows, using ALT-L. If you have trouble remembering the letter for a utility, simply hold down ALT. After a second or two, the main menu will reappear above your open window. All of SideKick's utilities can be stacked onto the display at the same time, but only the top utility will be active. The other windows will remain partially visible, but inactive. If you want to change the active window and work with another utility, press ALT and that utility's key, and SideKick will shuffle it to the top of the pile.

To leave multiple utilities you can press either ALT-CTRL or SHIFT-SHIFT to return you to your original application or to DOS. Or you can press ESC, which removes the active or uppermost utility from the screen entirely. Repeated use of ESC removes the utilities one by one until you reach the original application or DOS. Leaving utilities via ALT-CTRL gives you the option of using ALT-CTRL to return to SideKick, with all of the utilities just as you left them.

Help

Within each of SideKick's utility windows, you can perform a variety of functions with the special function keys. The keys generally perform similar functions no matter which window you're using. One key that always has the same function is F1. At any point, in the main menu or in one of the utility windows, pressing F1 opens a Help window full of command definitions and explanations (Figure 2-7). Each Help window is *context-sensitive;* that is, SideKick only provides information for the utility you are currently using. You can scroll through the Help pages by using the up- and down-arrow cursor keys. To leave Help, press ESC, which returns you to the previously active SideKick utility. Pressing ALT-CTRL has no effect and does not get you out of Help.

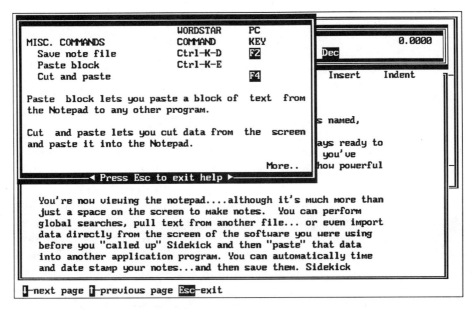

Figure 2-7. Example of SideKick's context-sensitive Help windows

Limited SideKicks

Sometimes a SideKick function requires more RAM than you have available. There are several solutions to this memory shortage problem, including changing your SideKick installation and using one of the limited forms of SideKick.

These limited forms, as mentioned in the previous section "Side-Kick Files and README," are

SK.COM   This is the complete SideKick and includes the Notepad, Calculator, Calendar, Dialer, and ASCII table.

SKN.COM   This limited SideKick includes the Notepad, Calculator, Dialer, and ASCII table.

SKC.COM   This limited SideKick includes the Calculator, Calendar, Dialer, and the ASCII table.

SKM.COM   This is the smallest SideKick and includes only the Calculator and the ASCII table.

For example, if you don't want the Calendar utility, use the SKN.COM file instead of the standard SK.COM. When you're ready to load SideKick into memory, just type **skn** and press RETURN, instead of typing the customary **sk**. The Calendar will be left out of the line-up, and additional RAM space will remain free for other operations.

If you don't want the Notepad, for instance, you can use the SKC.COM starter program; type **skc** and press RETURN to get this set of utilities. SideKick's smallest set, the SKM.COM program with its **skm** command, gives you only the Calculator and the ASCII table. The main menu for this last version is shown in Figure 2-8.

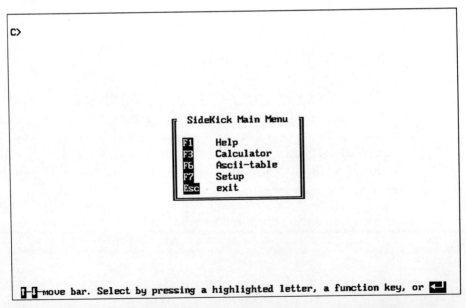

Figure 2-8.   Main menu for SKM.COM, the most limited version of SideKick

Unfortunately, you can't change your version of SideKick while SideKick is in RAM. You must reboot the computer by using the ALT-CTRL-DEL key combination to load a new version of SideKick, to change its setup, or to work with a different set of utilities.

If you use only one of the SideKick configurations regularly, you may want to delete the other starter program files from your active disk to save RAM. But be sure to keep a couple of copies of those other files on backup disks. You may want them later.

Removing SideKick

One way to unload SideKick is to turn off the computer. SideKick will vanish, but remain on disk, ready to be loaded again later. But if SideKick and some other TSR program seem to be interfering with proper computer operation (this shouldn't happen very often), or if you need more RAM freed for some operation, you may want to erase SideKick from RAM without turning off your computer or rebooting. This can only be done from a DOS prompt such as A> or C>.

To unload SideKick, press ALT-CTRL to call up the main menu and then press CTRL-HOME-END. SideKick will no longer activate when you press ALT-CTRL, because it has been removed from RAM. Be careful: If you haven't saved your data — such as the contents of the Notepad — to disk by pressing F2 , that data, too, will be lost when you remove SideKick. Saving data will be discussed in Chapter 3.

TSR Controllers

If you use a number of TSR programs along with SideKick, you may want to buy a special program that organizes these programs in memory. This type of program provides slots for TSR programs and keeps them from interfering with each other. It also sits between them and DOS and helps DOS understand how to work with RAM that may have empty locations resulting from removed TSR programs.

TSR controllers are helpful to avoid overcrowding your computer's RAM. This can happen when several TSR programs are watching for the same signals from the keyboard. If one program always responds to these signals first, the others will become mute and invisible because they never get their cue.

Installation for Customization

If you want more free memory, don't want to eliminate any SideKick utilities, and don't want to install a TSR controller, there's another option: SideKick's Installation program (SKINST.COM). The installation program lets you customize SideKick for your amount of RAM, your screen display, and so on. Figure 2-9 shows the screen display when you run SKINST.COM by typing **skinst** and pressing RETURN. The installation program can affect the following:

- Screen type

- Display colors

- Maximum notefile size

- Editing commands within the Notepad

- Right margin for text in the Notepad

- Modem type, port, and phone number format for the Dialer

- Commands used to activate SideKick

Any changes you make while running this program are recorded in the disk files, not in the SideKick stored in memory. To activate your changes, you must remove SideKick from memory and then reload it. You choose the item you want to change in SideKick by typing the letter corresponding to its name, much as you do in the main menu.

Notefile Size

For instance, SKINST.COM can change three areas of the Notepad. Type **N**, and you can choose the Notepad's file size. All your documents

```
          Installation program for SideKick 1.50

         Choose installation item from the following:

   Screen type | notepad Commands | Notepad size | right Margin

   Dialer      | cOlors          | Activate commands


            Enter S, C, N, M, D, O, A or Q to quit:
```

Figure 2-9.   SKINST.COM, the SideKick Installation program

are kept in RAM, so the smaller the size of the document, the less RAM SideKick will occupy. For example: Type **1000** (for 1000 characters maximum), press RETURN, and press **Q** to quit the installation process. Then reboot your system, load SideKick, and see how much of your free memory SideKick uses. Now run SKINST.COM, type **N** (to change the Notepad size), type **50000**, and press RETURN and then **Q** (to quit the Installation program). Then reboot and reload SideKick to see how much memory SideKick uses.

Note that although you set notefile size to 50,000 characters, you'll get little more than 45,000 characters into the Notepad. The Notepad document and the Notepad program code have to fit together into 64K — 45,000 characters is the limit. Since each character occupies a byte, if you try loading a file with more bytes than there are allowed characters, you'll get an error message.

You can also change the right margin and the Notepad commands, which will be discussed in Chapter 3. Installation of the Dialer will be described in Chapter 6.

Setting the Graphics

A brand-new copy of SideKick always uses the text mode for display. When you are running a graphics display and change to SideKick, the graphics may become strange-looking and change colors. If you are working on a SideKick-compatible system, the old graphics will return as soon as you deactivate SideKick and return to your application program.

To prevent eye strain, more recent versions of SideKick will blank the meaningless graphics behind the SideKick text screen. You can remove this feature with the Installation program if you want to see the odd effects.

Screen Type

The Installation program also lets you set SideKick for your type of monitor by means of the display shown in Figure 2-10. Note that you should use the default display mode for multidisplay adapters (those that are compatible with several standards) and that the monochrome display

```
Choose one of the following displays:

  0)  Default display mode
  1)  Monochrome display   (includes Hercules card)
  2)  Color display 80x25
  3)  B/W   display 80x25  (one-color monitor connected to color graphics card)

Which display? (0-3 or  ←  for no change): 0

Does your screen blink when the text scrolls? (Y/N,  ←  for no change): Y


Do you want to use Sidekick on top of graphics (Y/N,  ←  for no change): Y
```

Figure 2-10.   Installation display for setting the screen type

option includes the Hercules, AST Preview, and AST Monograph Plus boards. The black-and-white display option is used for systems that have a monochrome monitor hooked up to a color graphics adapter. SideKick does not yet support the highest-resolution, 43-line part of EGA (enhanced graphics adapter) graphics, but it does support the regular color modes of the EGA. SideKick, along with SuperKey and Turbo Lightning, supports 640 $\times$ 200 and 320 $\times$ 200 color, and Hercules graphics.

Finally, SideKick also lets you push your adapter card to produce as little "noise" or screen "snow" as possible.

As a special note, the Notepad also can be toggled with the CTRL-Q-G key combination to change from text to graphics mode and back. In the text mode, the window only displays the first 128 ASCII characters. In the graphics mode, you can see all 256 ASCII characters. This feature is useful for writing European-language character sets and for creating graphics with the special graphics characters. There is even a patch that will cause SideKick's Notepad to start in the graphics mode automatically.

Also, if you hold down ALT and type a decimal number between 0 and 255 within 1.5 seconds, that number will be translated into its ASCII equivalent and displayed in the Notepad window. (On the IBM AT and when using SuperKey, you must press SHIFT and ALT while typing the ASCII numeric equivalent.) Of course, SideKick offers an ASCII table for you to examine at any time. More on this feature in Chapter 3.

Colors

The Installation program allows you to pick your own colors and black-and-white attributes for color or monochrome screens for all parts of the SideKick displays. When you choose **O** from the Installation menu in Figure 2-9, you see the display shown in Figure 2-11. Although the initial SideKick colors have been selected as the most commonly clear colors, you may want some other setting. The menu at the bottom of the display shows the names of the various SideKick windows. You can use the arrow keys to move the highlighted area through this list to the window whose colors you want to change. When you have settled on your chosen window, the top line of the bottom window shows the numeric code for the foreground, background, and frame colors of that window.

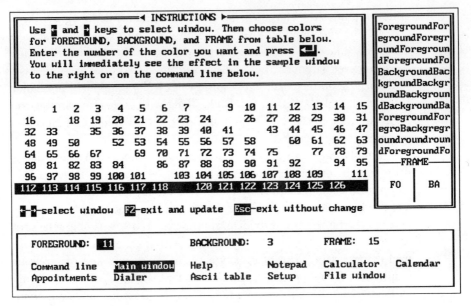

Figure 2-11.   Installation display for choosing screen colors

To change a color, enter a new color code number and press RETURN. The sample window shows the change. Repeatedly pressing RETURN cycles you through the foreground, background, and frame selections. The numbers from 1 (which shows as black on black and isn't available as an option) to 127 are translated into their representative colors in the middle of the display. The numbers from 129 to 255 represent blinking versions of the same colors you find from 1 to 127. Add 128 to any of the low numbers to get the code for its blinking analogue. When you change command line colors, the sample window disappears so you can see the Installation program's command line for comparison.

When you are finished, press ESC to reject your changes or press F2 to save them. Once again, to see the changes you must remove and reload SideKick.

Activation Commands

If you don't like either ALT-CTRL or SHIFT-SHIFT, the two commands that activate SideKick, or if you are using some other program that also uses

CTRL and ALT, the Installation program allows you to pick your own activation key commands. Choose the A option and follow the instructions on the menu at the bottom of the display. Your new choices will be saved to disk, ready for work the next time you load SideKick.

Setup

The SideKick main menu also offers an additional option called Setup (Figure 2-12). This option shows the size, directory, paste delay, and name for your notefile (the document manipulated by the Notepad window). It also shows the name for the active appointment calendar and its directory, and the name and DOS directory for the phone directory. You can change any of these names and directories (but not the Notepad size, which can be changed only from the Installation program) by using the up- and down-arrow keys to move to the item you wish to change and then typing the new value for the item. Setup is discussed in detail in the individual utility chapters.

Figure 2-12. The Setup option

You also can use the Setup window to save the current sizes and positions of the various SideKick utility windows. Any new pattern you save reappears automatically the next time you load SideKick. This works properly only if you load SideKick from the disk directory where the files were copied.

Summary

Now it's time to jump into an individual utility chapter. Don't worry if you aren't all installed and set up yet. You have plenty of time to mold SideKick over and over again until it fits your computer like a glove.

3

The Notepad: Opening and Setup

The Notepad is the most complex and powerful tool within SideKick. How to use it and customize it to your needs are topics too extensive for a single chapter. Therefore, this chapter covers preliminaries such as manipulating the window and loading and saving files. Information about moving the cursor, entering text, and modifying text, is presented in Chapter 4.

At its simplest, the Notepad is a bare-bones text editor or word processor for writing short letters, memos, and of course, notes. But in the hands of an experienced user, the Notepad becomes an extremely versatile tool. With it you can handle documents up to 20 pages long, and rapidly create, modify, and manipulate text and numerals. Although it lacks some of the fancier features of powerful word processors, the Notepad is a remarkably efficient word processor for several-page essays or entire chapters of books.

But the Notepad isn't only a text processor; it can be useful even for people who rarely write a word. Its features for cutting and pasting information between different applications and screens are nearly as important as its editing abilities. The cut-and-paste features allow you to move text or numbers from one application to another, providing a smooth and immediate conduit between programs that otherwise might not be on speaking terms without complex software and hardware interfaces. The Notepad can even sort material that has been taken from one program before sending it on to another.

Opening the Notepad

Open the Notepad from the SideKick main menu. The procedure for loading and starting SideKick is laid out in Chapter 2, but basically it consists of typing **sk** to load the program and pressing ALT-CTRL to open the main menu. (Make sure you are using a SideKick program that contains the Notepad, such as SK.COM or SKN.COM. Several limited versions —including SKC.COM and SKM.COM —leave it out.)

From the main menu (Figure 3-1), there are four ways to activate the Notepad.

1. Press N.

2. Press ALT and N.

3. Press F2.

4. Use the cursor arrow keys to move the highlight onto the Notepad line and then press RETURN.

The Notepad should appear as shown in Figure 3-2. The actual *notefile,* the text and numeric data that occupy the Notepad window in this figure will not appear on your screen. The first time you activate the Notepad after loading SideKick, the program always checks the Setup window for the name of the initial file to load. With a brand-new copy of SideKick, this file is called "Notes." You can change the Setup to call some other file or to see a directory of files from which to choose.

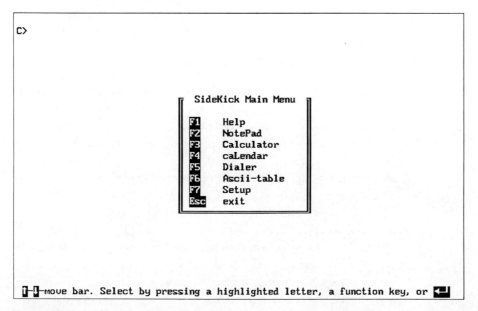

Figure 3-1.   The main menu

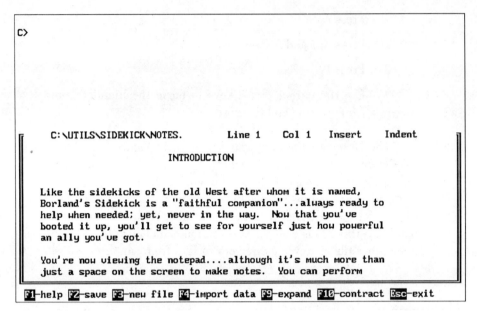

C>

C:\UTILS\SIDEKICK\NOTES.   Line 1   Col 1   Insert   Indent

INTRODUCTION

Like the sidekicks of the old West after whom it is named,
Borland's Sidekick is a "faithful companion"...always ready to
help when needed; yet, never in the way. Now that you've
booted it up, you'll get to see for yourself just how powerful
an ally you've got.

You're now viewing the notepad....although it's much more than
just a space on the screen to make notes. You can perform

F1-help F2-save F3-new file F4-import data F9-expand F10-contract Esc-exit

Figure 3-2. The Notepad window

If the Notepad finds a file on the disk drive specified in the Setup window, it will read that file and display it immediately. (In the initial Notes file, there is some short example text that tells about SideKick's features. You can delete this text if you wish.) If the Setup requires the Notepad to show you a directory (that is, if it has *.* for the file name), it will do so in a new, small window, and then will load the file you choose from that directory.

If the Notepad does not find a file specified in the Setup window, it opens a new file and assigns it the name "Setup." (This new file is not a disk file and won't appear in disk directories until you specifically save it to disk. Until you issue a *save* command, the file only exists in RAM.)

If you have used the Notepad during your current computing session, the file you last saw in the Notepad window reappears just as you left it. You can demonstrate this feature by pressing CTRL-ALT to get out of the Notepad and out of SideKick, and then pressing CTRL-ALT again to return. If you use ESC to deactivate the Notepad and SideKick, you'll return to the main menu when you press CTRL-ALT. One additional command allows you to get out of the Notepad: pressing CTRL-K-Q (you

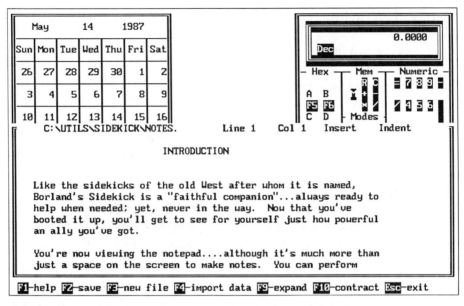

Figure 3-3.   Multiple windows: Notepad, Calendar, and Calculator

can also press CTRL-K and then press Q). This is a WordStar-style key command and is explained more thoroughly in Chapter 4.

Next, use any of the four methods listed previously to activate the Notepad and your file will reappear.

As mentioned in Chapter 2, you can call up the Notepad while other SideKick utilities are on screen. You can do this in either of two ways: First, you can press ALT-N when another SideKick utility window is displayed; the Notepad window will pop up on top of the other utility window. Second, you can press and hold down ALT for a second or two to return you to the main menu, and then you can use any of the four listed methods to call up the Notepad. Figure 3-3 shows the Notepad called up on top of the Calendar and Calculator windows.

If the Notepad window is already on the display but has been obscured by other, more recently activated SideKick tools (only one utility can be active at a time), follow the preceding instructions to bring the Notepad window to the top of the stack so that it becomes the active window. No matter how you bring the Notepad to the active position, you'll use the same editing commands to manipulate the text within it.

Notepad Window Anatomy

Figure 3-4 illustrates the parts of the Notepad window: two lines of information, a border, and a central area for displaying a notefile. The central area may not show the entire file; it is a "window" onto the file, showing as much as will fit in the area you have allotted for the window. As you'll see later in this chapter, you can change the size and position of the window without affecting the notefile itself.

At the top of the window a status line lists which notefile is in the Notepad, the disk and directory that file is taken from, the line and column position of the cursor within the writing area, and the status of the Insert and Auto-indent modes, which are explained later. Some of this information, such as the Insert, Indent, and Graph mode indicators, may not be visible if the window is too narrow for them to fit on the status line.

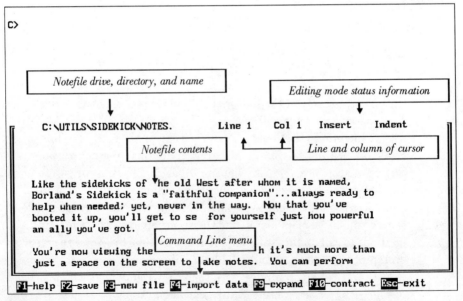

Figure 3-4.   The parts of the Notepad window

At the bottom of the window is a command line that lists your function key menu options. As you make choices from this menu or use editing commands within the Notepad, the menu changes to keep pace. Some keys, though, remain constant. Pressing F1 always brings you context-sensitive help; that is, information about menus and commands that relates directly to the part of SideKick you are using. Pressing ESC always causes you to exit a command or mode. (There are a few instances where ESC won't extricate you completely, which are discussed later in this chapter and in Chapter 4. But ESC is never assigned to another task.)

Moving and Resizing Windows

Before you begin using the Notepad you'll need to know some basic information that applies to any SideKick window. As already mentioned, there are several ways you can change the size and position of a SideKick window. You can enlarge or contract a window, slide it around on the screen, or change the color of the display. (For Notepad windows, you can also set right and left margins that will change the appearance of the notefile within the window, and you can choose to work in the Graphics mode or in the Standard Text mode. More on this later.) Here is a summary of the keys used to change windows:

SCROLL LOCK	Press this key to prepare the window for movement. Once the scroll lock is in place, you can use the cursor arrow keys to move the window.
F9	Press this key to prepare the window for enlargement. Then use the cursor arrow keys to expand the window. Press F9 again when you are finished changing the window's size.
F10	Press this key to prepare the window for contraction. Then use the cursor arrow keys to shrink the window. Press F10 again when you are finished changing the window's size.

UP ARROW
DOWN ARROW
RIGHT ARROW
LEFT ARROW

} Pressing any of these keys after one of those listed above actually changes the size or position of the window.

Moving a Window

To move a window press SCROLL LOCK. The words "Scroll Lock" appear at the far right of the command line beneath the window (Figure 3-5). You won't see any change in the menu on the command line: The same commands remain available. However, with SCROLL LOCK pressed, you can move the window up or down using the up- or down-arrow cursor keys or from side to side using the right- and left-arrow cursor keys. You can shift the position of the window until it runs into an edge of the display screen. At that point, SideKick ignores any further commands to move in the blocked direction.

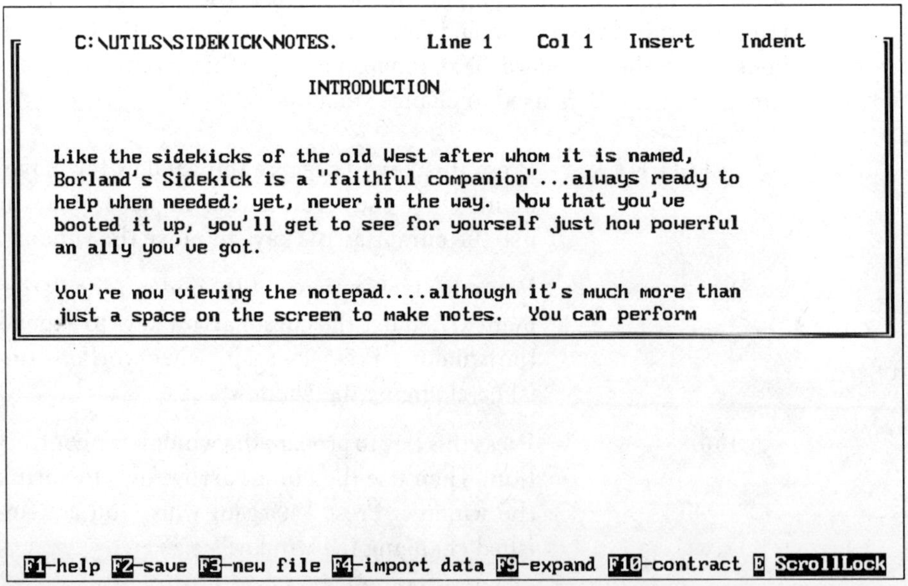

```
   C:\UTILS\SIDEKICK\NOTES.        Line 1    Col 1    Insert     Indent

              INTRODUCTION

   Like the sidekicks of the old West after whom it is named,
   Borland's Sidekick is a "faithful companion"...always ready to
   help when needed; yet, never in the way.  Now that you've
   booted it up, you'll get to see for yourself just how powerful
   an ally you've got.

   You're now viewing the notepad....although it's much more than
   just a space on the screen to make notes.  You can perform




   F1-help F2-save F3-new file F4-import data F9-expand F10-contract  ScrollLock
```

Figure 3-5. SCROLL LOCK set and Notepad window moved vertically

Note that the arrow cursor keys are in different places on different keyboards. On the original IBM PC, they were overlaid on the numeric keypad. If your cursor arrow keys are in that position make sure that NUM LOCK has not been pressed before you use them, because when NUM LOCK is pressed those keys act as numeric rather than arrow keys. A NUM LOCK sign shows just to the left of the SCROLL LOCK sign on the command line when NUM LOCK is active.

As you move a window, it covers up new areas of the display and uncovers areas it had blocked. Information is not lost or damaged when it is covered by a window. Material that is blocked by a window reappears exactly as it was before when the window is moved to another area. Try moving the Notepad window up and down to see this happen.

When you are done moving the window, press SCROLL LOCK again to lock it into position.

Enlarging a Window

The most common change to make to the original Notepad window is to enlarge it so you can see more of the active notefile at one time. Press F9 and notice the changed command line at the bottom of the window (Figure 3-6). Nearly all of the options disappear. F1 is there for help, and the only other choice listed is F9, which takes the window out of Enlarge mode and back to its standard state.

To enlarge the window you use the cursor arrow keys. If the window is already against the bottom of the screen, press UP ARROW, and the top line of the window will move one line upward. If you move the Notepad window all the way to the top, you can fit 22 lines into the editing area, nearly a full screen. Twenty-two lines by 78 characters is the maximum size of the Notepad window.

When you're finished enlarging the window, press F9 or ESC to return to the standard mode.

Shrinking a Window

You can shrink a SideKick window by using the Contract mode. To do so press F10, and you'll see a menu on the command line that offers two choices: F1 for help or F10 to return to standard mode. Experiment with

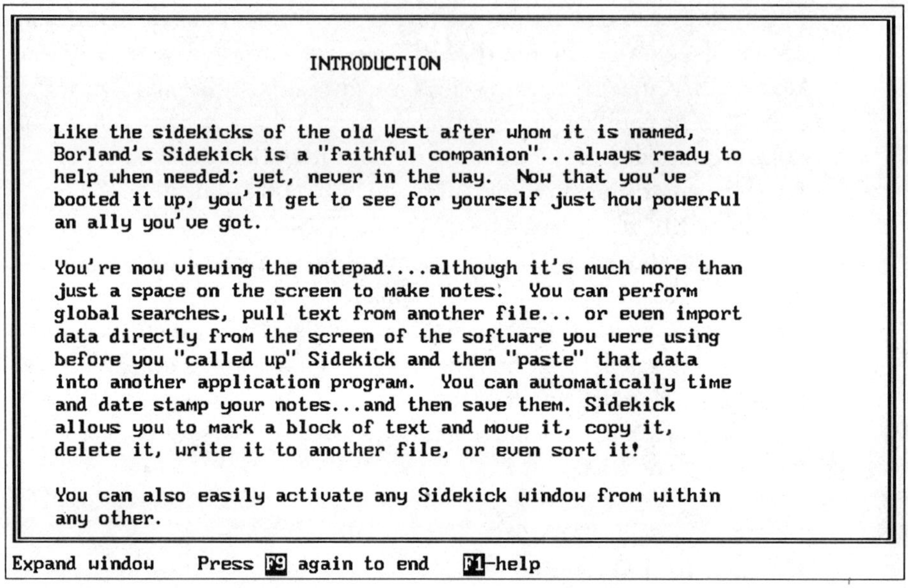

```
┌─────────────────────────────────────────────────────────────┐
│ ┌───────────────────────────────────────────────────────────┐ │
│ │                                                           │ │
│ │        INTRODUCTION                                       │ │
│ │                                                           │ │
│ │ Like the sidekicks of the old West after whom it is named,│ │
│ │ Borland's Sidekick is a "faithful companion"...always ready to│ │
│ │ help when needed; yet, never in the way.  Now that you've │ │
│ │ booted it up, you'll get to see for yourself just how powerful│ │
│ │ an ally you've got.                                       │ │
│ │                                                           │ │
│ │ You're now viewing the notepad....although it's much more than│ │
│ │ just a space on the screen to make notes.  You can perform│ │
│ │ global searches, pull text from another file... or even import│ │
│ │ data directly from the screen of the software you were using│ │
│ │ before you "called up" Sidekick and then "paste" that data│ │
│ │ into another application program.  You can automatically time│ │
│ │ and date stamp your notes...and then save them. Sidekick  │ │
│ │ allows you to mark a block of text and move it, copy it,  │ │
│ │ delete it, write it to another file, or even sort it!     │ │
│ │                                                           │ │
│ │ You can also easily activate any Sidekick window from within│ │
│ │ any other.                                                │ │
│ └───────────────────────────────────────────────────────────┘ │
│ Expand window    Press F9 again to end    F1-help              │
└─────────────────────────────────────────────────────────────┘
```

Figure 3-6.   Expanded Notepad window (maximum size)

the Contract mode by pressing the up- or the down-arrow cursor keys and then the right- or left-arrow cursor keys. You'll notice that the top and then the bottom line of the window move inward, collapsing the size of the central display area and uncovering some of the display that was underneath the window. When you press UP ARROW to move the bottom line of the window up, you'll notice that the command line stays at the bottom of the screen as shown in Figure 3-7. Figure 3-7 also illustrates the Notepad's minimum size: 3 lines by 40 characters.

Changing the Right Margin
Within the Notepad Window

There are two ways to choose a new right margin setting for text within the Notepad window: by using the Installation program or by using an editing command. The first method is described in "Changing the Right Margin" later in this chapter; the second is discussed briefly here, and covered more thoroughly in Chapter 4.

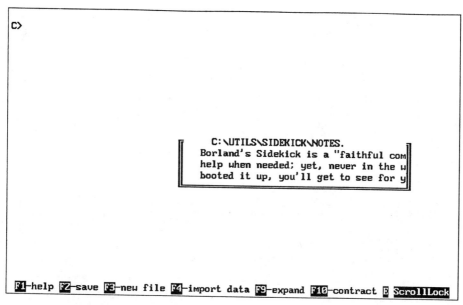

Figure 3-7. Contracted Notepad window (minimum size)

If you press CTRL-O-R, you'll be asked for a new right margin value. This value will be the column at which words that are too long to fit in the remaining space will *wrap,* or automatically move down to the next line in the Notepad window so that you don't need to press RETURN. The column can be any number from 1 to 250, but if it is larger than 78, your text will be too long for the window to accommodate, and will scroll horizontally before you reach the end of a line. If after setting a new margin you call the Setup window (using ALT-S from the Notepad) and press F3 or F4 to save your window setup, you'll also save the new margin setting.

Changing the Left Margin Within the Notepad Window

Early versions of SideKick didn't allow you to set a left margin, but that feature has been added to more recent versions. The left margin is a little different from the right margin, because it is not a *document-level* margin.

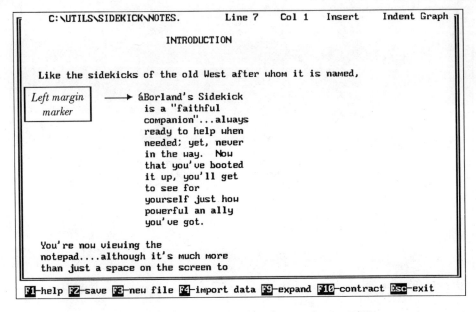

Figure 3-8.   Left margin marker displayed; right margin set at 40

It is a *paragraph-level* limit that applies to only one paragraph at a time.

The automatic setting for the left margin of any paragraph is column one. If you want a different left margin, place the cursor in the column where you want the left margin to be and press CTRL-P and the SPACEBAR. To start a new paragraph where the margin will return to column 1, just add a blank line.

To see where the left margin is, turn on the Graphics mode (described near the end of this chapter) by pressing CTRL-Q-G. The margin will be marked by ASCII character 160, which is a small "a" with an accent mark above it, as shown in Figure 3-8.

A Practical Example of Shifting
and Resizing the Notepad Window

Moving the window isn't merely for decoration. If you have a spreadsheet on your display before you bring up SideKick, and you want to write something about the information in that spreadsheet, it is handy to have at least part of the spreadsheet visible as you write. If you have a

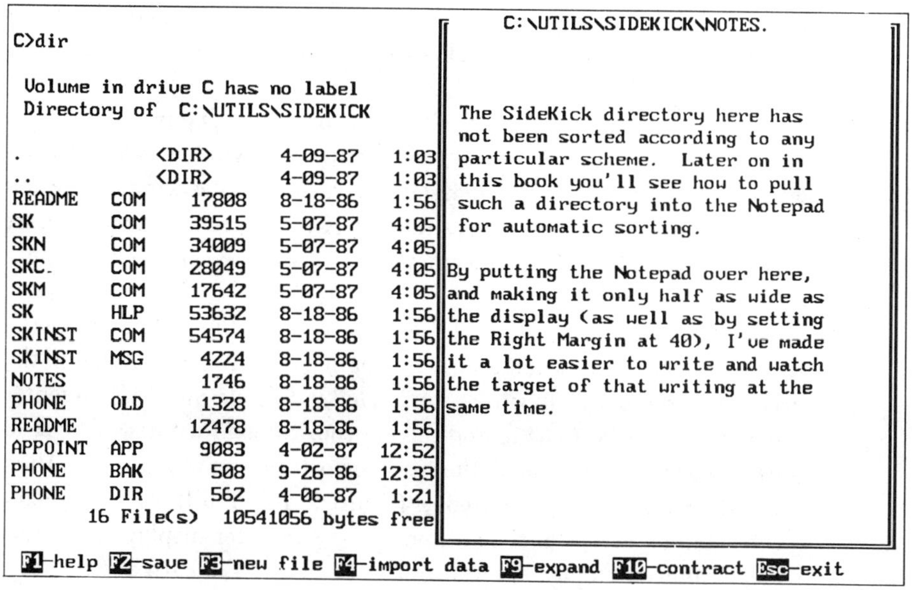

```
C>dir                                       C:\UTILS\SIDEKICK\NOTES.

  Volume in drive C has no label
  Directory of  C:\UTILS\SIDEKICK           The SideKick directory here has
                                            not been sorted according to any
.             <DIR>      4-09-87   1:03     particular scheme.  Later on in
..            <DIR>      4-09-87   1:03     this book you'll see how to pull
README   COM  17808      8-18-86   1:56     such a directory into the Notepad
SK       COM  39515      5-07-87   4:05     for automatic sorting.
SKN      COM  34009      5-07-87   4:05
SKC.     COM  28049      5-07-87   4:05     By putting the Notepad over here,
SKM      COM  17642      5-07-87   4:05     and making it only half as wide as
SK       HLP  53632      8-18-86   1:56     the display (as well as by setting
SKINST   COM  54574      8-18-86   1:56     the Right Margin at 40), I've made
SKINST   MSG   4224      8-18-86   1:56     it a lot easier to write and watch
NOTES          1746      8-18-86   1:56     the target of that writing at the
PHONE    OLD   1328      8-18-86   1:56     same time.
README        12478      8-18-86   1:56
APPOINT  APP   9083      4-02-87  12:52
PHONE    BAK    508      9-26-86  12:33
PHONE    DIR    562      4-06-87   1:21
      16 File(s)  10541056 bytes free

  F1-help F2-save F3-new file F4-import data F9-expand F10-contract Esc-exit
```

Figure 3-9. Practical example of changing window size and position

full-screen Notepad window, contract that window until it lets part of the spreadsheet show. If your Notepad window stretches across the bottom half of the screen, you'll be able to see the beginning part of your spreadsheet. If you need to see some details at the bottom of the spreadsheet, use SCROLL LOCK and move the half-screen Notepad window to the top of the screen. The bottom half of the spreadsheet display will be revealed, and your Notepad will still be available for writing or editing.

Or perhaps you have made a directory in DOS and want to write about it in SideKick. You can contract your Notepad window until it is only half the width of the screen, as shown in Figure 3-9. (In this case, to make editing easier and to avoid scrolling within the Notepad window, you'll probably want to keep the right margin at a low value.)

Saving Window Sizes and Positions

Once you change the position and size of your Notepad windows, they remain in the new setting until you turn off your computer or otherwise remove SideKick from RAM. If you use ESC or CTRL-ALT to leave SideKick temporarily, the windows will be as you left them when you return to SideKick.

If you want to save the new sizes and positions of your windows you can use the Setup option of the main menu. This window is specifically designed to help you save on disk such characteristics as window size and position. This operation changes the SideKick program so that the next time you load SideKick into memory, the new window positions reappear automatically.

Here's the procedure. Exit SideKick (using ALT-CTRL) and use the DOS DIR command to make sure the original SideKick program is in the drive and directory from which you loaded SideKick into RAM. Reenter SideKick (using ALT-CTRL) and reopen the Notepad window. Check to see that your window is set to the size and position you want to save. Then press ALT-S to get the Setup window (Figure 3-10). You'll see a new menu on the command line at the bottom of the computer display. With this window you can change the paste delay (which you'll learn about later), the file name, or the file's directory. You also can see the present setting for maximum size of the notefile. (This size can be changed with the SKINST program, which is described later in this chapter.) If you press either F3 or F4 at this point, your new window sizes and positions will be saved on the SideKick program file disk and can be used next time you load SideKick into RAM. If you don't want to save your window settings, just press ESC.

Choosing and Loading a File

The Notepad loads an entire notefile into RAM before working on it. (This system differs from many other word processors that load only part of a file into RAM, leaving the rest on disk.) Working directly from RAM makes SideKick a fast editor, and lets you take the notefile disk out of the drive while you are editing in the Notepad window. Unfortunately, this RAM scheme limits the length of your files to about 20 pages. Other word processing packages such as WordStar can handle files ten times that long; but they do not have the advantages of working directly from RAM.

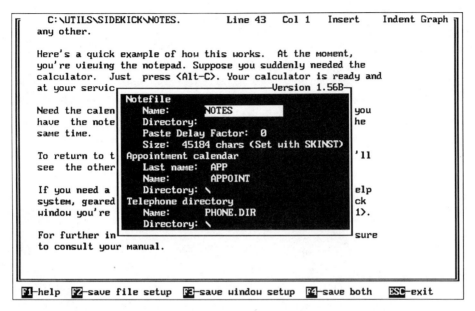

Figure 3-10. Setup window for saving Notepad window size and position

The scheme also puts your files at more risk, since any loss of power to your system will erase what's in RAM, therefore erasing the version of your notefile that is in RAM. Only the most recent version you have saved on disk will survive. Pressing F2 will save your work. This problem is easy to solve by regularly saving your work, a good policy when working with any word processing system.

Changing the Automatically-Loaded File

As mentioned, the first notefile automatically loaded into the Notepad window is typically called "Notes." If there is no Notes file, the Notepad opens an empty window and allows you to create a new Notes file.

You can change the name of the automatically-loaded Notes file by using the Setup window. The commands for this window follow.

F1 Help, as always in SideKick.

F2 Save File Setup. This command saves the names, directories, and paste delay setting that are currently in the Setup window. The values are changed in the SideKick main programs and become the standards the next time SideKick is loaded into RAM.

F3 Save Window Setup. This command saves the positions of all of the SideKick utility windows, the size of the Notepad window, and the right margin column value in the Notepad. The values are changed in the SideKick main programs and become the standards the next time SideKick is loaded into RAM.

F4 Save File and Window Setups. This key not only saves the names, directories, and paste delay setting (as does the F2 key), but it also saves the window positions, Notepad window size, and Notepad right margin (as does F3).

ESC Escape, or exit, from the situation. Press ESC to remove the Setup window from the screen.

Bring the Setup window to the screen by pressing ALT-S from the Notepad window. Use the arrow cursor keys to move the highlight to either the directory line or the file name line and type in the new directory and file you want automatically loaded into the Notepad. Press RETURN after typing the new names to make sure those names are recorded on the appropriate lines. Then, press F2 or F4 to save the new name and directory on the disk. The next time you load SideKick into memory and call up the Notepad, Setup will dictate which notefile is loaded automatically. If you use the F4 key you'll also save the current window positions and sizes for all of the SideKick utilities. It can't hurt to save these settings; if you don't like them next time, just change them again.

You can even arrange things so that SideKick automatically offers you a choice of files to be loaded if you use a DOS feature called *wildcards* on the name line.

Wildcard symbols act as variables in a file name. The question mark (?) indicates any single letter or legal character, while the asterisk (*) indicates any number of letters or legal characters up to the DOS-imposed limit of eight letters for the name and three for the extension. (The letters that correspond to the asterisk may not cross the period between file name and extension.) For example, entering *.TXT on the name line calls up a list of all files with a .TXT extension. When you activate the Notepad, you'll be shown a directory of all the file names that meet the wildcard criteria, and you can choose the file you want from that directory. Figure 3-11 is an example of such a directory.

Loading a New File

If you want to use a different file than the one already in the Notepad, press F3 (see the command line menu at the bottom of the screen). When

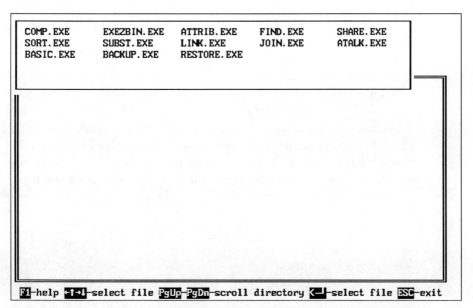

Figure 3-11.   Directory window for automatic file loading of Notepad

you do, you'll see the following prompt:

New Note File:

unless you have changed the notefile presently in the window without saving it. If you have, SideKick protects you from accidental data loss by asking:

Workfile b:*filename.ext* not saved. Save (Y/N)?

(The *filename.ext* position will show the name of the file currently in the window. If you press N, the file will be removed from memory. If you press Y the file will be saved to disk. If there is already a file with that name on the disk (as is likely if you have been working on the file), then the old file will be given the extension .BAK and the new file will be given the old extension.

Once you are confident that you won't lose your old file, you can load a new file by typing its name (including disk and directory) at the New File Name prompt and then pressing RETURN. (If you do not include disk and directory, the program will assume you mean the current disk drive.) Notice that the name of the active file is automatically inserted after the prompt, as soon as you press F3. If you type even one character at this point, that name disappears entirely. However, if you use BACK-SPACE, you can move back through the name and modify it.

If SideKick finds the named file you have chosen, it loads it into the RAM space for the Notepad and displays it within the window, with the top of the file on the top line of the window. The bigger the file, the longer it will take to load. If SideKick can't find the file you named in the specified directory (or on the current disk drive, if you don't specify a drive and directory) it starts a new, empty file and assigns it that name.

Viewing a Directory

If you are looking for a file that is on disk, and you can't remember its name, just type the drive and directory information at the New File Name prompt and press RETURN. You'll see a new, small window appear, which contains a list of the files in that drive and directory (see Figure 3-11).

There is a highlight at the top left corner of the window. To select a file from the list, use the arrow cursor keys to move the highlight until it is on the file name you want, then press RETURN. If the directory is too long to fit in the window, use PGDN and PGUP to move through the directory, which will be shown on consecutive window displays. All the commands for this directory search are shown in a small command line at the bottom of the directory window, as shown in Figure 3-11. Pressing ESC removes the directory window and returns you to your present notefile.

Using Wildcards

The DOS wildcard symbols (? and *) can be used after the New File Name prompt just as they can in the name line of the Setup window to get a focused list of files. For example, if you type **b: \catclub *.txt** at the New File Name prompt and then press RETURN, you'll see a list of only those files on drive B, in the Catclub directory, that have the extension .TXT.

This method of tailoring directory lists also works with the Notepad's Read File command, which is discussed in Chapter 4.

Changing Your Mind About
New File Command

If you choose the New File option, get the New File Name prompt, and then decide you don't want to change files yet, ESC cannot help you, but don't worry; two other methods can get you out of this situation. First, just press RETURN. You may have noticed that the New File Name prompt is followed automatically by the name of your current notefile. If you press RETURN, you'll simply reload that file from disk. If you saved your work just previous to the New File operation, you'll have to wait a bit for the file to load into RAM. Because of the safeguard mentioned earlier, where the program asks if you want to save a modified file before calling up a new one, this option is safe but slow. A faster method is to press CTRL-U, which will bring up the notice:

*** INTERRUPTED. Press <Esc>

When you press ESC, you'll return to your current notefile. (CTRL-U also works in some other tight situations, which you'll learn about later.)

Saving a File

Saving files comes logically after loading them, because knowing how to save a file is as vital to editing text as knowing how to brake is to driving an automobile.

There are five ways to save the text in your file: two are for use in all common situations; the other three ways are handy in an emergency, for example, if your system has crashed or for some reason is threatening to "dump" your notefile without letting you save it through normal channels.

F2

The first method for saving a file is to press F2. The file shown in the window is saved to disk with the drive, directory, and file name shown at the top left of the screen. While the computer is saving your file, you'll see a notice that reads

Saving *filename.ext*

replace the file name itself on the status line. The notefile in RAM is saved on disk, and any previous file with the same name is renamed *filename.bak*.

If you want to forgo .BAK files to save disk space, there is a special patch you can add to your SideKick program that eliminates the automatic .BAK process. See Appendix B for information on this and a number of other patches.

CTRL-K-D

The second method for saving a file is to press CTRL-K-D. This combination works the same as F2, but is easier to remember if you are used to WordStar commands. You'll hear a lot more about WordStar-style commands in Chapter 4. If you know WordStar, you'll be comfortable with these commands although some differ a bit from WordStar itself.

To use CTRL-K-D, press all three keys simultaneously, or press CTRL and K together, and then after releasing them, press D.

Write a Block

The third way to save a file is to use block commands to specify the entire file and then write that file under a new file name. This method is not as fast or as easy as the first two ways, but it does let you save a notefile to a new disk or directory without returning to DOS or going through lots of loading and unloading. To use this method, press CTRL-K-B or F7 to mark the beginning of the file, CTRL-K-K or F8 to mark the end, and CTRL-K-W to write the marked block to a new file. Then supply a new file name and press RETURN. (The section on block editing in Chapter 4 covers this procedure in detail.)

Hard Copy

Although it's usually important to save a file to disk, it is also useful in many instances to print a copy of the file to be kept as backup. To print a SideKick file, mark a block (with CTRL-K-B or F7 at the beginning and CTRL-K-K or F8 at the end) and press CTRL-K-P.

Cut and Paste

This last method saves only part of a file by pasting what is visible on the screen to some other application. Use the Block command described in Chapter 4 to outline a section of a SideKick file and then paste a copy of that section to another display. This technique can be used to save text from crashed SideKick applications and to move information out of SideKick, saving it elsewhere.

Changing the Notepad with the Installation Program

The SKINST.COM program is an installation program that lets you change screen colors, key commands, and many other features of Side-Kick. The parts of the program that affect the general setup and hardware compatibility of SideKick are described in Chapter 2. SKINST.COM can change three characteristics of the Notepad: the maximum file size, the right margin, and the editing commands.

Running SKINST

SKINST is not part of the main SideKick program. It is a separate
program that changes the settings of the SideKick main program.
SKINST does not stay in memory the way a TSR program like SideKick
does. SKINST only runs as a standard application.

To run SKINST, place SideKick in a drive. At the prompt for that
drive, type **skinst** and press RETURN. (You can perform this operation
whether or not SideKick is already in memory and active.) The display
shown in Figure 3-12 will appear. From this display you can choose
options by typing the significant letter from an option name. For
instance, to change the Notepad commands, type C; to change the right
margin type M.

Once you have chosen an option, you can make changes by following the on-screen instructions, which are discussed in the sections that
follow. When you've finished you'll return to this Installation menu, and
from here you press Q to quit the installation and return to the DOS
prompt.

```
              Installation program for SideKick 1.50

            Choose installation item from the following:

     Screen type | notepad Commands | Notepad size | right Margin

     Dialer      | cOlors           | Activate commands

              Enter S, C, N, M, D, O, A or Q to quit:
```

Figure 3-12.   SKINST.COM, the SideKick Installation program

You have installed new values into the main SideKick programs (SK.COM, SKC.COM, and so on). However, your changes will not affect the SideKick that is already in RAM. To see your changes, you will either have to remove SideKick from memory or reboot your computer and load SideKick from disk.

Notefile Size

Because SideKick keeps its active notefile in RAM, the computer needs to know ahead of time how much space to allow for it. The Notefile size setting is a maximum; you can load files smaller than the maximum, but you cannot load files that are larger than the limit. Once you have loaded SideKick into memory, notefile size is set in concrete. You can see what the limit is by checking the Setup window (Figure 3-13), but the only way to change the size limit is to run the Installation program and reload SideKick into memory (either by removing SideKick from memory with the CTRL-HOME-END command and then loading it again, or by turning

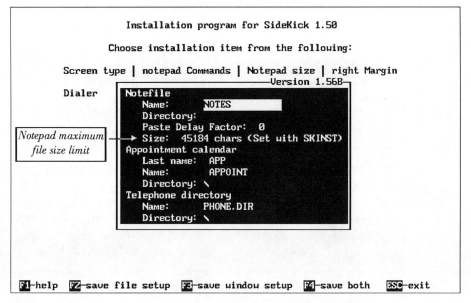

Figure 3-13.   Setup window display for checking notefile size limit

the computer off and starting from scratch). The original Notepad size setting is 4000 characters, which is about two pages of single-spaced text.

From the Installation program main menu, choose N. This message will appear:

"Size of notefile (1000 to 50000 characters, Return for no change):"

Just type the number of characters you want to use as a maximum for your file and press RETURN. The biggest number you can enter is 50,000; the smallest is 1000. If you don't want a new size, press RETURN to maintain the previous setting.

Choose the smallest size you think will fit your needs easily. The smaller the limit, the more RAM you'll have free after loading SideKick (more RAM always comes in handy). On the other hand, if you write a lot, you don't want to see the warning

"ERROR: Out of Space. Press <Esc>."

That message means you have to remove SideKick, install a larger notefile size, and reload it, or you have to use some other program to break your notefile into pieces. Even worse is to be working in the Notepad and suddenly see a warning such as that in Figure 3-14, where SideKick tells you that you're about to run out of RAM. In that position, SideKick keeps warning you as you clip away at the remaining several hundred characters of space. With so little RAM, the Notepad runs very slowly.

If you choose a 50,000-character limit, you won't actually be able to use that many characters with the regular SideKick Notepad; that is, if you load SideKick using the SK.COM program, you'll only be able to use about 45,000 characters. The SideKick program code itself and the notefile must all fit into 64K of RAM. The SK.COM version doesn't leave enough space for a full 50,000-character notefile. If you need that last 5000 characters, you can load the limited SKN.COM version, which leaves out the Calendar and has space for a full 50,000 characters.

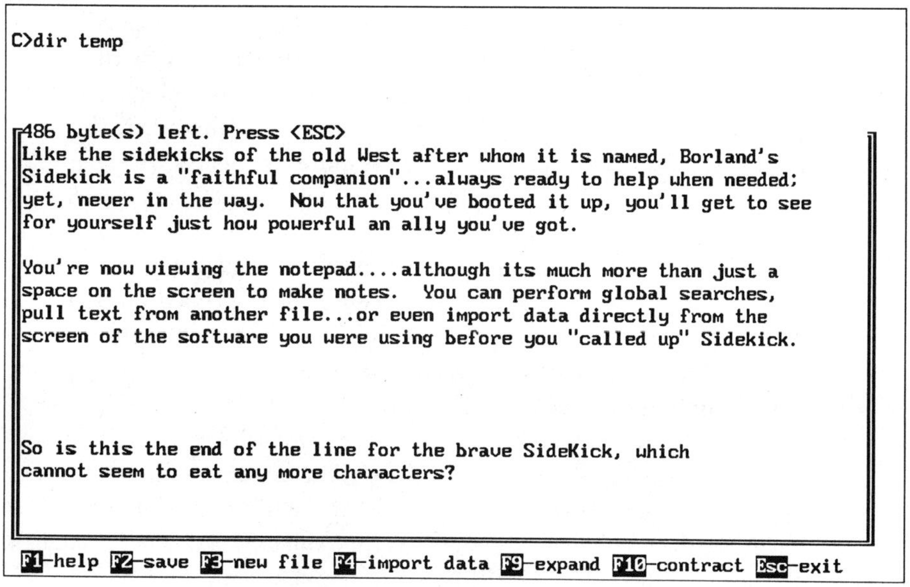

```
C>dir temp



486 byte(s) left. Press <ESC>
Like the sidekicks of the old West after whom it is named, Borland's
Sidekick is a "faithful companion"...always ready to help when needed;
yet, never in the way.  Now that you've booted it up, you'll get to see
for yourself just how powerful an ally you've got.

You're now viewing the notepad....although its much more than just a
space on the screen to make notes.  You can perform global searches,
pull text from another file...or even import data directly from the
screen of the software you were using before you "called up" Sidekick.




So is this the end of the line for the brave SideKick, which
cannot seem to eat any more characters?




F1-help F2-save F3-new file F4-import data F9-expand F10-contract Esc-exit
```

Figure 3-14.   Warning that notefile is approaching its maximum size limit

Changing the Right Margin

As mentioned previously, when you are entering text or editing a note-file, if you type enough characters on a single line, the words or characters at the end of the line will wrap to the next line. The word-wrap feature is common to most word processors. It saves the typist from having to hit RETURN at the end of each line. Changing the right margin changes the column at which words wrap as you enter text.

The Notepad's original right margin is set at 65 characters. If you choose the M option in the Installation program, you can enter a new right margin value of any number from 1 to 250. To set the new margin permanently, you must quit the installation procedure, remove Side-Kick, and reload it. If you decide not to change the right margin value, press RETURN to maintain the present value.

If you set the margin beyond the right side of the display screen, words will disappear off the right side of the screen. Moving the cursor toward the end of the line or typing characters beyond the edge of the screen causes the display to scroll horizontally. The characters that were on the far left of the display disappear as more characters are exposed on the right. When the line wraps, the scrolling automatically returns the cursor to the left margin of the file.

If you set the right margin to the maximum, 250 characters, word wrap won't work. SideKick can accommodate a maximum of 251 columns; when you come to that last column, you won't be able to enter another character. If this happens, you'll hear a beep indicating that you've run out of space.

Another way to change the right margin within the editor is by typing CTRL-O-R and entering the new right margin setting. To save a right margin set in this way, open the Setup menu window and press F3 or F4 to save the window setup. The next time you load SideKick from disk, the margin automatically will be set to the new value.

Changing Notepad Commands

Another thing you can change about the Notepad is the editing commands. (You probably won't want to do this until you have at least tried the built-in commands described in Chapter 4.) Most of the Notepad editing operations are executed by pressing certain keys or key combinations. These move the cursor, delete text, move text, and so on. There are two sets of editing commands: the primary set and the secondary set. Both sets are described in Chapter 4.

You can't change the secondary set, which copies the fundamental commands of WordStar and is compatible with the editor built into Borland's Turbo Pascal. These secondary commands are always available. But you can change the primary set. To do so, run the Installation program and press C. The display shown in Figure 3-15 will appear. One at a time, the Installation program displays the current commands and lets you select new combinations. (There are 53 commands, although some are alternate ways to perform the same function.)

Unfortunately, as you can see in Figure 3-15, the character sequence is somewhat confusing. Fortunately, you don't have to worry about reading those character sequences in the menu. Instead, simply

```
┌──────────────────────────────────────────────────────────────────┐
│              Installation program for SideKick 1.50                │
│                                                                    │
│            Choose installation item from the following:            │
│                                                                    │
│   Screen type | notepad Commands | Notepad size | right Margin     │
│                                                                    │
│       Dialer      | cOlors        | Activate commands              │
│                                                                    │
│                                                                    │
│              Enter S, C, N, M, D, O, A or Q to quit:               │
│                                                                    │
│                                                                    │
│                                                                    │
│                                                                    │
│ CURSOR MOVEMENTS:                                                  │
│                                                                    │
│   1:  Character left          <ESC> K  ->                          │
│   2:    Alternative           Nothing  ->                          │
│   3:  Character right         <ESC> M  ->                          │
│   4:  Word left               <ESC> s  ->                          │
│   5:  Word right              <ESC> t  ->                          │
│   6:  Line up                 <ESC> H  ->                          │
│   7:  Line down               <ESC> P  ->                          │
│   8:  Scroll up               Nothing  ->                          │
│   9:  Scroll down             Nothing  ->                          │
└──────────────────────────────────────────────────────────────────┘
```

Figure 3-15.   Using SKINST to change the keys for editing commands

decide what keys you want to press for an operation, and type those characters on the menu line. You can enter up to four key presses, including function keys. Then press RETURN.

As an alternative to typing the keys you want to use, you can type in ASCII values for the keys. Press ALT-A while in SideKick, and you'll see a complete, on-line chart of ASCII values and their equivalents, as is shown in Figure 3-16. (This chart is discussed in Chapter 7.) Type the ASCII values as numbers. If you type them in hexadecimal, put a dollar sign before each number. If there is to be more than one number at a time (up to four numbers), separate them by a space. Finally, press RETURN. Remember that you can't mix this ASCII entry method with the standard key press method on a single line for a single command.

Whichever method you use to change editing commands, you'll automatically move to the next line for possible alteration. If you don't want to change that command, press RETURN. To remove a command from the list, press the hyphen key. Press B if you want to go back in the list of possible changes. You can even jump from number 1 directly to number 53 at the end of the list, and then back through the list from

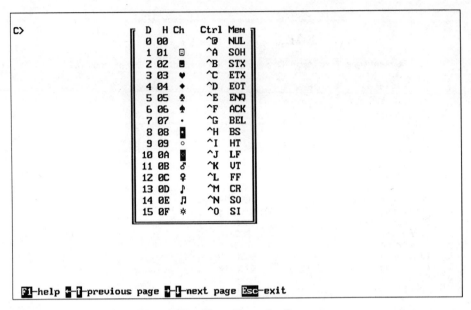

Figure 3-16. SideKick's ASCII table utility: the first page

there. If you define one of these primary commands with the same key sequence normally used by the secondary commands, the primary definition you have chosen will supersede the secondary command.

If you press RETURN after reaching the fifty-third line of the list, you return to the main Installation menu. If you're satisfied with your changes before that point, press Q to exit directly to the main Installation menu. Then press Q again to quit the Installation program. Your new commands will be implemented when you next load SideKick into RAM.

Editing Modes

The Notepad is primarily a "modeless" editor. That is, you can perform any of the editing functions at almost any point. However, there are some aspects of the Notepad's status that will affect your editing. Figure 3-17 shows the top right part of the status line, when the status of these few modes is indicated. The modes are explained here.

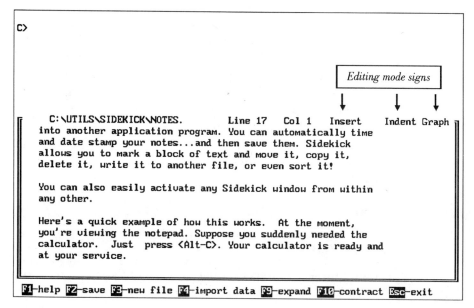

Figure 3-17.   Editing mode signs on status line

Text Mode Versus Graphics Mode

If the word "Graphics" appears near the right end of the status line above the Notepad window, the Notepad is in Graphics mode. Otherwise it is in Text mode. The characters used in Text mode are normally taken from a list of 128 ASCII codes. Each code is a 7-bit binary value. The complete ASCII list actually contains 256 codes of 8-bit values; the other 128 codes stand for graphics and foreign language characters. You can see the complete ASCII list by pressing ALT-A from the Notepad to access SideKick's on-line ASCII table.

SideKick normally works entirely in Text mode—the 128-character mode. But if you want to use the full 256-character set to work in a foreign language, work with graphics characters, reveal the left margin marker, see the high-order-bit marks left by a word processor such as WordStar, or for any other reason, you can switch SideKick into Graphics mode by pressing CTRL-Q-G. (Watch the "Graphics" sign appear on the status line.) Beware: Some manuals erroneously state that CTRL-O will activate the Graphics mode.

If you want to change your program permanently so that it automatically comes on with the Notepad in Graphics mode, use the patch for this purpose that is included in Appendix B. To enter the characters from the extended ASCII set, hold down ALT and type on the numeric keypad the decimal value of the character you want to see. (You can get this value from the ASCII table shown in Figure 3-16.) Figure 3-18 shows some graphics characters in a Notepad window.

If you're using an IBM AT or are working with an IBM PC or XT and SuperKey (or a similar keyboard program), you must press SHIFT-ALT instead of just ALT to enter extended ASCII characters.

Insert Mode Versus Overwrite Mode

If the word "Insert" appears near the right end of the status line above the Notepad window, then the Notepad is in Insert mode. Otherwise, the word "Overwrite" appears in that position. Insert mode causes newly entered characters to displace existing characters, pushing them further along the display. In Overwrite mode existing characters are obliterated when new characters are typed.

To switch between Insert and Overwrite, press INS or CTRL-V. (This procedure is reviewed in Chapter 4.)

Indent and Auto-indent

Another sign that normally appears on the status line is "Indent." When this sign is present, each new line begins in the column where the immediately previous line began. Although not as powerful as indenting features in most word processors, this automatic indent is very useful, especially in programming.

To turn Indent off, press CTRL-Q-I.

There are no real tabs in SideKick's Notepad, but Tab commands (either the TAB key or CTRL-I) work with Indent, returning the cursor to the same column on which previous text began. (If there is no text on the previous line, these commands will have no effect.)

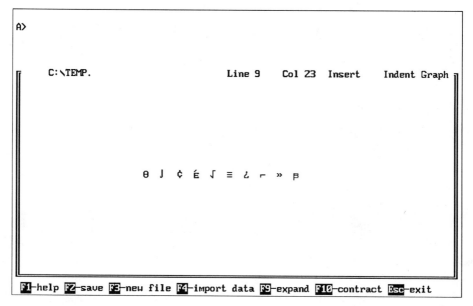

Figure 3-18.   Some characters from the extended ASCII set

Time and Date Stamping

You can customize SideKick so that it automatically inserts the time or date whenever you open a notefile. There are several ways to do this. Pressing either CTRL-Q-T or CTRL-Q-O takes the current date and time values from your computer's internal clock and inserts them into the Notepad window. The time is written in 24-hour military style and the date is written numerically in month/day/year format. Note that these values may be wrong if your system doesn't have a battery or if you don't enter the correct date and time when you start a work session.

Another way to get the time and date into your notefiles is to place the command .LOG at the beginning of each file. The period must be in column 1 of line 1, and the letters must be capitalized. Saving this command along with the notefile creates a LOG file. Thereafter, when

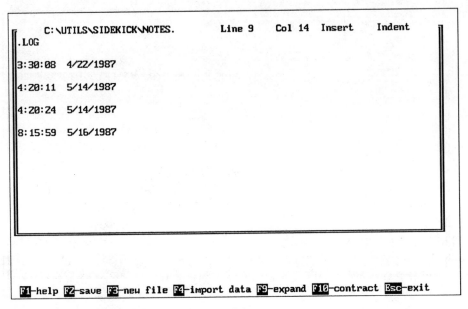

Figure 3-19.   .LOG file showing time and date stamps

you load that notefile into the Notepad window, SideKick leaps to the end of the file and automatically inserts the current time and date before accepting any other input (see Figure 3-19). This feature provides you with a complete record of the times you have entered and worked on a file.

4

The Notepad: Editing Commands

Chapter 3 thoroughly examined the Notepad's setup and installation: opening it, setting its window size and margins, choosing its text or graphics modes, and so on. Many of the commands and options mentioned can help you customize the Notepad for your own uses, but they aren't necessary if you just want to start writing notes or memos. This chapter describes the Notepad's editing commands.

WordStar-Style Commands

The Notepad has one main set of editing *functions*, but many of those functions can be executed by pressing either of two key combinations. One set of key commands uses the special function keys on the PC keyboard: the cursor arrow keys, HOME, END, PGUP, PGDN, INS, DEL, and so on. The other set uses combinations of CTRL plus other letter keys. For example, if you press CTRL and T at the same time, you'll delete the word in advance of the cursor's position.

These key combinations are "WordStar-like," that is, they follow the same key combinations first used by the classic WordStar word processing program. WordStar was one of the early, best-selling microcomputer word processing programs, and it largely depends on key combinations using CTRL. Other programs later included many of these commands because many users had learned them already and had gotten quick at using them. Although the WordStar combinations are more difficult to learn than the commands based on the special function keys and require some memorization for efficient use, they allow you to use the alphabetic keys, and so can be used at high speed by touch typists and other experienced users. The fundamental WordStar commands were included in the built-in editor of Turbo Pascal, Borland's first popular program, and they have been included in SideKick. Not all of the commands are the same in the three editors Turbo Pascal, WordStar, and SideKick, but the basics are nearly identical. If you have used Turbo Pascal or WordStar, you probably can get started editing without reading much more of this chapter. However, some of the Notepad's most powerful functions, such as pasting and importing text, are unavailable in WordStar or Turbo Pascal.

Opening and Exiting the Notepad

Once SideKick is loaded into memory, as described in Chapter 2, you can open the program's main menu by pressing ALT-CTRL or SHIFT-SHIFT. Then, you can open the Notepad window by pressing N or F2, as described in Chapter 3. To exit the Notepad, press ESC or ALT-CTRL or SHIFT-SHIFT. You also can use a command unique to the Notepad: CTRL-K-Q. (This is easy for WordStar users as it is also found in that program.)

Loading a File

The first time you start the Notepad, the Notepad window opens and a notefile called Notes is loaded. This file is on the SideKick disk. You can use the Installation program's Setup window to change which file loads automatically. You also can choose to open a new, empty file by pressing F3. (See Chapter 3 for more detail.)

Making a Practice File

Let's create a notefile that you can use to practice the editing commands described in this chapter. Here's how: load SideKick, activate it, and choose the Notepad (if you haven't done so already). Then press F3 to indicate that you want to open a new file. In response to this prompt:

New note file:

type **tempedit** and press RETURN. When the Notepad window reappears empty and lists your chosen working file at the top, press CTRL-K-R to "read" in a file. Type **notes** in answer to the prompt, and wait while your computer reads the Notes file into your Tempedit file.

Once it has been read, its contents appear inside the Notepad window, and the cursor is placed at the beginning of the file. The Notes file on the disk has not been disturbed by this reading process: a copy of the Notes file is created and placed in RAM for the active notefile.

Until you save the Tempedit file on the disk —complete with its Notes file text and any edits you add to that text —it won't appear on the disk directory. Now, save your notefile by pressing F2 or CTRL-K-D. Saving the file now prevents you from having to remake it later if it accidentally gets lost.

Now, enlarge the Notepad window so you can see as much of it as possible on the screen. To enlarge the window, press F9 and then repeatedly press UP ARROW until the Notepad window fills the screen. When you're done, press F9 again.

Your practice file contains text that Borland uses to introduce SideKick.

Editing Help

The rest of this chapter describes the commands you use to enter, move, and delete text within a notefile. Remember that at any point you can press F1 to view helpful information about what options and commands are available. Also, most of the commands described in this chapter are listed on the command card included with this book.

Adding Blank Lines

Let's make some more space before adding new text. To do so, insert three or four blank lines at the top of the Notepad window, pushing the Notes text down the window. You can add blank lines in a number of ways, but two simple methods are to press RETURN or CTRL-N. Using UP ARROW, move the cursor to the top of the text in the window. Then press RETURN to move the cursor down one line and press repeatedly to insert blank lines. CTRL-N leaves the cursor in the same position but adds one blank line beneath the cursor.

Adding Text

As you've seen, pressing CTRL-K-R reads files into the Notepad. After pressing CTRL-K-R, all you have to do is name the file you want to read in from the disk and then press RETURN.

Of course, you also can add text by typing. Try adding some text on the top line of the file —where your cursor already sits —by typing **This is a line of new text**. You don't need to press RETURN. The new text appears on that first line, with the cursor at the end. The line (Line) and column (Col) number indicators at the top of the window change as the cursor moves. If you continue to type the words **and I wonder when it will wrap to the next line**, all of your words that run past the original 65-column right margin setting wrap to the next line. You don't have to press RETURN. This *word wrap* is a common feature of word processors. If you wish, you can change the right margin by pressing CTRL-O-R, as discussed in Chapter 3. After pressing the key combination, type in the new right margin column number you want to use and then press RETURN.

The Insert Mode

Press UP ARROW to move the cursor to the first line of the Notepad window. If you then type **some more words**, they are inserted into the previous text as shown in Figure 4-1. Already typed characters are not deleted, they are moved to the right.

The text enters the Notepad window via the Insert mode. This is signaled by the word Insert at the top right of the screen. Press CTRL-V or INS (insert) to switch to the Overwrite mode, which is discussed shortly. Press CTRL-V or INS again to return to the Insert mode, and so on. When opening the Notepad, SideKick always defaults to the Insert mode.

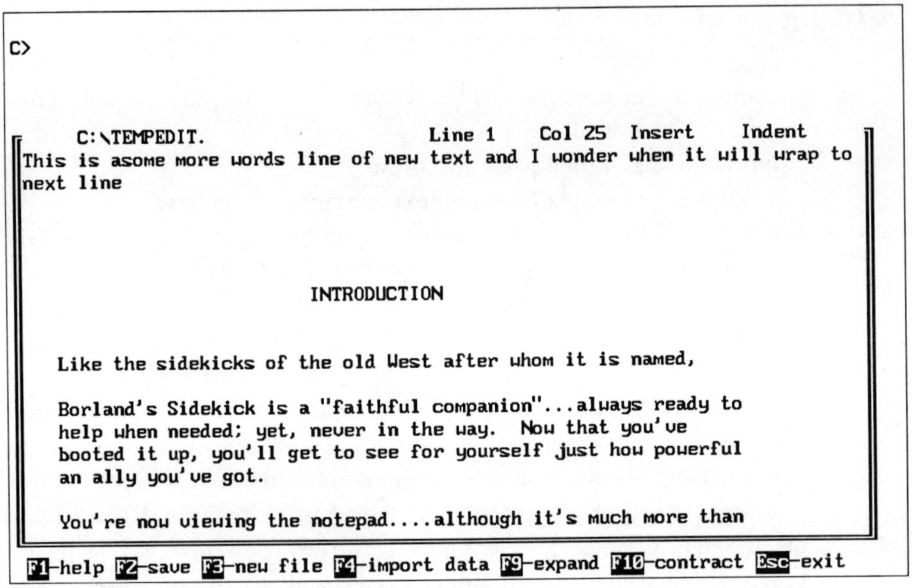

```
C>



    C:\TEMPEDIT.                    Line 1    Col 25  Insert    Indent
 This is asome more words line of new text and I wonder when it will wrap to
 next line




        INTRODUCTION


 Like the sidekicks of the old West after whom it is named,

 Borland's Sidekick is a "faithful companion"...always ready to
 help when needed; yet, never in the way.  Now that you've
 booted it up, you'll get to see for yourself just how powerful
 an ally you've got.

 You're now viewing the notepad....although it's much more than
```

F1-help F2-save F3-new file F4-import data F9-expand F10-contract Esc-exit

Figure 4-1. Notefile displaying inserted text

A Word About Reformatting Text

Word wrap is controlled by the right margin: any word that extends beyond the right margin is wrapped down to the next line and the text continues from that point. Although wrapping occurs automatically when you type beyond the end of a line, it doesn't occur automatically when you are editing in the middle of a line. For example, in Figure 4-1, the text that was pushed beyond the right margin didn't wrap automatically to the next line. To make it wrap, you must press CTRL-B. This reformatting affects all lines until a blank line is reached. After editing, you must reformat your paragraphs to fit within the margins. Unfortunately, you must issue a new CTRL-B command at the beginning of each paragraph. There is no global command to reformat the entire document.

However, it is easy to let the reformatting go too far. If you forget to put blank space between your paragraphs or if you make a long list of items with no blank line between each line (Figure 4-2), your reformatting will string the work together into a single paragraph (Figure 4-3). If you have a long file, reformatting may take some time. To interrupt reformatting, press CTRL-U and then ESC.

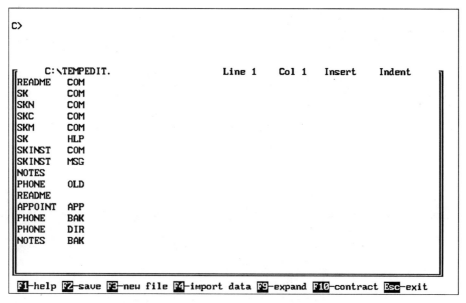

Figure 4-2.   Notefile before reformatting

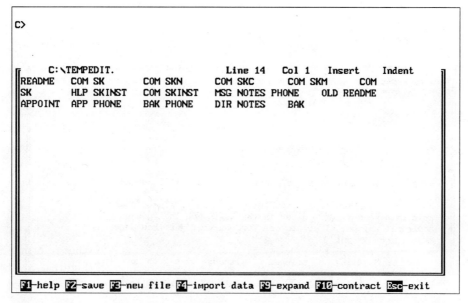

Figure 4-3.   Notefile after reformatting

A Word About Space

Remember, even blank space is considered text. When you press SPACE BAR you're entering a "space character." However, there are other spaces on the screen, such as those to the right of the right margin marker, that truly contain no text or space characters. SideKick clips off all trailing space to save room in memory. That is, although some word processors let you pad the ends of lines with space characters, SideKick cuts these off to leave a truly blank space.

The Overwrite Mode

Press CTRL-V or INS to switch to the Overwrite mode. The word Overwrite then appears at the top right of the screen.

Now switch to the Overwrite mode and type **a few more words**. The new text is entered in the place of previous text of the same length, and the old text is deleted permanently (Figure 4-4).

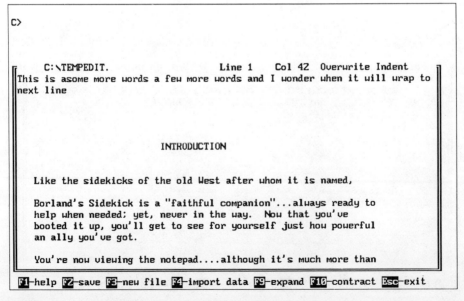

Figure 4-4.   Notefile displaying "overwritten" text

Deleting Text

Overwriting is only one way to eliminate text. There are also a variety of other deletion commands, which are described in the following sections.

Deleting Characters

From your current cursor position, try pressing DEL (delete). Each time you press DEL, the character on which the cursor sits disappears and characters to the right move in to fill the gap. CTRL-G, borrowed from WordStar, deletes characters in the same way as DEL.

Pressing BACKSPACE plays a similar single-character deletion role, but it moves the cursor to the left and erases the character on which it lands.

Deleting Words

You can delete an entire word to the right of the cursor by pressing CTRL-T. Try it a couple of times. This deletion also rearranges the rest of the file, which moves in to fill the gap left by the deleted word. The Notepad defines word boundaries by a space between characters or by many of the common punctuation marks. For example, Notepad treats a blank line as a word for this command: if you go to the end of a line that is followed by a blank line and press CTRL-T, you delete the blank line.

Deleting Lines

If you type CTRL-Q-Y you delete all of the text to the right of the cursor on the cursor's line. Try that now. You also can delete the entire line by pressing CTRL-Y. Press this a couple of times to delete all of the text you typed into Tempedit.

Deleting a Block

Finally, you can delete an entire block of text by marking the beginning and end of the block and then pressing the block delete command. Block delete is described in the section "Block Operations."

Undeleting or Restoring a Line

It's easy to delete something and then suddenly regret the deletion. In some cases you can restore what you deleted by pressing CTRL-Q-L. Type the first few lines of this paragraph into your Notepad. Then press UP ARROW once to move to a previous line. On that line, press CTRL-T twice and type the word **change**. You've modified the line. Now, if you press CTRL-Q-L, the line returns to its initial state, before you pressed UP ARROW. Any changes you make to a line can be reversed in this manner unless you leave the line. Once you leave the line, you cannot use the restoration command to return your original text.

Note: CTRL-Y completely eliminates a line and therefore automatically moves the cursor to a new line. Thus, you cannot use the restoration command after pressing CTRL-Y.

Moving the Cursor

In previous paragraphs we have pressed UP ARROW to move the cursor up on-line within the Notepad window. There are also many other cursor movement commands. SideKick's Notepad offers two sets of commands for moving the cursor: one using the arrow keys and the other using key combinations borrowed from WordStar. These commands are described in this section.

Arrow Keys

Within the Notepad, you can move the cursor by pressing UP ARROW, DOWN ARROW, LEFT ARROW, and RIGHT ARROW. These keys are typically found on the right side of the keyboard on either the numeric keypad or a separate keypad next to the numerals. Pressing any one of the cursor arrow keys moves the cursor one line (up or down) or one character (right or left) in the direction the arrow indicates.

The cursor cannot be moved to the bottom line of text within a window. Instead, the lines on the screen scroll up one position, letting the cursor move down a line and yet remain within the visible Notepad window.

For longer moves, you can use PGUP, PGDN, HOME, and END. PGUP and PGDN move your cursor a full page at a time, either up or down, within the text. The actual number of lines the cursor moves depends on the size of the Notepad window. A page is considered the number of lines that can appear in a given Notepad window. For example, a PGUP command in the minimum window size of 3 lines by 40 characters would move up the cursor only three lines at a time; if the window were 22 lines by 80 characters, the cursor would move up 22 lines.

Pressing HOME returns the cursor to the beginning —column 1— of the line it is already on. Pressing END moves the cursor to just after the last character in the line it is already on.

Pressing CTRL-RIGHT-ARROW moves the cursor one word to the right, with a word defined as a sequence of characters ending with a space or punctuation mark. CTRL-LEFT-ARROW moves the cursor left one word at a time.

CTRL-HOME moves the cursor to the top of the visible page, keeping it in the same column it is already in. Pressing CTRL-END moves the cursor to the bottom of the visible page, also keeping it in the same column it is already in.

CTRL-PGUP moves the cursor to the first column position at the top of the current file. CTRL-PGDN moves the cursor to the last occupied column position at the end of the file.

Tabs

The Notepad does not offer standard tabs. Instead, you generally have to add spaces with the SPACE BAR, such as at the beginning of a line. In some situations, however, the Auto-indent mode can do this for you automatically. Press CTRL-Q-T to activate the Indent mode (as described in Chapter 3). The word "Indent" then appears on the Notepad's status line, and the indentation of the current line is repeated on following lines until there is a blank line. An example is shown in Figure 4-5. Reformatting with CTRL-B aligns text with a uniform indent until the end of a paragraph.

If you are on the line following a line with an indent, press TAB or CTRL-I to move the beginning of the new line to the same beginning column as the line above.

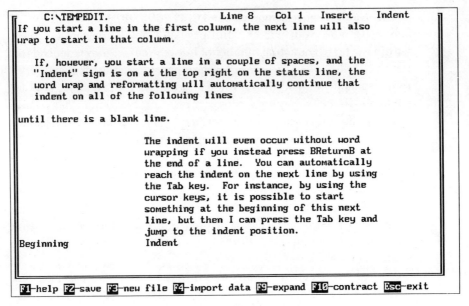

Figure 4-5. Example of automatic indenting

Sometimes if you read a file with tabs into the Notepad the tabs appear as highlight "I" characters. If you replace the "I"s with spaces, you can use the Find-and-Replace command to search out the highlight "I"s and replace them with a series of spaces.

WordStar-Style Cursor Commands: "Diamond" for Short Moves

The heart of the WordStar key commands is the WordStar "diamond," so named because its central keys are arranged in a rough diamond pattern. The position of the four major keys of the WordStar diamond is meant to relate directly to the cursor movement direction. Pressing CTRL-E moves the cursor up one line; pressing CTRL-X moves the cursor down one line. Pressing CTRL-D and CTRL-S, respectively, moves the cursor a single character position to the right or left.

The next level of the WordStar diamond, just outside the previously mentioned commands, lets you move a full word at a time, instead of a character at a time. Pressing CTRL-F moves the cursor one word to the right; pressing CTRL-A moves the cursor one word to the left. (The cursor moves to the beginning character of the word.) A word is defined as a set of characters that begins or ends with one of the following characters:

$$<>,;.()^{\wedge}{}'{*}{+}{-}\$$$

The cursor can move up or down one line if you move left from the first word or right from the last word in a line. The cursor also can pass over a blank section on the screen to the next section of text.

CTRL-W is next to CTRL-E and offers a similar function, although, instead of moving the cursor within the text, this command moves the text within the window. The cursor remains in the same position, and the window moves up one line (or the text scrolls down one line, depending on your point of view). Pressing CTRL-Z scrolls the Notepad window in the opposite direction. These moves occur regardless of the cursor position in the window.

More WordStar-Style Cursor Commands: Long-Distance Moves

Rounding out this second layer of the WordStar diamond are CTRL-R and CTRL-C. Pressing CTRL-R moves you up a page (the same as PGUP). Pressing CTRL-C moves you down a page (the same as PGDN).

There are also some WordStar-style commands that require a three-key combination, where you must press CTRL-Q and then another key. Try experimenting with these commands. Once you learn them, they are much faster than using the arrow and special function keys.

These three-key commands can move the cursor quite a few positions at a time. Pressing CTRL-Q-S moves the cursor to the beginning of the line it is in. Pressing CTRL-Q-D moves it to the end; the end is defined here as the position just to the right of the last character. (As mentioned earlier, SideKick always strips out trailing blanks to save space in storing the files.) Both CTRL-Q-S and CTRL-Q-D simulate the action of repeated CTRL-S or CTRL-D commands.

Some of these three-key commands relate to HOME and END. Pressing CTRL-Q-E moves the cursor to the same column position at the top of the window, and pressing CTRL-Q-X moves the cursor to the same column position at the bottom, just as CTRL-HOME and CTRL-END would do.

Pressing CTRL-Q-R moves the cursor to the beginning of the file, just as CTRL-PGUP would do. Pressing CTRL-Q-C moves the cursor to the end of the file, just as CTRL-PGDN would do.

Pressing CTRL-Q-P moves the cursor to its previous position. This command is handy after a long find-and-replace operation or a similar function where you might lose your place in the file.

Fast Moves to Markers

The last four commands described here don't fit in easily with the others because they move the cursor farther and in more specific ways. Pressing CTRL-Q-B moves the cursor to the *block beginning marker* (which is entered in the file by CTRL-K-B). Pressing CTRL-Q-K moves the cursor to the *block end marker* (which is entered in the file by CTRL-K-K). Block editing is explained in more detail in the next section.

Although these commands sometimes are called "move to beginning of block" and "move to end of block," both block limits don't have to be set to use either command. Also, it doesn't matter if the block is hidden or displayed. Some people just use these commands as temporary bookmarks in a file. If you're at one position and want to scroll through the file, and then return to the original position, just press CTRL-K-B to set the beginning marker and then scroll away. When you're ready to return, press CTRL-Q-B. The beginning and end markers give you two place holders that you can use at any one time.

Block Operations

If you could work on only one word or one line at a time, editing would take forever. Some editors lead this sort of restricted life. Not SideKick's Notepad. Like WordStar and other word processing software, the Notepad has *block* commands that let you mark a block of text and then manipulate that text all at once. You can read, write, delete, move, copy, print, and even sort blocks. Remember, you can abort any block operation by pressing CTRL-U.

Reading a Block

The SideKick manual refers to the "Read Block from Disk" command. Actually, this command — CTRL-K-R — reads an entire file from the disk. After you press CTRL-K-R, you type the name of the file you want to read. If you use wildcard symbols, a small file directory window appears from which you can choose a file (use the cursor arrow keys and then press RETURN). The entire file is then inserted into your Notepad window, starting at the cursor's present position. It appears "highlighted," and it is treated as a marked block of text until you unmark it. (All other block operations require that you first mark a block, then specify the operation. Block marking is described in the next section.)

If you read a block that contains lines too long for the Notepad — lines that extend beyond the 255-column limit — the warning

Line too long — CR inserted. Press <Esc>

is displayed. Here you must press ESC to continue editing.

Marking a Block

Marking the section of the file you want to manipulate is the first step in block editing. Move the cursor to the beginning of the section you want to mark and press CTRL-K-B or F7. The beginning marker is not visible. The beginning of your block includes the character the cursor was on when you pressed CTRL-K-B. Then move the cursor to the end of the section you want to mark and press CTRL-K-K or F8. The end marker also is not a visible marker. The end of the section is the character just to the left of the cursor when you pressed CTRL-K-K. The block section consists of all of the information between the two markers: everything to the right of the beginning marker on its line, the lines in between, and everything to the left of the end marker on its line. The marked block appears in highlight or color, depending on the type of display you're using.

You also can mark a single word at a time by pressing CTRL-K-T. The word the cursor is within is marked; or if the cursor isn't within a word, the word to the left of the cursor is marked.

Once a block is marked, you can "hide" the marking by pressing CTRL-K-H. The highlight or color then disappears. But the marking is not forgotten — press CTRL-K-H again to "display" the marked block.

The block manipulation commands — copy, move, delete, write, and print — only can be used on a displayed, marked block. You can mark only one block at a time in a file. The marking remains if you exit the Notepad window and then return.

Deleting a Block

The simplest manipulation of a marked block is to delete it. Once you have marked a block and displayed it with the highlight apparent, press CTRL-K-Y. The marked block disappears, even if another part of the file is shown in the window. The deletion does not leave behind blank lines; the text beneath or after the marked block moves up to fill the gap, shortening the entire file. Block deletions are not reversible.

Writing a Block

You also can write a marked block — that is, you can create a new disk file of the block's text. Just mark the block and press CTRL-K-W. The following prompt appears:

Write block to file:

which asks you to assign a file name to the block. Type in a file name and press RETURN. If there is already a file with that name on the disk, the warning

Overwrite old "filename" (Y/N)?

appears. If you press N, the original prompt returns and again asks you for a new file name. If you press Y, the old contents of the file are eliminated, and the file now contains only the marked block's text. You cannot interrupt this prompt with CTRL-U: you must choose Y or N. You can interrupt the "Write block to file" prompt by pressing CTRL-U.

After writing the new file to the disk, the marked block remains in the Notepad. The disk file just contains a copy of the block.

Sometimes when you try to write a file, you may see a warning that the disk is full. This could be true, but it may just be that you've tried to use an illegal disk drive, path, or file name. Check them and try again.

Copying a Block

Once you have marked a block, you can make another copy of the block within the Notepad window. Just move the cursor to the position where you want the copy of the block to be and press CTRL-K-C. The new copy will be inserted into the file beginning at the cursor's position. The new copy also becomes the marked block; the original block loses its markings.

Moving a Block

Once you have marked a block, you can move it to another position within the Notepad window. Just move the cursor to the position where you want the block to be and press CTRL-K-V. The block is moved from its old position, which is filled in by the succeeding text just as if it were deleted, and then is inserted into the file beginning at the cursor's position. The moved block remains marked.

Printing a Block

You can direct your printer to print a copy of a marked block by pressing CTRL-K-P. If you use this command when no block has been marked and displayed, the entire file is printed. You can insert control characters to format the printed copy. Printing is discussed in the section called "Printing a File."

Pasting a Block

Pasting a block stands somewhat apart from other block operations, and it is one of the most important features of the Notepad. You can *paste* a marked block from the Notepad into another window or application —

which is a key element in SideKick's ability to work with, and not just alongside, other programs.

Pasting a block is different from writing a block to a disk. When you write, you are creating a file on disk, a file that contains the block's text. But when you paste, you can copy a marked block and inject that marked block directly into the file of another program, such as a communications program, a word processor, or a spreadsheet. You mark the block, assign it to a single key, and then use that key to paste or write the entire block, whether or not you are in SideKick. The Calculator utility also has a Paste feature, but it only allows you to paste a single number. The block you paste with the Notepad's feature can be many lines long.

Choosing the Paste Key

To paste a block, you first must mark a block. Just move the cursor to the beginning of the block and press CTRL-K-B, then move the cursor to the end of the block and press CTRL-K-K. The block becomes highlighted. Then, press CTRL-K-E. The following prompt then appears:

Press the key to paste with:

Answer this prompt by pressing the key you want to assign the block to. You have 40 possibilities: you can use any of the programmable function keys (F1 through F10) or any of those keys in combination with SHIFT, CTRL, or ALT. Also, you can press ALT simultaneously with any other key on the keyboard.

Block or Line Mode

Once you answer the preceding prompt with your key assignment, the prompt

Block or Line mode (B/L):

appears. You must press either B or L. If you press B, you are choosing the Block mode, which pastes the entire marked block at once. After you make this choice, whenever you press your assigned paste key, the block

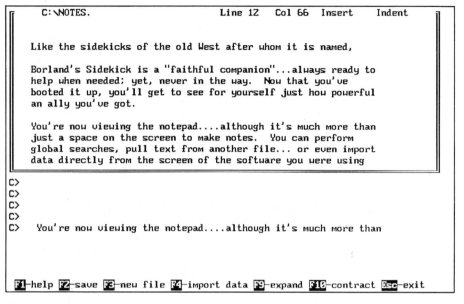

Figure 4-6.   Example of block pasting

writes quickly to wherever you have the cursor positioned. The pasting won't stop until all of the characters have been pasted. Figure 4-6 shows an example of a block paste.

On the other hand, if you press L in response to the prompt, you are choosing the Line mode, which pastes the marked block a single line at a time. At the end of the pasted line, SideKick will not send a CR (carriage return) control character, which means it won't automatically return the cursor to the beginning of the next line.

In the Line mode, each time you press the assigned Paste key, one line of the marked block is written to the cursor's position. The first time you press the assigned key, the first line of the block is pasted; the second time, the second line is pasted; and so on until all of the lines have been pasted or until you choose not to paste any more of the block.

When you use the Line mode, you should mark your block by placing the cursor at the end of the final line of the text, instead of at the beginning of the next line. If you place the cursor at the beginning of the next line, a blank line is pasted at the end of the paste operation.

Repeated Pasting
of the Same Marked Block

When you have pasted the entire block using either Block mode or Line mode, you still can continue to paste. In the Block mode, pressing the Paste key again pastes another complete copy of the block. Pressing the Paste key again in the Line mode pastes another copy of the first line; press it again, and the second line is pasted again; and so on.

Pasting of Multiple Blocks

An assigned Paste key only works if a block is marked and displayed, not hidden. If the block is deleted or hidden, the Paste key cannot paste anything. *If you mark a new block in Notepad, that new block still is pasted with the previously assigned Paste key.* The key is not assigned to a specific block — it is simply the official Paste key for any marked block in the Notepad window.

Paste Limits

The Paste key function takes precedence over other SideKick functions. In other words, if your chosen Paste key has another SideKick function, it is superseded while the paste assignment is in effect. Thus, you must choose a key or key combination carefully, opting for one that you won't want to use for anything else. Also, you can assign only one Paste key at a time, as discussed previously. And you cannot paste a block within the Notepad: use the block copy command CTRL-K-C to copy a block.

The Block mode is clearly the fastest way to paste text, and it works fine when pasting to most word processors. However, if you're using an application such as a spreadsheet, you should use the Line mode, which does not try to force a return to the beginning of a new line (something the spreadsheet may not immediately understand).

Finally, some programs cannot accept the pasted information as fast as SideKick can send it. Don't worry. SideKick has an adjustment that lets it work with just about any program, which is discussed in the next section.

Paste Delay

SideKick can paste characters at a rate of nearly 1000 characters per second. Some programs cannot accept characters that quickly, as just mentioned. When they can't take them in, the program may beep an error message to you, and it even may lose some characters. To solve this problem, you can slow down SideKick's transmission. The Notepad only pastes after checking the *Paste delay* factor in the Setup window. The Paste delay is the time SideKick waits after sending each character. Figure 4-7 illustrates the Setup window with the default Paste delay of 0. The default Paste delay works with many programs; but if you're having trouble, try moving the cursor to the Paste delay line in the Setup window, type **2**, press RETURN, and press F3 or F4 to save the new value to disk. Then try pasting again. If it still doesn't work, increase the delay.

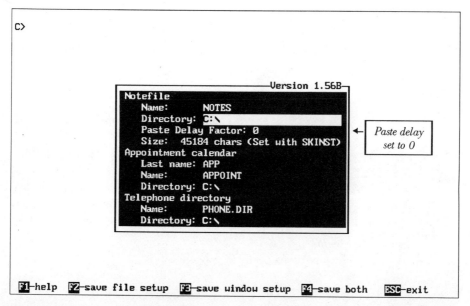

Figure 4-7. Setup window showing the Paste delay factor line, here set to the default Paste delay factor of zero

Most troublesome programs can function when given a Paste delay factor between 3 and 10. You can set the factor as high as 99, but the greater the number, the slower your pastes — so you should start low and climb until you reach a minimum value that works. Use your adjusted Paste delay factor for all of your pasting to all programs, unless it is just too slow for the easily pasted occasions. Note: the actual delay time caused by a certain delay factor is not always the same. It depends on the program you're pasting to.

Deleting a Paste Key

This is known as "Remove Paste" in the SideKick manual. If you don't like your Paste key assignment, or if you need to reassign your Paste key for any reason, you can delete the assignment by pressing CTRL-K-E-DEL. (You can press all four keys simultaneously, or you can press CTRL and while holding it down press K, E, and DEL in sequence.) The only other way to delete a Paste key is to make a new Paste key assignment to some other key.

Importing Data

The ability to import data is another vital feature of SideKick's Notepad. The Import Data feature can be combined with the Paste feature to *cut and paste* information between two outside programs. The Import Data function lets you move text from one activated display on the screen and copy it into a Notepad notefile. Although SideKick cannot capture graphics, only characters, this feature allows you to share information between two programs that otherwise might not be on any sort of "speaking" terms.

The following steps perform this operation:

1.   Open the Notepad window.

2.   Move the cursor to where you want the imported data to start. (You can do this after finding and clipping the text to be imported, using the following steps, but it is helpful to decide ahead of time where you want to put it.)

3.   Press F4.

4.   The Notepad window then vanishes, leaving you a view of the display underneath. Imagine that a rectangle contains the display text you want to import.

5.   Use the Notepad's cursor movement commands to move the cursor to the top left corner of that rectangle and press CTRL-K-B.

6.   Then move the cursor to the bottom right corner of the rectangle and press CTRL-K-K. The Notepad window now reappears.

7.   Make sure the cursor is positioned where you want the imported text to start and press CTRL-K-C. The Notepad window briefly disappears, and you'll see the cursor scurry through the other display, copying the text you zoned off. The Notepad window then reappears, and a copy of the text is inserted at the cursor's location.

Notice that the block marking and copying commands are the same as those used to mark and copy text within a single notefile.

Example of Importing

For instance, you run the directory of a certain DOS disk and then want to include that directory in a note you're writing to explain which files are your most recent ones. In DOS, type **dir** to call up the drive and directory you want to inspect. Then use CTRL-ALT to bring up SideKick. Press ALT-N to open the Notepad window, presumably a notefile you're already working with. Move the cursor in the Notepad window to the point at which you want to include the DOS directory information. Then press F4. As the menu notes, this function key is for "import data." The Notepad display then disappears, returning you to the DOS directory display. Use the SideKick cursor command keys to move the cursor to the top left corner of the data you want to capture. Then press CTRL-K-B, just as if you were marking a block within a SideKick file. Use the cursor command keys again to move the cursor to the bottom right corner of the section you want and press CTRL-K-R or ESC to mark the end of the block.

```
      C:\TEMPEDIT.                  Line 2    Col 1    Insert    Indent

README    COM    17808    8-18-86    1:56p
SK        COM    39515    6-02-87    8:52a
SKN       COM    34009    5-27-87   11:26a
SKC       COM    28049    5-27-87   11:26a
SKM       COM    17642    5-27-87   11:26a
SK        HLP    53632    8-18-86    1:56p
SKINST    COM    54574    8-18-86    1:56p
SKINST    MSG     4224    8-18-86    1:56p
NOTES            1747     6-02-87    8:29a
PHONE     OLD     1328    8-18-86    1:56p
README          12478     8-18-86    1:56p
APPOINT   APP     9083    4-02-87   12:52p
PHONE     BAK      508    9-26-86   12:33p
PHONE     DIR      562    4-06-87    1:21a
NOTES     BAK     1865    5-14-87    4:21a




  F1-help  F2-save  F3-new file  F4-import data  F9-expand  F10-contract  Esc-exit
```

Figure 4-8.   Example of a block of text to be imported

You can adjust your positioning carefully by moving one character at a time, if you wish. Figure 4-8 illustrates the type of block you can mark: notice that you could adjust the text width to move only the file names, the file names and sizes, or the dates and times of file creation.

The SideKick Notepad window reappears automatically at this point. Use the cursor command keys again to make sure the cursor is located where you want to include the marked block (although the cursor should be in the same position as it was before you pressed F4) and type CTRL-K-C. This command copies the block from the display outside SideKick to the designated Notepad notefile. The outside display remains unchanged, although you can watch the SideKick cursor flash through the display as it reads the block prior to copying.

You can perform this "import data" function from a wide variety of outside programs, including any sort of ASCII data.

Sorting a Block

SideKick also has the ability to sort lines, a feature lacking in many word processors. This type of sorting can be quite handy as an intermediate stage for text you want to import from one application and then paste to another. It is also useful in making lists within the Notepad itself.

To sort lines, you still have to mark out a block. The following steps explain how to sort a block, using the example file directory block imported in the previous section.

1. Use the cursor command keys to move the cursor to the top left corner of the directory block inside the Notepad window. Press CTRL-K-B to mark the block's beginning.

2. Use the cursor command keys to move the cursor to the bottom right corner of the block or to the first column of the line after the block. Press CTRL-K-K to mark the block's end. The block is marked and appears highlighted on the screen.

3. Press CTRL-K-S to perform the actual sort. The following prompt appears:

    Enter first column of sort key:

    Then enter an appropriate number, as discussed in the next paragraph.

SideKick sorts the blocks line by line, according to the alphabetic order of the characters in the columns. But you must specify which columns it should use as a guide. If you instruct SideKick to sort only by column one, it uses the characters in that column for an alphabetic sort; if any lines begin the first column with the same character, they are grouped but are left in their previous order within that group. If you specify the sorting to take place beyond column one, you can have several levels of sorting: thus, if two or more lines begin with the same letters in several columns, they can be sorted alphabetically using the first column in which they differ. The alphabetic sorting of characters and numbers follows the ASCII code (which places the numerals 1 through 9 before the alphabetic characters). Also, all other special characters available in SideKick have ASCII code equivalents and, therefore, sorting priorities. If you want to view on-screen how the sorting will work, press ALT-A to open the SideKick ASCII Table utility (which is discussed in Chapter 8).

4. After you answer the first prompt, the following prompt appears:

   Enter last column of sort key:

   Enter an appropriate number.

5. If you don't want to continue with the sort, just press CTRL-U and then ESC, and you return your notefile to the main Notepad window and commands.

6. If you press RETURN, the marked block is sorted.

```
      C:\TEMPEDIT.                    Line 3    Col 1    Insert     Indent

 APPOINT   APP      9083    4-02-87   12:52p
 NOTES              1747    6-02-87    8:29a
 NOTES     BAK      1865    5-14-87    4:21a
 PHONE     OLD      1328    8-18-86    1:56p
 PHONE     BAK       508    9-26-86   12:33p
 PHONE     DIR       562    4-06-87    1:21a
 README    COM     17808    8-18-86    1:56p
 README            12478    8-18-86    1:56p
 SK        COM     39515    6-02-87    8:52a
 SK        HLP     53632    8-18-86    1:56p
 SKC       COM     28049    5-27-87   11:26a
 SKINST    COM     54574    8-18-86    1:56p
 SKINST    MSG      4224    8-18-86    1:56p
 SKM       COM     17642    5-27-87   11:26a
 SKN       COM     34009    5-27-87   11:26a




 F1-help  F2-save  F3-new file  F4-import data  F9-expand  F10-contract  Esc-exit
```

Figure 4-9. Example of a sorted block: directory sorted by file name

The directory example sorted by columns 1 through 5 results in a list of the files sorted alphabetically by file name (Figure 4-9). If instead you choose to sort by columns 17 to 21, you can sort the example directory by file size. If you choose to sort by columns 24 through 31 you can sort the directory by date of file creation (Figure 4-10).

Determining the column numbers is easy: move the cursor into the block and set it on the first (and last) column you want to sort by. The Col indicator on the Notepad window's status line lists the column number you need to input after the first (and second) sort prompts.

Searching Operations: Find and Find and Replace

One of the features that moves SideKick's Notepad beyond the bare-bones text editor category is its ability to search for or to search for and then replace specified character patterns within a file. In the Notepad,

```
   C:\TEMPEDIT.                    Line 3    Col 1    Insert    Indent

APPOINT   APP     9083    4-02-87   12:52p
PHONE     DIR      562    4-06-87    1:21a
NOTES     BAK     1865    5-14-87    4:21a
SKC       COM    28049    5-27-87   11:26a
SKM       COM    17642    5-27-87   11:26a
SKN       COM    34009    5-27-87   11:26a
NOTES             1747    6-02-87    8:29a
SK        COM    39515    6-02-87    8:52a
PHONE     OLD     1328    8-18-86    1:56p
README    COM    17808    8-18-86    1:56p
README           12478    8-18-86    1:56p
SK        HLP    53632    8-18-86    1:56p
SKINST    COM    54574    8-18-86    1:56p
SKINST    MSG     4224    8-18-86    1:56p
PHONE     BAK      508    9-26-86   12:33p

F1-help F2-save F3-new file F4-import data F9-expand F10-contract Esc-exit
```

Figure 4-10.   Example of a sorted block: directory sorted by date

the operations are similar but separate: Find and Find and Replace. Both operations rely on WordStar-style key commands.

Find

By pressing CTRL-Q-F, you can search for any character or string of characters in a Notepad file. (A *string* of characters is one or more characters in sequence. A word is string, as is a phrase, as is a dozen blank spaces followed by an exclamation mark.) You can press the three keys simultaneously. Or you can press CTRL, then while holding CTRL down, press Q and then F; you can release CTRL before you press F, if that is easier for you to do. The prompt

> Find?

appears at the top left of the Notepad window, temporarily covering up the status line. After the prompt, you must type in what you want SideKick to search for or you must terminate the operation (which is discussed in the next section). Try experimenting a little using the practice file Tempedit that you used earlier in the chapter.

(If you don't know how to do this, check the section called "Making a Practice File" in this chapter. To reiterate briefly, open the Notepad, press F3, type **tempedit**, press RETURN, wait for the new, empty file to open in the Notepad window, press CTRL-K-R, type **notes**, press RETURN, and wait for the Notes text to appear in the Tempedit file.)

Now you're ready to experiment with the Find operation. After you press CTRL-Q-F, you must enter the text to be found. In this example case, just type **Sidekick** (for this first trial, don't capitalize the middle "k") and press RETURN. The second prompt of the Find operation then appears:

> Options:

At this point, you can type in single-letter codes that specify how you want to run the Find operation, or you can terminate the operation.

For now, just press RETURN to try Find without any special options. (The various option codes are discussed in the section called "Options.")

The Notepad then begins searching for the "Sidekick" characters you entered, starting from the cursor's current position and working toward the end (bottom) of the file. If the operation locates such an occurrence, it stops and places the cursor just after the last letter or character of the sequence (Figure 4-11). Unless you want SideKick to repeat its Find operation for the same character sequence, which is discussed in the section "Immediately Repeating a Find," the Find operation is over. You can resume your writing, editing, and so on.

Interrupting a Find

If you decide that you don't want to complete the Find operation, you can press CTRL-U after viewing either the "Find?" or the "Options:" prompts. The prompt

      *** INTERRUPTED. Press <Esc>.

```
  C:\TEMPEDIT.                    Line 7    Col 22  Insert    Indent

                      INTRODUCTION


  Like the sidekicks of the old West after whom it is named,

  Borland's Sidekick█is a "faithful companion"...always ready to
  help when needed; yet, never in the way.  Now that you've
  booted it up, you'll get to see for yourself just how powerful
  an ally you've got.

  You're now viewing the notepad....although it's much more than
  just a space on the screen to make notes.  You can perform
  global searches, pull text from another file... or even import
  data directly from the screen of the software you were using
  before you "called up" Sidekick and then "paste" that data
  into another application program. You can automatically time
  and date stamp your notes...and then save them. Sidekick
  allows you to mark a block of text and move it, copy it,
  delete it, write it to another file, or even sort it!

  You can also easily activate any Sidekick window from within

 F1-help F2-save F3-new file F4-import data F9-expand F10-contract Esc-exit
```

Figure 4-11.   Example of a Find operation

then appears. Press ESC, and you return your notefile to the main Notepad window and commands.

Immediately Repeating a Find

If you want SideKick to repeat its Find operation immediately for the same characters used in the previous example ("Sidekick"), the Notepad provides a simple command: CTRL-L. This command is quite useful, because many times you want to search through a file, in a single run, checking for the number of incidences of a character sequence. In this case, if you press CTRL-L, the cursor moves down to the next instance of "Sidekick," which occurs at the end of the eighth full line of text (see Figure 4-11). If you wish, you can keep pressing CTRL-L to find other occurrences of the phrase.

Search String Not Found

If the Notepad cannot find a single occurrence of your chosen Find characters from the cursor position to the end of the file, or if you press CTRL-L and it cannot find another occurrence after the previous finding, the cursor moves to the bottom of the file (which is displayed on the screen). The warning

Search string not found. Press <Esc>.

appears. Here you must press ESC. Then you must use the cursor commands to return to your previous position in the file or to any other chosen location in the file.

Limits on Find

Find can be used to search for any letters, words, phrases, punctuation marks, and even control characters. Your only restriction is that the character string you type in at the "Find?" prompt cannot exceed 30 characters in length. If you're entering a long phrase, you can use the word-left, word-right, character-left, character-right, BACKSPACE, and DELete commands to edit and move around within that phrase. To enter a

```
┌Find: ^M^J─────────────────────────────────────────────────────────┐
│                      INTRODUCTION                                    │
│                                                                      │
│  Like the sidekicks of the old West after whom it is named,          │
│                                                                      │
│  Borland's Sidekick is a "faithful companion"...always ready to      │
│  help when needed; yet, never in the way.  Now that you've           │
│  booted it up, you'll get to see for yourself just how powerful      │
│  an ally you've got.                                                 │
│                                                                      │
│  You're now viewing the notepad....although it's much more than      │
│  just a space on the screen to make notes.  You can perform          │
│  global searches, pull text from another file... or even import      │
│  data directly from the screen of the software you were using        │
│  before you "called up" Sidekick and then "paste" that data          │
│  into another application program. You can automatically time        │
│  and date stamp your notes...and then save them. Sidekick            │
│  allows you to mark a block of text and move it, copy it,            │
│  delete it, write it to another file, or even sort it!               │
│                                                                      │
│  You can also easily activate any Sidekick window from within        │
└──────────────────────────────────────────────────────────────────┘
 F1-help F2-save F3-new file F4-import data F9-expand F10-contract Esc-exit
```

Figure 4-12.   Searching for control characters

control character, press CTRL-P and then, while still holding down CTRL, press your chosen control character letter. For instance, to search for a line break, press CTRL-P CTRL-M CTRL-P CTRL-J after the "Find?" prompt (which appears as $^\wedge$M$^\wedge$J after the prompt, as is shown in Figure 4-12).

Wildcards

You can add a wildcard character to your search phrase. A wildcard character is a symbol that can be interpreted by the operation as any character. *Don't* use the asterisk (*) and question mark (?) characters that are the DOS wildcard characters. If you do use those characters, your Find operation will search specifically for asterisks and question marks. Instead, insert CTRL-A after the "Find?" prompt (which appears as $^\wedge$A) at any point or points you want in the search phrase. Remember, you must press CTRL-P and then A, as discussed in the preceding section. The Find operation treats CTRL-A as "search for anything here." For instance, searching for "tr$^\wedge$A$^\wedge$At" would locate both "treat" and

```
C>

┌Find: tr^A^At
│                     INTRODUCTION
│
│   Like the sidekicks of the old West after whom it is named,
│
│   Borland's Sidekick is a "faithful companion"...always ready to
│   help when needed; yet, never in the way.  Now that you've
│   booted it up, you'll get to see for yourself just how powerful
│   an ally you've got.
│
│   You're now viewing the notepad....although it's much more than
│   just a space on the screen to make notes.  You can perform
│   global searches, pull text from another file... or even import
│   data directly from the screen of the software you were using
│   before you "called up" Sidekick and then "paste" that data
│   into another application program. You can automatically time
│   and date stamp your notes...and then save them. Sidekick

 F1-help  F2-save  F3-new file  F4-import data  F9-expand  F10-contract  Esc-exit
```

Figure 4-13.   Using wildcard symbols in a search

"trout" if those two words were in the file (Figure 4-13); otherwise the "search string not found" message would appear.

Options

There is even more power to the Find command than the preceding paragraphs reveal. You can specify options after the "Options:" prompt that can speed or streamline your searching task. For instance, you may have noticed that the Find operation carried out in the preceding example didn't find the word "sidekicks" in the first full line of text (see Figure 4-11). The word "sidekicks" was passed over because the Find operation was searching specifically for "Sidekick" (with an uppercase "S"). The word "sidekicks" (with a lowercase "s") didn't qualify. If you try the Find operation using the word "sidekick," the first instance can be located, but the second is passed over.

What if you want to find all instances of the word "sidekick," no matter what the capitalization? After the "Options:" prompt just press u (it doesn't matter whether you use an uppercase or a lowercase letter when entering options). Then press RETURN. The Find operation now can ignore the differences in upper- and lowercase letters: it treats an uppercase letter the same as its lowercase counterpart.

After pressing u, you may have noticed that the word "sidekicks" was found, when you were looking for the singular "sidekick." The Find operation doesn't understand meanings, it just looks for series of characters. However, it does know that spaces indicate separate words, and it offers an option to look for whole words only. If you press w after the "Options:" prompt and then press RETURN, only separate occurrences of your search phrase are located: you won't be led to places where your phrase occurs within some other word. For instance, in the preceding case, you would skip over "sidekicks" in the first line.

If you know there is going to be more than one occurrence of your search phrase, and you want to skip over some of the early instances without bothering to stop and CTRL-L past them, you can use the numeric option. Here, you type in a number n after the "Options:" prompt, press RETURN and the Find operation skips over $n-1$ instances of the phrase, locating its nth occurrence. For example, if you press 9 after the "Options:" prompt and then press RETURN, the cursor will land either on the ninth occurrence of the phrase or arrive at the end of the file without having found the ninth occurrence.

Generally, if you want to search the entire file with a Find operation, you first must move the cursor to the file's beginning (press CTRL-Q-R to do this). But there is another option: you can type in b after the "Options:" prompt and then press RETURN to search backward from the cursor's position. This option lets you search from the end of the file to the beginning or just search from the cursor to the beginning of the file.

The following list summarizes the Find options available within the Notepad. If you need Help, press F1 after the "Options:" prompt for information on the options available.

U   Ignores case of letters. Treats uppercase and lowercase letters the same during the search, no matter which is in the search phrase.

W   Whole words only. Finds only the search phrase by itself. Doesn't pay attention to cases where the search phrase is buried within a longer word.

B   Search backward. Search backward from the cursor's position toward the beginning of the file (upward in the Notepad window). (The default searches forward toward the end of the file, which is the bottom of the Notepad window.)

n   The n stands for any number. Finds the nth matching example from the current cursor position. *Do not* type in the letter "n."

The next time you specify a Find operation, the same option(s) you used previously appear automatically after the "Options:" prompt line as defaults. (Multiple options are discussed in the following section.) You can press RETURN to use the option(s) listed, or you can type in any new set of defaults you wish.

Multiple Options

The Find options don't exclude one another. For example, you can search for the word "you" from the midpoint of the Tempedit file and add the options uw4b. Type all your chosen options in a row, spaces aren't necessary, and then press RETURN. In this case, the Notepad searches backward (toward the beginning of the file) for the fourth, single, separate, capitalized or uncapitalized occurrence of the word "you."

Find and Replace

In many word processors the SideKick Find-and-Replace feature is called the "search-and-replace" feature. This feature allows you to go beyond merely locating character strings in your text to replacing those strings with a specific new set of characters. For example, you could use this feature to change all the periods to question marks or change every occurrence of the word "Sidekick" to the spelling "SideKick."

Like the Find operation, the Find-and-Replace operation borrows its command key from WordStar: CTRL-Q-A. You must press CTRL and Q simultaneously, and you then can press A with CTRL still down or with it released.

To illustrate how Find and Replace works, again create the file named Tempedit (its creation is discussed in the previous section called "Find"). With the Tempedit file displayed in the Notepad window and the cursor placed at the beginning of the file, press CTRL-Q-A, which calls up the following prompt:

Find?

The prompt temporarily covers up the Notepad status line. Your responses and restrictions are the same as with the Find operation: enter a string of up to 30 characters; use word-left, word-right, character-left, character-right, BACKSPACE, and DELete commands to edit the string; enter control characters by pressing CTRL-P and then holding down CTRL while pressing your chosen control character; and enter wildcard characters using CTRL-A (pressing CTRL-P and then holding down CTRL while pressing A). If you wish further review on these subjects, you should refer to the section called "Find."

Enter the text to be found and replaced after the "Find?" prompt. In this example, imagine that Borland has decided to name its program "Helper!" instead of "SideKick." Find the word "SideKick" wherever it appears in the Tempedit file and replace it automatically with "Helper!" To start the operation, type in the word "SideKick" after the "Find?" prompt and press RETURN.

The second prompt now appears:

Replace with:

Enter the word "Helper!" and press RETURN. A third "Options:" prompt appears, which is discussed in the following section called "Options."

If you decide you don't want to complete the Find and Replace after viewing either the "Find?" or the "Replace with:" prompts, you can press CTRL-U to interrupt the operation, as discussed in the previous section "Interrupting a Find."

Replacement Limits

The Replace phrase has all of the same restrictions as the Find phrase (described in the previous section "Limits on Find") except that the Replace phrase cannot hold a wildcard symbol. To edit your replacement phrase, you can use the character-left, character-right, word-left, word-right, DELete and BACKSPACE commands.

You also can search and replace graphics characters —that is, extended ASCII characters, which are described in Chapter 8. To search and replace these characters, press CTRL-Q-G to change the Notepad into the Graphics mode. Then you can enter graphics characters after the prompts by pressing ALT and the ASCII value of the character you wish to find or replace.

Options

As mentioned earlier, the Find-and-Replace operation involves a third prompt: "Options:". Before discussing the option codes, try the Find-and-Replace operation without any special options.

After working through the "Find?" and "Replace with:" prompts (as already explained), press RETURN in response to the "Options:" prompt. The Notepad now searches for the characters you entered ("SideKick") starting from the cursor's current position and working toward the end (or bottom) of the file. If the Find portion of the operation discovers an occurrence of the phrase, it stops and places the cursor just after the last letter or character of the sequence. The prompt

Replace Y/N

then asks you if you want to replace this occurrence ("Sidekick") with your previously-entered replacement string ("Helper!"). The prompt appears in the upper left corner of the Notepad window. The cursor will bounce back and forth between its position at the end of the replaceable phrase and at the end of the questioning prompt.

If you type Y at this point, the string is replaced, and the operation is over. You return your notefile to the main Notepad window and commands. When replacements are made, they are inserted into the text, pushing other text further down in the file. The replacements do not overwrite any text other than the string that was searched for and chosen for replacement.

If you press N, the operation also ends immediately, but nothing in your text is changed.

As with the Find operation, Find and Replace also offers options other than RETURN. After the "Options:" prompt, you can type in any one or several of the options listed on pages 111-112. Then press RETURN.

(Like the Find operation, multiple options are allowed.) If you need Help, press F1 for information on the available options. In addition, Find and Replace offers two options not available to the Find operation. These options are listed here:

N   This *N* is actually the letter *N*, rather than the unknown number (*n*) option (see the Find options list). *Do not confuse the two options*. When you type N, lowercase or uppercase, the Find-and-Replace operation replaces any occurrences of the replaceable phrase without asking you to answer Y or N at each occurrence.

G   Global. Finds and then replaces all occurrences in the text, no matter where the cursor is positioned.

After a Find-and-Replace operation is completed, you can use the CTRL-L command to repeat the operation. The procedure is the same as that discussed for the Find operation.

Fast Replace

Once you have started the Find-and-Replace operation, you can watch the cursor move down the page, through the file, and perform its duty. If you wish, you can have your replacements inserted more quickly: press any key after you have pressed RETURN to begin the Find-and-Replace operation. The remainder of the operation then occurs without displaying its intermediate work. This function is particularly helpful if you are using the global, no-ask option, "gn."

The key you press will be inserted into the file at the end of the Find-and-Replace operation. Thus, you should choose a key that cannot alter your text, such as the DOWN ARROW.

Resuming Work After Find or Find and Replace

A special cursor command — CTRL-Q-P — moves the cursor back to its previous position. This command can be quite handy if you start a Find or Find-and-Replace operation from somewhere in the middle of a file and then want to return to that spot after searching through to the beginning or end of the file.

Printing a File

There are two methods you can use to print a SideKick file. First, from DOS you can use the DOS command

    type filename >prn

which directs a simple printing of the file's text to whatever is attached to the printer port.

However, SideKick has a built-in command that lets you print files without exiting to DOS. This command was previously mentioned in the section "Printing a Block." When a block of text is marked in the Notepad window, you can press CTRL-K-P to print that block (assuming your printer is hooked up and attached to the printer port). The block prints as straight ASCII text, without any special commands or printer format controls such as skipping page perforations or printing page numbers on the bottoms of pages. If there is no marked block, SideKick prints the entire Notepad file when you press CTRL-K-P. Again, it is printed as straight ASCII text characters. If you want to include some printer format controls, you must insert the proper control characters into your file. Control characters are discussed in the next section.

Print Control Characters

Most characters that are sent to a printer by a computer are interpreted by that printer as "text" —letters, numerals, graphics shapes, and so on. But a computer also can send control characters to a printer, which tell the printer how to print. (For more information on control characters, see Chapter 8. The first page of the ASCII Table utility shows a handful of control characters. These are listed in the "Ctrl" and "Mem" columns of Figure 4-14.) There are many different sets of control characters used by many different computer systems, although some sets have been adopted as "industry standards" because they were used on very popular printers. Thus, many printers may use many of the same control charac-

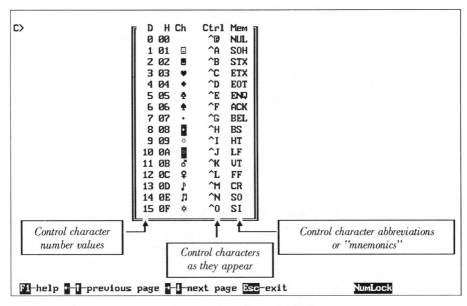

Figure 4-14. Some examples of control characters (page 1 of the ASCII Table utility)

ters to mean the same printing command.

To insert a control character instead of a regular character, use the CTRL-P key combination: press CTRL-P and then type in the control character you want to send. Your printer manual should contain a list of these characters, including those for form feed (moving to the beginning of a blank page of printer paper), line feed (moving one blank line down on the printer paper), and so on. Many printers even offer different print styles. Table 4-1 lists some of the control characters available for the Epson FX-80 printer.

Insert some control characters into your text, and then you can try the CTRL-K-P command.

Turbo Lightning

Another Borland program that you should consider using in concert with SideKick, and particularly with the Notepad, is Turbo Lightning. Lightning can add *word power* to your computing, and because it deals

Table 4-1.   Some Epson FX-80 Printer Control Characters

ASCII Values	Control Characters	Description
7	^G	Buzz. Makes a buzz sound for 0.1 seconds.
8	^H	Backspace. Empties the printer buffer then backspaces the print head one space.
9	^I	Horizontal tab. Empties the printer buffer then moves the print head to the next tab stop.
10	^J	Line feed. Empties the printer buffer then moves the printer paper down one blank line.
12	^L	Form feed. Empties the printer buffer then advances the paper to the next logical Top Of Form (top of a page).
13	^M	Carriage return (CR). Prints the buffer's contents then moves the print head to the left margin.
14	^N	Shift out. Activates the Expanded mode for the length of the line.
15	^O	Shift in. Empties the printer buffer and activates the Compressed mode.

with words, this chapter on the Notepad is an appropriate place to discuss it.

Word power? Yes, because Turbo Lightning is a TSR program (it stays in RAM memory, like SideKick) that gives you instant access to both a spelling dictionary and a thesaurus. It not only can check your spelling or offer synonyms, it can even monitor the keyboard to check your spelling continuously as you type. You can instruct it to "beep" at you as soon as you mistype a word —that is, a word that Lightning cannot find in its dictionary. You also can check the spelling of a single word or a full screen of text. If the dictionary does not contain words you want to use, you can add them to the dictionary. Once Lightning alerts you to a misspelled word, you can use the program to find correct spelling of the word and to replace it automatically.

The thesaurus can help you find synonyms as you write, and it can insert those synonyms into your text.

Turbo Lightning uses the *Random House Dictionary* and the *Random House Thesaurus* for its data sources.

If you follow the instructions in the Turbo Lightning manual to load it along with SideKick, you almost can consider Lightning as an additional SideKick utility. However, Lightning's command keys and menus are slightly different than the original SideKick set.

Hardware Requirements and Suggestions

You can use Lightning on any PC-compatible floppy-disk system that has at least 256K RAM, but it is recommended that you use a hard-disk system with additional RAM. The dictionary and the thesaurus take up a fair amount of disk space, and if you team up SideKick with other TSR programs (see Chapter 2 for an explanation of these other programs), you need more than the minimum amount of RAM. If you use Lightning on a floppy-disk system, you must keep the dictionary disk in one of your floppy-disk drives.

Installation

Lightning comes on three disks and has more files and larger files than has SideKick. You don't need all of the files for any one installation. For example, smaller dictionaries are available for systems with less RAM or floppy-disk systems, and larger dictionaries are available for systems with more memory. The Lightning manual describes how to choose the best set of files for you using the LIGHTINS program.

First, create working and backup copies of all three disks, as described for non-copy-protected disks in Chapter 2. You then can choose to activate Turbo Lightning from a floppy-disk or a hard-disk directory. This procedure is described in detail in the Lightning manual, and again uses the LIGHTINS program. To run this program, type **lightins** and press RETURN. A menu and command instructions then appear. These instructions should be self-explanatory.

Once you have activated LIGHTINS, placed the files where you want them, and the DOS prompt for that drive and directory are showing, you're ready to load Lightning into memory. You always should load Lightning before SideKick: in fact, SideKick always should be the last TSR program you load into memory. (If you are going to use SuperKey as well, it is best to load it before loading Lightning. SuperKey is described in more detail in Chapter 11.)

To load Lightning, type **light** and press RETURN. A loading display appears similar to that shown in Figure 4-15.

The Main Menu

Now that Lightning is loaded, there are two methods available to activate Lightning commands: first, you can press specific key combinations called *hot keys*. (Various hot keys are mentioned throughout the rest of this chapter and are discussed further in the section called "Options." See also Figure 4-22 for a summary of the hot keys.) Second, you can

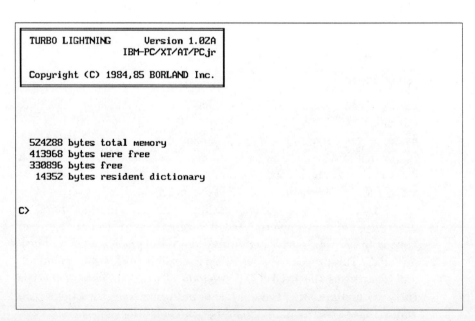

Figure 4-15. Turbo Lightning's loading display

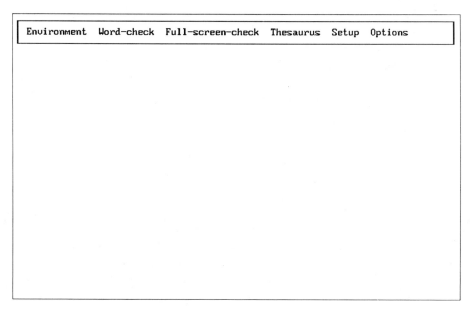

| Environment Word-check Full-screen-check Thesaurus Setup Options |

Figure 4- 16. Turbo Lightning's main menu display

work through a series of Lightning menus. To call up the main menu, press the hot key SHIFT-F8. The Lightning's main menu display then appears (Figure 4- 16). If you don't like the SHIFT-F8 combination, you can change it to whatever you wish by using the Lightning Options menu, which is described in the section "Options." You can activate Lightning at any time, even if SideKick is not loaded into memory.

The Lightning main menu is a horizontal listing of five command groups. Each of these groups —Environment, Word-Check, Full-Screen Check, Thesaurus, Setup, and Options —hides a *pull-down menu* of related commands. You can view a pull-down menu either by typing the first letter of the group name or by using the cursor arrow keys to move the highlight to that group name and then press RETURN. For instance, to open the Environment menu, press E.

To exit from any pull-down menu, press ESC, just as in SideKick, to return to the main menu. Also, to exit from Lightning entirely, press ESC after returning to the main menu.

Help

Just as in SideKick, Lightning contains a context-sensitive Help that is available at any time. Press F1, and you can view helpful command and options information that relate directly to your present position within Lightning.

Auto-Proof Mode

When you load Lightning into memory, it is automatically in the Auto-Proof mode, where it monitors what you type at the keyboard and beeps a warning message to you when it doesn't recognize a word from its dictionary. If you exit Lightning entirely and have left on the Auto-Proof mode, Lightning continues to beep at you if you mistype a word. (Note: Auto-proofing is contained in a smaller RAM-based dictionary, not in the larger disk-based dictionary.)

You can have Lightning present some alternative spellings by using one of the spelling-check commands such as Word-Check (which is discussed in the section called "Word-Check"). Or you can turn off the Auto-Proof mode at any time, by using the Options menu (described in the section called "Options").

Environment

Lightning can check your spelling in any program or SideKick utility — the Notepad, another word processor, DOS, a spreadsheet, and so on. Lightning also can let you substitute a preferred spelling or a synonym for any word. But not all application programs handle text in the same way. Some programs use control characters and others don't.

The first menu group is called Environment. You have to let Lightning know which "environment" it must work in, so it can interact smoothly with the other program. From the main menu, press E or move the highlight bar to that selection to call up the Environment pull-down menu (Figure 4-17). This menu lists the programs that Lightning is most able to work with. It can, however, work with many other programs not listed, so don't worry if your program isn't on this list. If the program you are working with appears on the list, press its corresponding letter key. If the program you are working with is not on the list, pick one that seems close to it and try editing that environment (described in the following

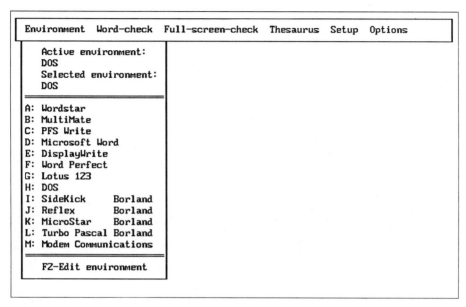

Figure 4-17. Turbo Lightning's Environment pull-down menu

section), or call Borland for advice on which selection to choose.

At the top of the pull-down menu is a brief description of your present Environment. The active environment is the one that appeared on the screen when you activated Lightning. The selected environment is the one that you last chose from this menu.

The Notepad and DOS are two special cases for Lightning: the program doesn't need to be alerted that they are the present environment. That is, no matter what other environment you choose, Lightning can recognize when you are using a DOS command or a Notepad command—and it adjusts automatically to work with these programs. This tight coupling of Lightning with the Notepad is one reason that you should consider trying Lightning.

Editing an Environment

At the bottom of the Environment pull-down menu is the option "F2-Edit Environment." If your program isn't listed or if you have a modified version of a program, you should consider editing one of the listed

```
┌─────────────────────────────────────────────────────────────────┐
│ Environment  Word-check  Full-screen-check  Thesaurus  Setup  Options │
├──────────────────────┬────────────────────────────────────────────┤
│   Active environment:│                                            │
│   DOS                │                                            │
│   Selected environment:│                                          │
│   SideKick    Borland│                                            │
│ ═══════════════════════                                          │
│ A: Wordstar │A: Change name                                      │
│ B: MultiMate│B: Right arrow key 1 RGT                            │
│ C: PFS Write│C: Right arrow key 2 CtrlD                          │
│ D: Microsoft│D: Left arrow key 1   LFT                           │
│ E: DisplayWr│E: Left arrow key 2   CtrlS                         │
│ F: Word Perf│F: Left arrow key 3   None                          │
│ G: Lotus 123│G: Backspace key 1    BKS                           │
│ H: DOS      │H: Backspace key 2    CtrlH                         │
│ I: SideKick │I: Delete key 1       DEL                           │
│ J: Reflex   │J: Delete key 2       CtrlG                         │
│ K: MicroStar│K: Insert toggle 1    INS                           │
│ L: Turbo Pas│L: Insert toggle 2    CtrlV                         │
│ M: Modem Com│M: Get words from     Screen                        │
│ ════════════│N: Piping delay       000                           │
│    F2-Edit e│O: Auto proof         ON                            │
│             │P: Insert/Overwrite setup                           │
└──────────────────────┴────────────────────────────────────────────┘
```

Figure 4-18.   Turbo Lightning menu for editing an environment

environments or creating a new environment. To do so, move the highlight to the listed environment that you want to edit and press F2. A new menu appears, as is shown in Figure 4-18. The Lightning manual describes in detail how to use this menu.

Word-Check

To reach the second selection on the Lightning main menu — Word-Check — you can press W or move the highlight bar to that selection and then press RETURN. There are only two options in this pull-down menu: "Check word at cursor," and "Check last bad word." The first option instructs Lightning to check the spelling of the word directly under or just to the left of the cursor. The second option instructs it to search through the last few words typed to look for the last misspelled word. (This is sometimes necessary when you are using the Auto-Proof mode, because you may type several words beyond the word that caused the misspelling "beep.")

When Lightning finds a misspelled word, it suggests a list of likely replacement spellings. If the word is spelled correctly, Lightning still lists possible alternatives. It chooses all likely replacements on the basis of what "sounds" similar when spoken, because that is how most people spell words that they aren't sure of.

To choose one of the two Word-Check options, you can move the highlight bar to your chosen option and press RETURN, or you can press the letter that precedes the option ("A" or "B"). You also can direct Lightning to "Check word at cursor" by pressing the hot key ALT-F9 or to "Check last bad word" by pressing the hot key ALT-F10.

Full-Screen-Check

The Full-Screen-Check pull-down menu also encompasses two options. To reach the menu from the Lightning main menu, press F or move the highlight bar to that selection and press RETURN. The "Do full-screen-check" option checks the spelling of all words on the display when you activated Lightning. You should still be able to see almost all of these words, because Lightning only appears as the menu line at the top of the screen (plus the pull-down menu if you're using one). Lightning highlights all of the words it questions, and you then can move the cursor to any word (highlighted or not) one at a time. At each word, you can make your own corrections, ask Lightning to check the word and suggest alternatives, or you can ignore the highlight tag. The second option, "Review last full-screen-check," lets you skip back to the last spell check to review the highlights on any words that it still considers misspelled.

You can choose either option by moving the highlight bar to your chosen option and press RETURN, or press the letter that precedes the option in the pull-down menu ("A" or "B"). You also can press the hot key ALT-F8 for "Do full-screen-check" or the hot key ALT-F7 for "Review last full-screen-check."

Correcting words is discussed further in the section "Correcting a Word." Also, you can instruct Lightning to recognize additional words by adding words to an "auxiliary" dictionary. Thus, Lightning no longer will highlight these new terms, saving you a little time. Adding words to the Auxiliary dictionary is discussed further in the section "Adding a Word to a Dictionary."

Checking a File

Turbo Lightning by itself cannot check the spelling of an entire file in memory or on disk. The most it can check is a single screen at a time. But if you're willing to do some programming, you can use Borland's Turbo Word Wizard, Turbo Editor Toolbox, and Turbo Pascal language to extend Lightning's powers. For instance, in the Turbo Editor Toolbox there is an editor (word processor) along with an example program code called SPELL.MS that shows how to have Lightning check the spelling of an entire file in memory. This code could be extended to work with a file on disk.

There is also a public-domain (free) program called LSPELL.COM that does this same thing. You might want to get this program from a user group or an electronic bulletin board, but check first to ensure that the program is compatible with your system.

Correcting a Word

Once Lightning has highlighted a word that it cannot find in the Dictionary (either in its RAM-based or disk-based dictionaries), it presents you with a list of possible alternative spellings. You can substitute one of these spellings in the place of the previous word by pressing the letter that precedes your chosen alternative (Figure 4-19) or by moving the highlight bar to the alternative of your choice and then pressing RETURN.

Adding a Word
to the Dictionary

Lightning also lets you add words to the Dictionary, to customize it with stored samples of your own spellings. These spellings typically are proper names, professional terms, and so on. When Lightning reveals a list of alternative spellings to you, you are given the option to add the present spelling of the word to the "auxiliary" dictionary. Just press the last letter option on the list to add your word.

Later, you can load the Auxiliary dictionary (called AUXI.DIC) into SideKick's Notepad and edit it —add new spellings, modify others, delete some words so the dictionary doesn't take up too much time or

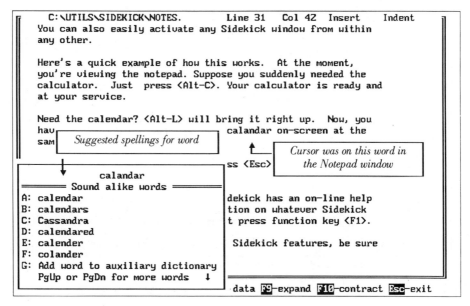

Figure 4-19. Turbo Lightning suggested spellings

memory. After editing AUXI.DIC, you must use the Lightning Setup menu to reload it, to get the new version into RAM. From the Setup menu, just choose the Auxiliary dictionary line and type the dictionary name again, even if it is the same name. When you exit the Setup menu, Lightning loads that file into memory. The Setup selection is discussed further in the section called "Setup."

Thesaurus

You can choose the Thesaurus option from the main menu by pressing T or by moving the highlight bar to that word and pressing RETURN. You also can press the hot key ALT-F6 to call up the Thesaurus option. Lightning then looks up synonyms for the word underneath or to the left of the cursor. You can only search for synonyms of a single word at a time.

After you choose the Thesaurus, a message tells you that Lightning is searching for synonyms, then a list of synonyms appears, such as that

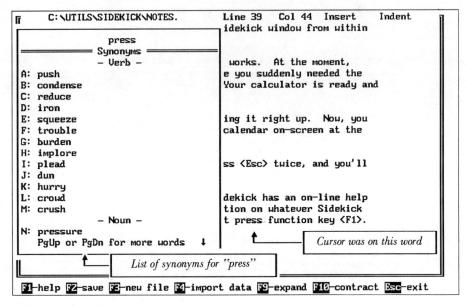

Figure 4-20.   Turbo Lightning example from Thesaurus listing

shown in Figure 4-20. (If no synonyms are found, Lightning lets you choose to see a list of alphabetically similar words.) The synonyms are divided into verbs, nouns, and so on.

To replace your original word with one of the synonyms, press the letter that precedes that synonym or move the highlight bar to the word and press RETURN.

Setup

The Lightning Setup selection operates like the SideKick Setup window: it lets you choose which data files to use while working with the program. These files include the Auxiliary dictionary, the Disk dictionary, and the Thesaurus (Figure 4-21). You can create several auxiliary dictionaries for use in various applications. The Disk dictionary is used when you invoke a full-screen-check. Single-word checks use the smaller dictionary already loaded into RAM.

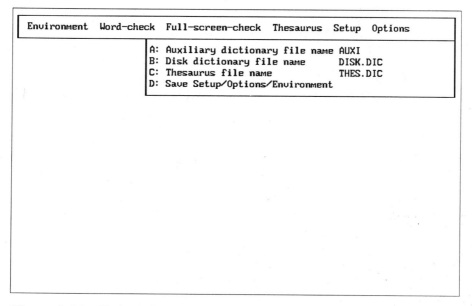

Figure 4-21.   Turbo Lightning's setup pull-down menu

To view the Setup menu, press S from the main menu or move the highlight bar to the Setup option and then press RETURN. The last item within the Setup menu — "D: Save Setup/Options/Environment" — is the one you should select if you want to save to the disk any changes you have made in the dictionaries or the Thesaurus.

Options

Press O from the main menu or move the highlight bar to Options to open the Options menu. This pull-down menu lets you manipulate a number of aspects of Lightning's performance (Figure 4-22). You can modify these options at any time. For example, if you press A or ALT-F5 you turn off Auto-Proof mode; press A or ALT-F5 again to turn Auto-Proof back on. A can be used to save an on or off setting of Auto-Proof as the default. ALT-F5 can be used only to toggle between on and off. In the same manner, you can turn off and on the Confirm window by pressing

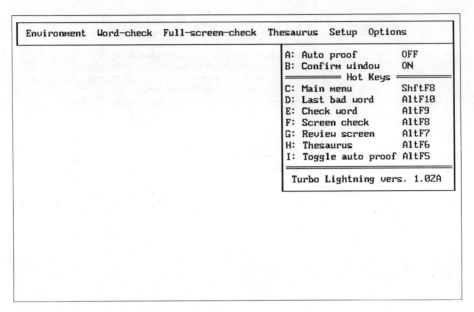

Environment Word-check Full-screen-check Thesaurus Setup Options

A: Auto proof	OFF
B: Confirm window	ON
══════════ Hot Keys ══════════	
C: Main menu	ShftF8
D: Last bad word	AltF10
E: Check word	AltF9
F: Screen check	AltF8
G: Review screen	AltF7
H: Thesaurus	AltF6
I: Toggle auto proof	AltF5
Turbo Lightning vers. 1.02A	

Figure 4-22.   Turbo Lightning's options pull-down menu

B. The Confirm window comes into play when you ask Lightning to check a word that is spelled correctly. Lightning then displays a small notice that says it doesn't find an error and offers you a list of similar word spellings anyway. If you turn off the Confirm window, that display won't appear. Instead, when you ask Lightning to check a word that is spelled correctly, it just beeps twice at you.

The options menu also lets you alter the hot keys. To do so, type in the letter that precedes the hot key command you want to change and then type in the new key combination you want to assign to that command (see Figure 4-22). Make sure that any new hot key assignments don't overlap with commands you use in SideKick or even in SuperKey, or you'll run into problems later.

When you're done making changes to the Options menu, you should open the Setup window and press D to save all selections.

For Future Reference

The same basic program routines that let Turbo Lightning use the *Random House Dictionary* and the *Random House Thesaurus* today will in the future be able to use almost any reference work. Borland is working on a data compiler that will be able to squeeze electronic versions of reference works into files that the Turbo software can handle. With that capability, you'll be able to use the Turbo software to work with medical dictionaries, law references, and all sorts of texts.

5

The Calculator

SideKick's Calculator utility is included in all versions of SideKick, even the smallest version, which uses the least RAM memory. The Calculator is similar to a pocket calculator except that it displays on your computer screen and uses the keys on the computer keyboard.

The Calculator utility is actually two calculators in one. The first is a standard, four-function arithmetic calculator that can add, subtract, multiply, and divide. It is handy for quick figuring, such as balancing a checkbook. The second calculator is a programmer's calculator that can convert decimal numbers to the number systems used by digital computers, binary and hexadecimal, and can perform computer-math operations in those number systems. These capabilities are especially important for the software developer working in assembly language or machine language, but also can assist any PC user who sometimes needs to decipher error messages and memory addresses.

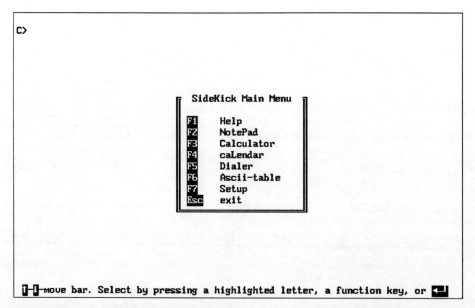

Figure 5- 1.   SideKick's main menu

Loading and Activating SideKick

As described in Chapter 2, the first step to using any of the SideKick utilities is to load SideKick itself into memory. To load SideKick, type **sk** and then press RETURN at the appropriate DOS prompt. For floppy-based systems, the prompt will be the letter of the floppy drive containing the SideKick disk —typically A>. For hard-disk systems, the prompt will be the drive and directory containing the SideKick files —typically C: \sk>. Once SideKick is loaded into memory, press ALT-CTRL to activate the program. The SideKick main menu will appear as shown in Figure 5-1.

Choosing the Calculator

To choose the Calculator utility from the main menu, use any one of these four methods:

- Press F3.

- Press C.

- Press ALT-C.

- Use the up-arrow and down-arrow cursor keys to move the highlight on the main menu to the Calculator option. Then press RETURN.

Any one of these methods will open the Calculator window, shown in Figure 5-2.

To exit the Calculator, either press ALT-CTRL again or press ESC. If you have exited from the Calculator with the ALT-CTRL command rather than using ESC, and have not turned the system off or removed SideKick from memory, you can return directly to the Calculator by pressing either of the SideKick activation commands: ALT-CTRL or SHIFT-SHIFT. If you exit the Calculator by using ESC, SideKick routes you through the main menu the next time you call up the Calculator.

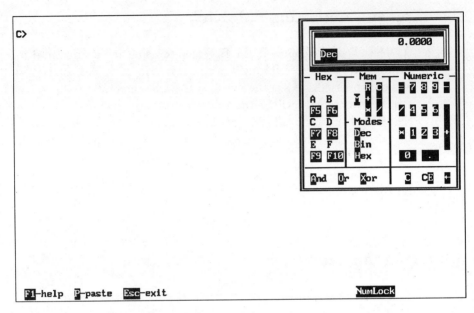

Figure 5-2.   The Calculator window

The Calculator Window on Top of Another SideKick Window

If you want to use the Calculator when you already have some other
SideKick window on the screen, you have two options: first, you can
press ALT-C , and the Calculator will appear on top of the other SideKick
window. Second, you can hold down ALT for just over a second, and the
main menu will appear on top of the other SideKick window. You can
then press F3 , C, or ALT-C to activate the Calculator window on top of the
other SideKick window. When the Calculator window is on top, it is the
active window —the one that responds to commands.

You can return to your previous utility by removing the Calculator
(press ALT-CTRL or ESC) or by bringing the other utility's window to the
front. To do so, press any of the commands that would normally activate
that window (such as ALT-N for the Notepad window).

Moving the Calculator Window

To move the Calculator window anywhere on the screen, press SCROLL
LOCK and use the cursor arrow keys to position the window where you
want it; then press SCROLL LOCK again. Unlike the Notepad window, the
Calculator window cannot be enlarged or contracted. You can save the
new position of the Calculator window in memory, so that it will appear
automatically the next time you run the Calculator. To do so, press ALT-S
to open the Setup window (Figure 5-3), and then press F3 to save your
new window position.

Fundamental Calculator Commands

When SideKick is active, the SideKick command line is displayed at the
bottom of the computer screen. This line contains the three following

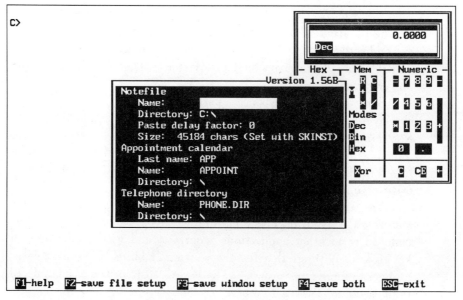

Figure 5-3.   The Setup window for saving Calculator's window position

commands:

F1   Accesses a Help display showing context-sensitive information about Calculator commands and options

ESC   Exits the Calculator and removes the Calculator window
from the display

P   Accesses the Paste commands so that the user can assign the
value in the Calculator display to a Paste key or can clear all Paste
key values

Pressing F1 brings up a Help display of basic information on using
the Calculator. F1 always provides help in SideKick —help that relates
directly to the utility and command you are using.

Pressing ESC performs its usual SideKick function —removing you
from the active utility. If another utility window is on the display, you'll
be moved to that utility, otherwise you'll be transferred to DOS or to any
other application that is running.

When you activate the Calculator, the Num Lock sign on the bottom
right of the screen will appear (Figure 5-2). The computer assumes that
you'll want to use the keyboard's numeric keypad with the Calculator.
On the standard IBM PC, this keypad is part of the keyboard but is
overlaid with the cursor arrow keys. The numeric values of the keys are
available only in Num Lock mode. Press the NUM LOCK key to access the
numeric values.

Some computer keyboards, particularly on portable computers,
overlay the numeric keypad on certain alphabetic keys. When you press
NUM LOCK and the Num Lock signal appears, these keys produce
numbers rather than alphabetic characters. When you leave the Calculator, Num Lock automatically turns off and the keys revert to their
original function.

The final selection on the Calculator's menu is P for Paste. This
feature allows you to move long numbers from the Calculator to the
Notepad or to other applications accurately and with a minimum of
keystrokes. Without this feature you are liable to miscopy a large
number to some other program. The Paste feature is described in detail
in the section "Pasting Numbers."

Four-Function Arithmetic

The right side of the Calculator window looks like a pocket calculator. The functions it offers are addition, subtraction, multiplication, and division, along with memory. To use this part of the Calculator, simply type numbers and operations in as you would key them into a calculator.

Decimal Number Limits

An important difference between a standard calculator and the SideKick Calculator is that the SideKick Calculator can handle larger numbers. (*Program Note:* the Calculator uses BCD arithmetic to ensure accuracy.) Although it does not offer exponents, the SideKick Calculator can work with 18-digit numbers. Four of those digits are to the right of the decimal point. The Calculator's range stretches from $-99,999,999,999,999.9999$ to $99,999,999,999,999.9999$. If you enter numbers beyond that range, the Calculator won't accept them. If you perform an operation that creates a number outside the range, the Calculator displays an "Overflow" warning (Figure 5-4). The only way to recover from an overflow is to clear the display, which is explained shortly.

Entering Numbers

To use the Calculator, type the numbers as if you were writing them on paper. If you make a mistake, use BACKSPACE to back over the error and delete it. To enter a fractional number, press the period (.) and type up to 4 numerals. You can use the keys on the numeric keypad or the number keys at the top of the alphabetic keyboard.

Simple Operations

Once you have entered a number, you can add another number to it by pressing the plus (+) key. You can use the + key on the numeric keypad or use SHIFT to get the plus sign from the alphabetic keyboard. Then type the number you want added. Finish the operation either by pressing

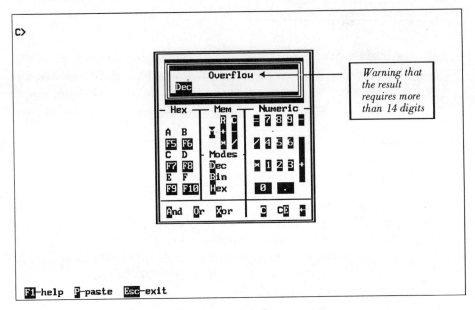

Figure 5-4. The Calculator showing an overflow warning

RETURN or the equal (=) sign. The result shows in the display. You can subtract, multiply, or divide using the same steps by substituting the appropriate symbol for the plus sign. Multiplication uses the asterisk (*), and division the forward leaning slash (/).

Each time you enter a number, you must press RETURN or type one of the operation symbols to tell the Calculator that your number is complete. If you want to use a negative number, you must subtract it from zero; you can't type a negative sign and then the digits. To perform a sequence of operations, enter another operation symbol instead of a RETURN or =. The Calculator can retain an intermediate result and use it in the next operation. For example, to multiply

        44.5
        97.73
        12

type **44.5**, *, **97.73**, *, **12**, RETURN (don't type the commas). After you type the second * symbol, the result of the first multiplication will appear in the display window, and so on.

Parentheses

You can perform more complex operations by using parentheses in your calculations. The Calculator can handle up to six levels of parentheses. Operations within parentheses are performed before those outside parentheses, so this can change the order of multiple operations, and sometimes the result. For example, if you entered

8*7—6/2

the result would be 25. Each operation would be performed in order, from left to right. The sequence would look like:

8*7—6/2
56—6/2
50/2
25

Parentheses can change this operation completely. For example, the operation

(8*7)—(6/2)

works like this:

(8*7)—(6/2)
(56)—(3)
53

yielding a result of 53, quite different from the previous outcome. This organization of parentheses

8*((7—6)/2)

leads to yet another answer.

8*(1/2)
8*0.5
4

This concept, called *operation precedence*, can be explored further in any algebra book. In brief, however, the rules are: left to right, multiplication and division before addition and subtraction, operations inside parentheses before operations outside parentheses.

If you enter multiple parentheses in an operation, all the left parentheses display (see Figure 5-5), until you enter a right parenthesis; then the enclosed operation is performed immediately, the result appears in the display, and that set of parentheses disappears.

Clearing the Display or the Calculator

There are four commands that clear the Calculator display. They are

BACKSPACE   Pressing the left-pointing arrow typically found at the top right of the keyboard moves the cursor one position to the left in the display, deleting the number that previously occupied that position.

E   Clears the Calculator display and the most recent number entered. Does not clear the memory or interim calculation results.

C   Clears the Calculator display and any interim results. Does not clear the memory.

M, C   Pressing M and then C clears the value in the memory cell and sets that cell to zero.

Note that three of these commands are displayed at the bottom right of the Calculator window.

Pressing C clears everything in the Calculator except the memory storage. Use this key to erase everything in the display as well as any intermediate results. To protect intermediate results and erase only what is in the display, press E (for entry). For example, imagine that you have added this set of numbers:

12345
23456
34567
45678

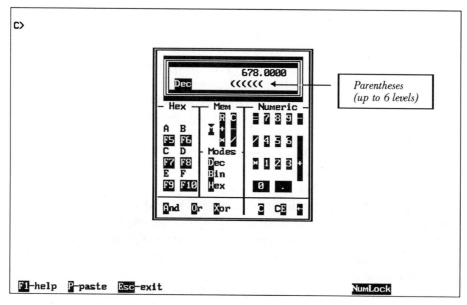

Figure 5-5. Parentheses in the Calculator display

and then you type **56788** instead of **56789**. If you press C, you'll lose all of your addition up to this point. If you press E, you'll erase only the incorrect entry, and can type the correct entry, **56789** and then press RETURN to see the final result. There's a simple solution in this situation, however: use BACKSPACE to erase the final digit. All you have to do then is type **9** and press RETURN to get your result.

Modes: Hexadecimal and Binary

The other dimension of the Calculator is a programmer's tool that can work with different number bases. The four-function Calculator works in decimal mode (base ten), the number system we use in everyday transactions. But computers operate in binary mode (base two), a system that is built exclusively of 1s and 0s. Because long strings of 1s and 0s are visually confusing, and because binary converts quickly and simply to the hexadecimal (base sixteen) system, programmers more often work with hexadecimal than with binary.

Hexadecimal requires 16 number symbols, and decimal only offers ten (0 through 9), so hexadecimal users have improvised, using the letters A through F for the values 11 through 15. SideKick's Calculator works in decimal, binary, and hexadecimal modes, and it can convert numbers between them.

Say you enter the decimal value **100.25**. You'll see the DEC symbol displayed as in Figure 5-5. If you press B, the DEC symbol will change to BIN (Figure 5-6). The Calculator is now in binary mode, and 100.25 changes to its binary equivalent, 1100100. (The binary and hexadecimal modes cannot accept fractions. If you try to convert a decimal number that has a fractional part, that part is deleted.) The number's value remains the same, but it is now written using only 1s and 0s. Press H, and this value will change to hexadecimal, 64. You can convert back to decimal by pressing D. As you make these changes, note that any number held in the Calculator's memory is also converted to the new number base.

The binary range extends from 0 through 11111111111111111111 (20 digits). The hexadecimal range extends from 0 through FFFFFFFFFFFF (12 digits).

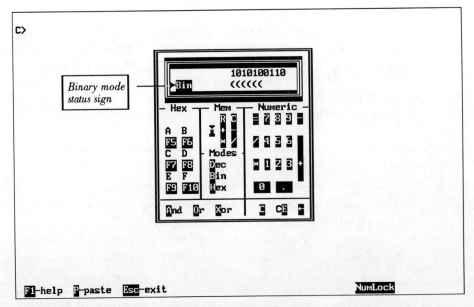

Figure 5-6.   The Calculator in binary mode

In binary mode, you can enter only 0s and 1s. In the hexadecimal mode, you can enter any numeral and can use the function keys F5, F6, F7, F8, F9, and F10 to enter the hexadecimal numerals A, B, C, D, E, and F. Do not use the regular alphabetic keys, because they have previous definitions (such as C for clear and B for binary).

The hexadecimal mode is useful when there is a question of memory. If you have an error message that says

Stack Starts at FFF0

you can press H to get into hexadecimal mode, type **FFF0** (three presses of F10 and one press of 0) and then press D to convert to the decimal mode equivalent, 65520. That is near the 64K point in RAM.

Logical Operations

Three logical calculation functions are listed at the bottom left of the Calculator window: AND, OR, and XOR. You use these as you do the functions of addition, subtraction, multiplication, and division. Type the first letter of the function you want (**A** for AND, **O** for OR, **X** for XOR) between two values and press RETURN to see the result.

A complete description of these operations can be found in any beginners' programming book. In simple terms, they compare numbers in binary form position by position from right to left (even if it is necessary to convert to binary during an operation and then reconvert the results). AND returns a 1 in the position of the result only if both the numbers compared had a 1 in that position. OR returns a 1 if either number had a 1 in that position. XOR (short for exclusive-or) returns a 1 only if one or the other but not both numbers had a 1 in that position. Figure 5-7 shows some simple examples of these operations.

Memory

The Calculator has a memory, often called a *cell*, that can hold one number. You can get around this limitation by using the Paste function described later in this chapter, but you can't operate as freely on

And

```
      0            0            1            1
AND   0      AND   1      AND   0      AND   1
     ___          ___          ___          ___
      0            0            0            1


      1000         1011         1111
AND   0101   AND   0011   AND   1111
     _____        _____        _____
      0000         0011         1111
```

Or

```
      0            0            1            1
OR    0      OR    1      OR    0      OR    1
     ___          ___          ___          ___
      0            1            1            1


      1000         1011         1111
OR    0101   OR    0011   OR    1111
     _____        _____        _____
      1101         1011         1111
```

Xor

```
      0            0            1            1
XOR   0      XOR   1      XOR   0      XOR   1
     ___          ___          ___          ___
      0            1            1            0


      1000         1011         1111
XOR   0101   XOR   0011   XOR   1111
     _____        _____        _____
      1101         1000         0000
```

Figure 5-7. Computer logic operations

numbers stored using Paste, as you can on the one in the regular memory. A set of memory operators lets you work directly with the value in the memory cell. These are located in a block at the center of the Calculator window. The following list summarizes the Calculator Memory Commands:

M   Moves the Calculator to the Memory Command mode. That is, it tells the Calculator that the next command will be a memory command. You must use this command before using any other memory command.

=   Places a copy of the number in the display in the memory cell, overwriting whatever the cell contained previously.

R   Recalls a copy of the number stored in the memory cell and puts it in the display, overwriting any existing display.

+   Adds what is in the display to what is in the memory cell and puts the result in the memory cell. Does not affect the display.

—   Subtracts what is in the display from what is in the memory cell and puts the result in the memory cell. Does not affect the display.

×   Multiplies the value in the display by the value in the memory cell and puts the result in the memory cell. Does not affect the display.

/   Divides the value in the memory cell by the value in the display and puts the result in the memory cell. Does not affect the display.

Each time you want to work with the value in memory, you must press M and then one of these operator keys. An M appears in the Calculator display whenever there is a value other than zero in the memory cell (see Figure 5-8). To put a number into memory, enter the number into the display, press M and then press =. To add a number to the value in memory, type the number into the display, press M, and then press +. You can use these instructions with different operator keys to subtract, divide, or multiply. The result is stored in the memory, but the display does not change. If you want to erase the display value, press

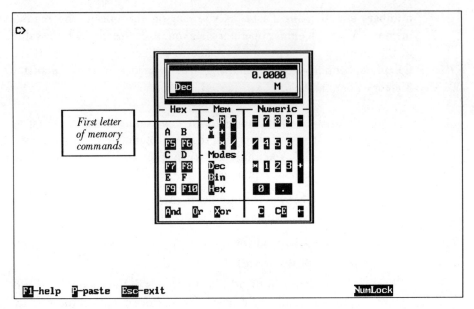

Figure 5-8.   Memory command box

either E or C. Neither of these clears the memory. To display the memory value, press M and then R (for recall). The value stored in memory will appear on the display.

To clear the memory (change it to 0), press M and then C.

The Calculator memory can be used in decimal, binary, and hexadecimal modes. The value in memory converts automatically each time you change modes.

Keeping a Tape

In some circumstances you will want a way to keep track of your Calculator commands and results as a tape does in a desk calculator. Here the SuperKey program proves its worth. The TapeOn and TapeOff feature that comes with SuperKey can act as a tape for SideKick's Calculator. See Chapter 11 for a discussion of SuperKey.

Pasting Numbers

It would be easy to work through a long calculation with SideKick's Calculator and then make a mistake entering the result into some other application or into a Notepad file. The Paste function solves this problem. It allows you to assign the value in the display to a single key or short sequence of keys on the keyboard. That key or sequence of keys then can be used to recall the entire number, even if it is 18 digits long.

Here is the procedure for pasting a number:

1. Activate the Calculator on top of the utility or application you want to paste to.

2. Enter the number you want to paste in the Calculator display.

3. Press P.

4. Choose a Paste key or key combination to stand for the number you've entered and press the keys of that combination.

5. Repeat steps 2 through 4 to create multiple Paste key assignments. Use a different Paste key or key combination each time.

6. Press ALT-CTRL to exit the Calculator and return to the utility or application you want to paste to.

7. Move the cursor to the place where you want the value pasted.

8. Press your Paste key or key combination. The number will appear, beginning where the cursor is positioned.

9. Press ALT-CTRL if you want to return to the Calculator.

When you want to paste a number, type the number into the Calculator's display. Then press P from the Calculator's command line menu. The prompt "press key to paste with" appears at the bottom of the display, on the Calculator command line. You can use any key to paste with, but you must be careful because the key's regular function will disappear temporarily. For instance, imagine that you are writing in the Notepad and activate the Calculator to calculate some numbers. You end up with an 18-digit result, and want to paste that number in a half-dozen places in your Notepad document. With the Paste function you can transfer your calculations quickly and accurately, but you must choose your Paste key with some thought. If you choose the S key, for example, you wouldn't be able to type an *s* in the Notepad. Each time you pressed S, you would get the Paste number assigned to that key. Similarly, although it's tempting, you should never use the P key alone as your Paste key, because P is used to get into the Paste mode, and the two definitions will conflict.

To avoid this kind of problem, the best Paste key choices are ALT and CTRL combinations that don't overlap with other commands. ALT-P is a good choice in many circumstances. If you're pasting a series of numbers, you might want to organize a series of keys such as CTRL-1 , CTRL-2 , CTRL-3 , and so on. Figure 5-9 illustrates a long number pasted from the Calculator into the Notepad window.

You can assign Paste values to any keys and can build a large "memory" of pasted values. You can use the keys you've assigned to reproduce their Paste numbers for as long as your computer is turned on

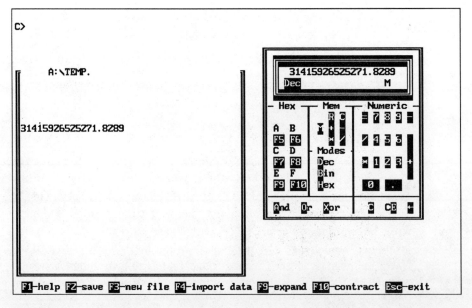

Figure 5-9.   Example of a long number pasted from the Calculator to the Notepad

and SideKick is in RAM. A SideKick window doesn't have to be displayed for the Paste function to work. To clear the value from a Paste key, however, you must activate the Calculator window, press P (to get into the Paste mode), and then press C. This clears all paste values; you cannot clear them one at a time.

Using the Calculator with the AT

You may have heard that the Calculator doesn't always run correctly on the IBM PC AT and its compatibles. An obscure bug is responsible. For instance, if you use the Calculator to divide 93,500 by 31,167 on an IBM PC (or a compatible with the 8088 central processor chip), you will get a correct result of 3.0. But if you perform the same calculation on an IBM AT (or compatible with the 80286 chip), you will get an incorrect result of 2.4.

A *patch*, a slight program change, will eliminate this problem. This patch is listed and explained in Appendix A. If you do make the patch to your copy of SideKick, it won't affect the way the program performs on a PC or XT.

6

The Calendar

Many computer users must keep a calendar of appointments, both planned and met. SideKick eases this task by including the Calendar utility, a computerized calendar and appointment book. You can use the Calendar to check the day of the week for any date both future or past. You also can use the Calendar to record appointments and daily use of time. If you are or become a frequent user of the Calendar, you will appreciate the extra power of Traveling SideKick, which is described in more detail in Chapter 10.

Opening the Calendar

To open the Calendar window from SideKick's main menu, you may use any of the four methods listed:

1.   Press F4.

2.   Press L (or l), which is highlighted within the Calendar option of the menu. You don't have to use the capital form of the letter. (The Calendar is the only utility that isn't designated by its first letter, because it conflicts with the Calculator, which is called up by the C or c.)

3.   Press ALT-L.

4.   Use the up- and down-arrow keys to move the highlight to the Calendar option and press RETURN.

After following any one method, the Calendar window appears, similar to that shown in Figure 6-1.

To exit the Calendar, press either ALT-CTRL or ESC. If you have used the Calendar previously without turning off the system or removing SideKick from memory and exited with the ALT-CTRL command (rather than the ESC command), you can return to the Calendar directly by pressing either of the SideKick activation commands, ALT-CTRL or SHIFT-SHIFT. It is only if you exit by pressing ESC that SideKick routes you through the main menu again.

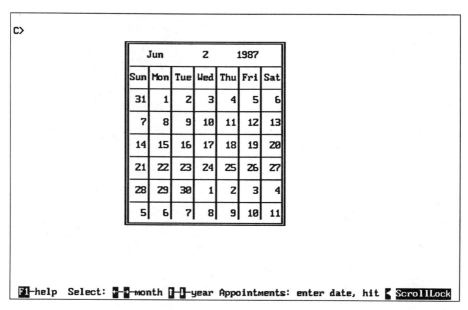

Figure 6-1.   Calendar window

Opening the Calendar on Top
of Another SideKick Utility

There are two ways to open the Calendar when you are working in another SideKick window on the screen. First, you can press ALT-L , and the Calendar appears on top of the other window or application. Second, you can hold ALT down for a second, and the main menu appears on top of the other window or application. You then can press F4, L, or ALT-L to open the Calendar window on top of the other SideKick window or application. Either method activates the Calendar.

To remove the Calendar and return to your previous utility or application, press ALT-CTRL or ESC or bring the other window to the front (by pressing any of the commands used to open that window, such as ALT-N for the Notepad window). Figure 6-2 shows an example of this multiple SideKick window arrangement.

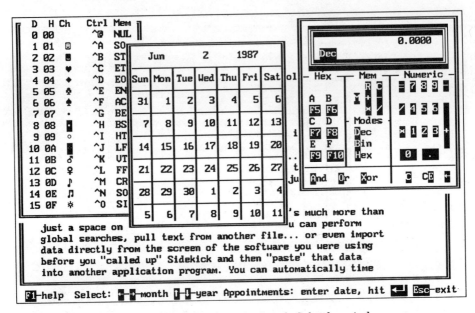

Figure 6-2. Multiple SideKick windows displayed, Calendar window on top

Moving the Calendar Window

You can position your Calendar window anywhere on the screen by pressing SCROLL LOCK and then using the cursor arrow keys. When you have positioned the Calendar where you want it, press SCROLL LOCK again. Unlike the Notepad window, the Calendar window cannot be enlarged or contracted. If you want SideKick to remember the new position and use it automatically next time you run SideKick, press ALT-S to open the Setup window. Then press F3 or F4 to save the new window setup. (F4 also saves your current files setup.)

Monthly Calendar Anatomy

When you first open the Calendar, a single-month calendar is shown, with a month, day, and year indicated across its top (Figure 6-1). The days within the displayed month are highlighted slightly; dates before and after the listed month are dimmer. The listed day is highlighted differently from the other days.

The command line across the bottom of the computer display lists a menu of commands that refers to the Calendar window, even though the window may not be touching that line. These commands are listed:

F1	As always in SideKick, this is the Help key. If you press it while using the Calendar, a description of commands and options specific to the Calendar is displayed.
ESC	At the other end of the command line is ESC, which exits you from your current operation or utility. Pressing ESC repeatedly moves you to DOS or whatever application you're running.
RIGHT ARROW, LEFT ARROW	The right- and left-arrow keys let you change the listed month. Pressing the right-arrow key moves you up a month, such as from January to February. (The listed month changes automatically.) Pressing it again moves you up another month, and so on. The months are cyclical, so when you move beyond December, for example, you get to January of the next year. (The listed year also changes automatically.) The left-arrow key moves you back a month, such as from February to January.
UP ARROW, DOWN ARROW	The up- and down-arrow keys let you change the listed year. Pressing the up-arrow key increases the year by one. Pressing it again increases the year again. The single-month calendar display also changes along with the changing years. The down-arrow key decreases the year by one. (Some versions of the SideKick manual and even the Help files mix up the functions of the arrow keys. Don't worry, it won't take you long to see how they work.)
RETURN	Pressing RETURN opens the Daily Schedule window for the day listed at the top of the monthly calendar. The Daily Schedule is described more fully later in this chapter.

To change the date, just type in the date. If the number you try doesn't exist within that month (such as February 30), the Calendar still accepts your date temporarily until you try to look at that day's schedule. This is described in more detail in the section "Opening a Daily Schedule."

The Monthly Calendar's Date Limits and Initial Setting

The SideKick Calendar utility works for the years 1901 to 2099 and includes the peculiarity of leap years. When you first open the Calendar, before you use the cursor arrow keys to change the month and year, the Calendar automatically displays the month it finds in the PC's internal clock. You set this date typically each time you start the computer with DOS and fill in the time and date. DOS uses the date and time to *stamp* new files. You can see these stamps when you call up a DOS directory of files (Figure 6-3). Some computer systems have a battery that saves the date even when the computer is turned off, and so automatically lists the right date without asking you for the information.

If you don't have a computer with an internal battery and didn't set the date when you started the computer, chances are the clock thinks the date is 1-4-80 (January 4, 1980), which is the default in most DOS versions. If SideKick finds this date or any date previous to this date, it automatically starts up the Calendar with 1-4-80.

If you use the cursor arrow keys to choose a month and year within SideKick, that date is not communicated to DOS or put into the DOS calendar. SideKick provides for the fact that the dates you choose are not necessarily the present date; they are often future dates for which you are storing appointments or past dates for which you are looking up appointments.

Also, if you return to DOS and change the date and then call up the Calendar again, this date does not change the Calendar's date. (To change the DOS date, see the next section.) The Calendar only reads the DOS date the first time the computer system is turned on.

The DOS Date Clock

The DOS date clock has the same units as the SideKick Calendar and can be changed in one of two ways. To change the DOS date, turn on your

```
FORMAT   COM      6016   3-08-83   12:00p
COMP     COM      2523   3-08-83   12:00p
GRAPHICS COM       789   3-08-83   12:00p
SORT     EXE      1280   3-08-83   12:00p
FIND     EXE      5888   3-08-83   12:00p
BACKUP   COM      3687   3-08-83   12:00p
BASIC    COM     16256   3-08-83   12:00p
BASICA   COM     25984   3-08-83   12:00p
DISKCOPY COM      2444   3-08-83   12:00p
DISKCOMP COM      2074   3-08-83   12:00p
TREE     COM      1513   3-08-83   12:00p
RESTORE  COM      4003   3-08-83   12:00p
ASSIGN   COM       896   3-08-83   12:00p
CRUISE   COM     14208   1-01-87   12:01p
AUTOEXEC CRZ        25   1-01-87   12:14p
SUPERDRV COM      3771   4-12-83    1:00p
SUPERSPL COM      6021   4-12-83    1:00p
LABEL    EXE      6784   4-10-84    1:37p
XTALK    EXE     60416  11-19-83    1:59p
CONFIG   QA         22  10-05-86    7:22p
CONFIG   TMP        22   8-26-86    9:33p
RAMCLEAR COM        67   3-24-83   10:57p
        39 File(s)    8689664 bytes free

C>
```

Figure 6-3. DOS directory displaying time and date stamps

computer system with your DOS disk loaded. The following display appears:

> Current date is Fri 1-04-1980
> Enter new date (mm-dd-yy):

Then enter the date in mm-dd-yy fashion and press RETURN. Use two digits each for month, date, and year:

> 11-28-87

You can abbreviate the date to one digit, if it is less than 10. You also can type the entire four digits of the year, if you wish. If you don't want to change the date, press RETURN twice.

Using the second method, call up the DOS prompt A> or C> (depending on whether you have a hard-disk system), then type **date**. The preceding display then appears, and you enter the date as described previously.

Opening a Daily Schedule

Once you have chosen a year, month, and date and displayed them on the monthly calendar, you can utilize a powerful feature: Calendar's daily schedules. From the monthly calendar, press RETURN. A new window opens on top of the monthly calendar with a schedule for the date you had listed (Figure 6-4). If you list a nonexistent date, such as February 30, for example, the monthly calendar remains on the display with the date set previous to your new entry, and the Daily Schedule window does not appear.

Anatomy of the Daily Schedule Window

When it is open, the Daily Schedule window is the active part of the Calendar utility. To return to the monthly calendar, you must press ESC.

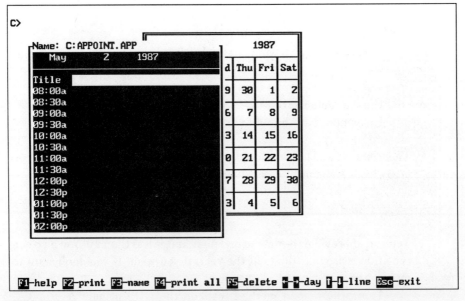

Figure 6-4.   Daily Schedule window: Page 1

If you press ALT-CTRL, all Calendar and other utility windows disappear from the display, and you exit SideKick entirely. If you press ALT-CTRL again, the entire set of windows returns, with the Daily Schedule window still active.

You can move the Daily Schedule window by pressing SCROLL LOCK and using the cursor arrow keys. This procedure is described earlier in reference to moving the Calendar window and is also detailed in Chapter 2. Be sure to press SCROLL LOCK again when you are finished moving the window.

The Daily Schedule window divides a day into half-hour blocks from 8 A.M. to 8:30 P.M. Figure 6-4 shows the morning hours. Figure 6-5 displays the afternoon and evening hours and doesn't allow a view of the morning hours; it almost can be considered a separate window.

To move from the morning half of the schedule to the afternoon half, press PGDN or the down-arrow key. PGDN jumps right to the afternoon half, and it moves to the same relative spot on the schedule.

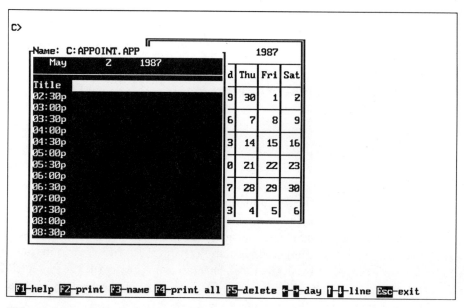

Figure 6-5.   Daily Schedule window: Page 2

The down-arrow key requires repeated presses to make the same move; the afternoon appears only when you move down past the last line of the morning half (2:00p). To move from the afternoon half to the morning half, press PGUP or press the up-arrow cursor key repeatedly.

The title and date information are listed at the top of the window and are the same in each display. Each half-hour has a line next to it for entry of appointment or scheduling information. There is also an empty title line above the 8 A.M. mark so you can give your day a name, if you wish. The command line at the bottom of the display offers a set of commands; these are listed and described in the section "Daily Schedule Commands."

Appointment Files

You probably heard the disk drive whir a little when you chose a particular daily schedule. That's because the information stored in that day's schedule isn't kept in RAM; it's kept on disk. Each time you open a day, SideKick must find the day's schedule on the disk. Although you're working with the Calendar, it's a good idea to leave the SideKick disk in the disk drive (or to work from SideKick on a hard disk), so the daily information is on hand.

Changing Appointment Files

Initially, the file in your Daily Schedule window is called APPOINT.-APP. You can change this file by pressing F3 (as is discussed shortly). Being able to change files allows you to switch back and forth between appointment files as different people make and change appointments. You also can set up several schedules for different tasks, although these schedules cannot be integrated by SideKick later.

To select a different appointment file from the one currently displayed in the Daily Schedule window, press F3. (Some earlier versions of SideKick and the SideKick manuals say to press F2. Newer versions have been changed to make the Calendar more consistent with the Notepad, where F3 is used to open a new file.) The top of the Daily Schedule windows displays the prompt:

New Name:

Type a name of up to eight letters and numbers, without spaces (following the DOS rules for naming a file), then press RETURN to load the new file into the Daily Schedule window. A typical format is to use the name or initials of the person whose appointments you are manipulating. SideKick automatically adds the extension .APP to these files when saving them, so don't add an extension yourself.

You can use wildcard characters in response to the "New Name:" prompt. Wildcard characters are explained in more detail in Chapter 2, but basically they let you use the question mark (?) for any single character and asterisk (*) for any sequence of characters. The Calendar looks for files that match the pattern you enter and displays any files that meet the requirements in a directory window (for example, Figure 6- 6). From the directory window, you can use the arrow keys to move the cursor to the file you want and then press RETURN to load the new file.

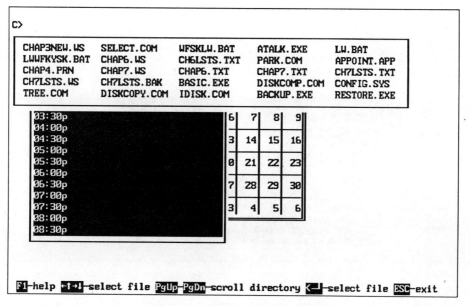

Figure 6-6.   Directory window of appointment files

Changing the Default Appointment File

You can use the Setup window to change the file that is selected automatically when you first open the Daily Schedule. To open the Setup window from the Daily Schedule window, press ALT-S. The Setup window is then displayed (Figure 6-7). (You also could hold down ALT until you see the main menu and then use any of the standard main menu options to open the Setup window.) Then press the down-arrow key three times to enter the section of the window devoted to the Calendar. You can select a new file extension name (that will be used for all Calendar files), a new default filename, and a new directory (that will be used for all Calendar files). Enter whatever values you select on the lines indicated and press RETURN after each of the three entries. If you don't press RETURN, the new value will disappear when you move to the next line. When you are finished, press F2 or F4 to save the changed files setup (F4 also saves your current window position). Your new values appear automatically the next time you start SideKick and open the Calendar Daily Schedule window.

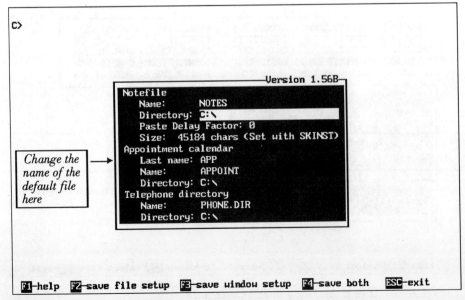

Figure 6-7.   Setup window for changing the default appointment file

Daily Schedule Commands

When you have the Daily Schedule window you want to look at or enter information in, you're ready to work with a day's events. Here are the commands:

F1	Help. Pressing F1 opens a small window of information about how to use this part of the Calendar.
ESC	Pressing ESC exits you from the current operation or utility. Pressing ESC repeatedly returns you to DOS or whatever application you're running.
F2	Print. Pressing F2 lets you print a portion of the Calendar's appointment files. After you press F2, you are asked to specify the beginning and ending dates for the portion of the calendar to be printed. Printing is discussed further in the section "Printing Schedules."
F3	Name. Pressing F3 lets you change the appointment file that is displayed in the Daily Schedule window. After you press F3, you are asked to name the new file to display. You may use wildcard characters if you want to see a small directory of files and choose a single, new appointment file from it.
F4	Print all. Pressing F4 allows you to print all of the appointments from the file currently displayed in the Daily Schedule window.
F5	Delete. Pressing F5 deletes a portion of the appointments from the file currently displayed in the Daily Schedule window. After you press F5, you are prompted to specify the beginning and ending dates for the portion of appointments you wish to delete.
RIGHT ARROW, LEFT ARROW	Day. Pressing the right-arrow key moves the Daily Schedule window back in time by one day, and the window then displays the appointments stored for that day. Pressing the left-arrow key moves the

	Daily Schedule window forward in time by one day, and then displays the appointments for that day.
UP ARROW, DOWN ARROW	Time. Pressing the up-arrow key moves the cursor and highlight bar up through the Daily Schedule display. Pressing the down-arrow key moves the cursor and the highlight bar down through the schedule. Each press moves one half-hour —one line —up or down the schedule.
PGDN	Pressing PGDN moves you from the first page of the Daily Schedule window to the second page.
PGUP	Pressing PGUP moves you from the second page of the Daily Schedule window to the first page.
BACKSPACE	Pressing BACKSPACE moves the cursor back one position on the line it is on and erases whatever character was in that position.
RETURN	Pressing RETURN saves information on a line and moves you down to the next line. If you move down a line without pressing RETURN, such as by using the down-arrow key, any new information or changes you made to that line are lost.

For each half-hour of the day and for the day's title, you can type up to 26 characters (letters, numbers, and so on). Figure 6-8 shows an example Daily Schedule window with some appointment information. Information is entered on the highlight line. Also, lines don't wrap to the next line; when you hit your 26-character limit, the cursor stops and doesn't enter further characters.

Modifying and Deleting Information

You can enter new information on a line by moving the cursor to that line and pressing BACKSPACE to delete the old information. Then type your new text and press RETURN to save the new text. You must use BACK-

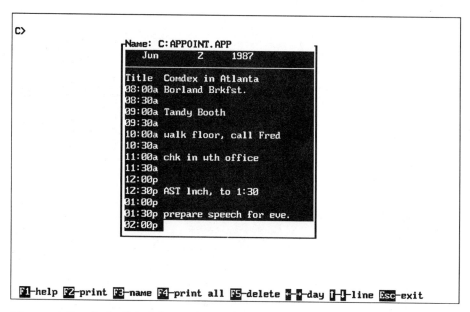

Figure 6-8.   Daily Schedule window with example appointments

SPACE to delete text, because when you move the cursor to the line to be altered, it automatically jumps to the end of the line of old text. If you want to delete everything on a line, simply move to that line, press BACKSPACE accordingly, and press RETURN. There is also a more powerful delete command, which is discussed in the next section.

Deleting Entire Sections of a Calendar

As you can see from the command line in Figure 6-5, F5 offers a delete function. You can delete information within any period ranging from one day to your entire schedule file (one file with one file name, not all schedule files simultaneously). To choose the material to delete, you must specify the beginning and ending dates of the period.

For example, to delete a single day (such as 12-6-86), press F5 and

First month to delete:

is displayed at the top of the Daily Schedule window (Figure 6-9). Type **12** and press RETURN. A similar prompt is displayed:

First day to delete:

Type **6** and press RETURN. Finally, a prompt for the year appears:

First year to delete:

Type **1986** and press RETURN. You must enter all four digits for the year; two does not work.

If you make a mistake, use BACKSPACE to delete a few characters and then start again. If you don't want to continue the operation, press ESC; CTRL-U doesn't work to interrupt this operation.

Now you must work through the prompts for the end of the period to be deleted. If you want to delete the single day, answer the following

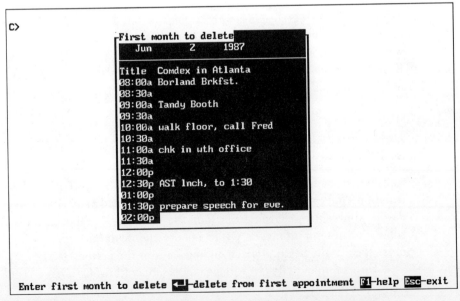

Figure 6-9. Daily Schedule window with delete specification prompt

prompts with the same dates you used for the period's start:

Last month to delete:

Type **12** and press RETURN:

Last day to delete:

Type **6** and press RETURN:

Last year to delete:

Type **1986** and press RETURN. (Of course, if you want to delete a longer period than just the one day, you must enter your dates accordingly.)

The information stored within the period you indicate is erased, although the Daily Schedule window's structure for the day remains. You do not delete an actual day from the Calendar, just the previously entered appointments for that day.

Deletion Defaults

If you press RETURN in response to the prompt:

First month to delete:

without entering a number for a month, SideKick assumes you want to delete all appointments starting from the earliest appointment in the file. The next prompt to appear is

Last month to delete:

You now have two options: you can enter a specific value here, press RETURN, and delete all appointments between your chosen final date and the earliest appointment in the file. Or you can just press RETURN, without entering any numbers, and SideKick will delete everything up through "yesterday." (Yesterday calculated by assuming whatever date is showing in the Calendar's Daily Schedule window is today.)

Printing Schedules

You can print schedules for a single day or an entire section of the
appointment file. From the Daily Schedule window, press F2 and respond
to the prompts that appear at the top of the window. These prompts are
almost identical to those for the deletion defaults. The first prompt is

>   First month to print:

to which you should enter the beginning month of the period you want to
print and press RETURN. The next prompts are, respectively:

>   First day to print:

and

>   First year to print:

to which you should enter the relevant information, pressing RETURN
after each entry is completed. The year must be entered with all four
digits; two doesn't work. If you make a mistake, press BACKSPACE to erase
the incorrect digits and then type in the correct ones.

To define the end of the print period, answer the following prompts,
pressing RETURN after each entry is complete:

>   Last month to print:

>   Last day to print:

and

>   Last year to print:

If you want to print a single day, the month, date, and year will be the
same for the beginning and ending printer prompts. If at any point you
decide you don't want to print anything, press ESC.

Defaults for Printing

If you press RETURN in response to the "First month to print" prompt,
without entering a specific month, SideKick assumes you want to start
printing with the earliest or first appointment in the appointment file,

however far back that goes. If you press RETURN in response to the "Last month to print" prompt, without entering a specific month, SideKick likewise assumes you want to print up to and including the last appointment in the file (the one with the furthest forward date).

If you simply want to print everything in one appointment file, without specifying any starting and ending dates, you can press F4 , which "prints all."

Print Formatting

The Calendar's printing function prints one day per page of printer paper. A full day of appointments occupies 28 lines. At the end of each day's printed appointments, the Calendar sends a *form feed* command to the printer, which tells the printer to move to the beginning of the next page. If you want to squeeze more days onto each page, you can change the page length setting on your printer. For instance, if your printer lets you set each page to 33 lines, then the standard 66 lines of an 8 1/2" x 11" sheet of paper could fit two days of printed schedules.

Borland also has published a *patch* to change the form feed to a line feed. This patch is included in Appendix B.

Traveling SideKick

If you want yet more control over all aspects of your scheduling, you should look at Traveling SideKick. Traveling SideKick is not just another version of SideKick; it is an independent program made for people who handle complicated schedules, telephone lists, and address lists. It is made to work with SideKick's Calendar and Dialer utilities. This program offers a wide range of Calendar printing commands that let you reorganize and format the Calendar's information in many ways. It also comes with a special binder and paper for printing and carrying long and complex appointment files. Chapter 10 describes Traveling SideKick in more detail.

7

The Dialer and Phone Directory

The SideKick Dialer utility is not a complete telecommunications program, but it does offer three useful functions. First, it can pick out telephone numbers from displays in other programs and dial them. Second, it can search through its own phone directory for a telephone number and dial it. Third, its phone directory can be used as a phone number and address database, even if you don't need any dialing.

What is dialing, and how is it different from a telecommunications program? A standard telecommunications program allows your computer to work through a modem to dial phone numbers, but it also allows your computer to translate computer files and programs into data that can be sent to or received from another computer. A standard telecommunications program lets your computer connect to other computers and then talk to those computers. It lets you send and receive files and work with on-line services. Although many such programs let you build short lists of commonly used telephone numbers, they don't provide a true database function for these numbers, with searching and sorting, nor can they store many numbers.

Although less powerful than a standard telecommunications program, a dialer program, teamed with a simple database manager, is a worthwhile tool —with quite a different aim than a standard telecommunications program. SideKick's Dialer utility is such a dialer program. It does not give your computer the ability to talk to other computers, but it does offer a much more extensive telephone number store-and-retrieve function: a database or directory for phone numbers.

Dialing means letting your computer do the work of punching in a phone number into a telephone. If you hook up your modem to the phone lines, then when you want to make some calls, you can have SideKick's Dialer dial or *tone* the number. You can hear your modem dial a chosen number, and when all the digits have been dialed, all you have to do is pick up your telephone receiver, press SPACE BAR, and start talking. The Dialer may be merely a minor convenience if you only make a few local calls, but it is a major advantage if you make a lot of long-distance calls using different phone services and even credit card numbers. Computerized dialing can rescue you from making dialing errors and can save you time.

The Dialer Requires Immediate Installation

The Dialer is different from the other SideKick utilities as far as installation is concerned. Using SKINST isn't just a convenience for customization — it is a necessity. Until you use SKINST, the Dialer can only function in the third of its three employments: as a phone and address directory.

Using SKINST

Reboot your computer or turn it on for the first time. (If you are already using SideKick during this computing session — SideKick is in memory — you can still install the Dialer. You just have to reboot it after you're done.) If you must reboot, make sure you save whatever SideKick files you're currently using, such as the notefile in the Notepad window, before you reboot. If a SideKick window is on the display, exit SideKick by pressing ESC.

From the DOS prompt (A:> if you're using a floppy-disk system with SideKick in drive A or C:> \sk if you're using a hard-disk system where all of the SideKick files are in the file directory sk in the C drive), type **skinst** and press RETURN to call up the Installation program's main menu. To make installation changes to the Dialer, press D, and a Dialer installation menu appears (Figure 7-1).

Modem Type

The Dialer default modem type can be any of the modems in the top section of the display: Hayes SmartModem 1200 or 1200B, AST Reach, ProModem 1200, Racal-Vadic Maxwell 1200 or 1200PC, US Robotics Password, Ven-Tel's PS Modem Plus, or any Hayes-compatible modem running at 300 baud. Most personal computer modems are Hayes-compatible. If your modem is in this first set or you're not sure what type of modem you have, press H. If you haven't run this part of the

```
Press H to select one of the following modems:

        Hayes SmartModem 1200 / 1200B
        AST Reach
        ProModem 1200
        Racal-Vadic Maxwell 1200 / 1200 PC
        US Robotics Password
        Ven-Tel's PS Modem Plus
        or any other Hayes compatible modem (300 Baud)

Press J to select the IBM PCjr modem (300 Baud)

Press V to select the VOAD Keyboard Phone (9600 Baud)

Press A to select the AT & T 4000 modem (1200 Baud)

Modem selected (H/J/V/A, ◄┘ for no change):  Hayes etc.

Select Tone or Pulse dial (T/P, ◄┘ for no change: T

Minimum number of digits (1-80, ◄┘ for no change):   6

Required character (up to 10 characters, ◄┘ for no change):  -()

Modem port (0 for no modem, 1 for COM1:, 2 for COM2:, ◄┘ for no change):  0
```

Figure 7-1. Dialer installation menu

installation program before, the default value H is indicated already. You only have to press RETURN to verify the choice.

There are only three other selections here: the IBM PCjr modem in an IBM PCjr, the VOAD Keyboard Phone, and the AT&T 4000. If you know that your modem is one of these, then press the appropriate letter (J, V, or A). You don't need to press RETURN.

Tone or Pulse Dialing

After you choose the type of modem, you must specify whether you're going to use pulse or tone dialing. Pulse is the older form, like that produced by telephones with a rotary dial. Tone is the newer form, the "beep" sounds often made by pushbutton phones. You should select pulse or tone based on the phone you're using. Don't worry about this choice. You still can use either tone or pulse after you get the Dialer installed; you simply insert a T or P code into the phone number you are going to dial. This installation option just sets the default that is used when no code is indicated in the number. When dialing, a prompt such as the following appears:

Select Tone or Pulse dial (T/P, Return for no change): T

instructing you to press T or RETURN for tone dialing or to press P for pulse dialing (Figure 7-1).

Telephone Number Recognition

The Dialer can dial numbers automatically from other applications or windows (such as the Notepad or a database display), because it can search through a display and find sequences of characters that could be phone numbers. How, for instance, can it tell a phone number from a price? The Dialer applies a couple of rules: these rules have default values, but you can change the values to fit your own needs.

Number of Digits   The first rule is the minimum number of digits. As you can see from Figure 7-1,

Minimum number of digits (1-80, Return for no change): 7

this is the next selection in the Installation program. It sets the minimum number of digits that are recognized as a phone number. You should set it for the smallest phone numbers you will use. For example, you might set it for 10 (by pressing **10** and then RETURN), because standard United States phone numbers with area codes have 10 digits (such as (408) 438-8400). However, what if a phone number is indicated inside the Dialer user's own area code (thus does not use an area code for dialing)? Without the extra three digits, the number is only seven digits long and would not be found by the Dialer and therefore could not be dialed. You can set this selection value from one to 80 digits, but the seven-digit default works well in most circumstances. The only reason to choose higher values is to be more selective: to eliminate shorter numbers from consideration as phone numbers. You might consider such a selection if you're working with a display that mixes a few longer phone numbers in with many short numbers that aren't phone numbers.

Special Characters   The Dialer also looks for special characters to help it distinguish phone numbers from other numbers and text. The prompt

Required character (up to 10 characters, Return for no change) : - ( )

is the next prompt on the installation display (Figure 7-1). The default characters are the hyphen (-) and the right and left parentheses. If you press RETURN without entering any new characters, the default characters continue to define the rule. The Dialer only locates phone numbers that have at least one of these characters. Also, the numbers may not be interrupted by other characters such as periods, slashes, or other characters that are used in dates, amounts, and other numeric information. You can include one of these other characters by creating a new installation list after the prompt. The new installation list must include each character, including the hyphen and the right and left parentheses. Even if more than one special character is listed in the installation line, as in the default example, the Dialer can find a phone number that has only one of the special characters. As the prompt suggests, you can enter as many as 10 characters. The inclusion of characters in the phone number doesn't change the number of digits specified by the previous rule. The number

408-4388400

and this number

(408) 438-8400

both have 10 digits.

Modem Port

The final prompt of the Dialer installation menu is

Modem port (0 for no modem, 1 for COM1:, 2 for COM2:, Return for no change) : 0

This is the only prompt that you *must* answer, and it is the reason you need to install the Dialer before using it (unlike the other SideKick utilities that are ready for use without any installation).

As you can see in Figure 7-1, the default is 0—which means no modem is attached. If you press RETURN, you are returned to the Installation program main menu. But you won't be able to have SideKick dial any numbers automatically: the Dialer will be useful only as a phone and address file.

To be able to use the Dialer for automatic dialing, you must attach a modem to either the COM1 or COM2 ports and to your telephone line. The COM ports are your computer's serial ports. Most PCs have at least one, and it is almost certainly the COM1 port. However, it probably doesn't have any sort of label. At most it will have a "Serial" or "Com" label. If you have more than one serial port, one of them is COM1, and one is COM2. COM1 is the primary port. If you don't know which port is COM1, you can experiment by trying the installation for COM1 and then seeing if your modem works. If it doesn't, try the other port. You also can ask someone more expert in computers to tell you which port is which. Remember: you can always call Borland (as mentioned in Chapter 2) for help.

The same rule applies if you have an internal modem: try one port in the following installation, then try the other port. If neither works, talk to a local expert or call Borland.

In most cases, you'll be able to specify your single serial port as port 1 and attach your modem to it. But because modems aren't the only devices that attach to serial ports —printers, plotters, mice, and many other peripherals can be attached —you may need some expert advice on setup.

Hooking Up Your Modem and Phone   Most modems have two telephone jacks, often labeled TEL and LINE. Plug the telephone line into TEL and the line that runs to the telephone box on the wall into LINE.

Finishing Installation   When you have worked through all of the prompts for installation (Figure 7-1), you are returned to the main Installation program display. Press Q to quit. If SideKick isn't in memory, load it. If SideKick is in memory, reboot your computer and load SideKick into RAM. Your installation changes are now ready to use.

Opening the Dialer Window

To choose the Dialer from the main menu, you can use any of the four methods listed (the fastest options are the first three given):

1. Press F5.

2. Press D or d (which is the highlight within the Dialer option of the menu). SideKick doesn't care whether you opt for the uppercase "D" or the lowercase "d."

3. Press ALT-D.

4. Use the up- and down-arrow keys to move the highlight line to the Dialer option. Then press RETURN.

After any one of these four commands, the Dialer is active and immediately looks for a possible phone number to dial. To exit the Dialer, press ESC.

The Dialer identifies phone numbers by searching for a certain number of digits in a row along with at least one special character and not other characters (such as periods or slashes), as defined by the installation process.

The default looks for strings of at least six digits with at least one hyphen or parenthesis. Longer strings of numbers or numbers with more special characters also are recognized.

If the Dialer finds a telephone number, it highlights the number on the screen. If it finds more than one telephone number, it highlights only the first number (from top to bottom and left to right). If it doesn't find any number, it opens the Telephone Directory window (Figure 7-2). If your Dialer is not attached to a modem, as defined in the installation procedure, then the Telephone Directory window pops up automatically, without doing any searching for telephone numbers.

All of the preceding material is discussed in greater detail as you work through the chapter.

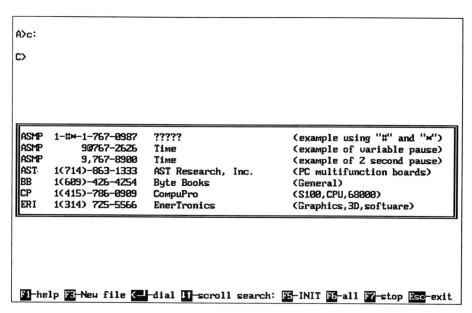

```
A>c:

C>




ASMP  1-#x-1-767-0987   ?????            (example using "#" and "x")
ASMP      90767-2626    Time             (example of variable pause)
ASMP     9,767-8900     Time             (example of 2 second pause)
AST.  1(714)-863-1333   AST Research, Inc.   (PC multifunction boards)
BB    1(609)-426-4254   Byte Books       (General)
CP    1(415)-786-0909   CompuPro         (S100,CPU,68000)
ERI   1(314) 725-5566   EnerTronics      (Graphics,3D,software)




F1-help F3-New file ⟵-dial ↕-scroll search: F5-INIT F6-all F7-stop Esc-exit
```

Figure 7-2.   Telephone Directory window

Picking and Dialing a Number
from Another Program

The simplest way to use the Dialer is to have it select and dial a single number from another program's display. Figure 7-3 illustrates a DOS display with a telephone number. (The Dialer can work with numbers from any sort of display: DOS, application, or another SideKick utility.) With this telephone number on the screen, SideKick loaded into memory, and the Dialer installed for use with a COM port, activate SideKick by pressing ALT-CTRL or SHIFT-SHIFT and open the Dialer using any of the methods described previously. Dialer highlights the telephone number.

Figure 7-3 also shows the Dialer's menu on the command line at the bottom of the display. To dial the highlight number, press RETURN. When you hear the modem finish dialing, pick up your telephone receiver, press SPACE BAR, and wait for the connection.

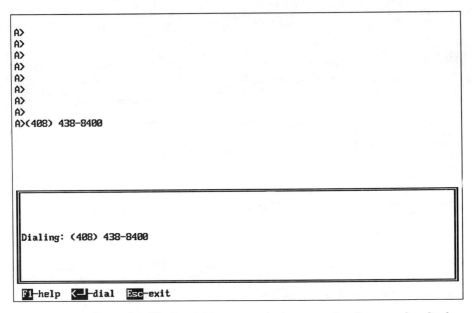

```
A>
A>
A>
A>
A>
A>
A>
A>
A>(408) 438-8400




 ┌────────────────────────────────────────────────────────────┐
 │                                                              │
 │                                                              │
 │ Dialing: (408) 438-8400                                      │
 │                                                              │
 └────────────────────────────────────────────────────────────┘
 F1-help  ←┘-dial  Esc-exit
```

Figure 7-3.   Example of Dialer picking out a telephone number from another display

If you don't want to dial this number, you have two choices. You can press ESC (ALT-CTRL won't work in this case) and return to your other application (in this example, to DOS). Or you can press SPACE BAR to open the Dialer's Telephone Directory window, as shown in Figure 7-2. Use of this phone directory is explained in the following sections of this chapter.

If you need information about how to use the Dialer, press F1 or ALT-H, just as you can in any SideKick utility.

You may have noticed the one other option on the command line: the RIGHT ARROW. You can use this option if you have a display that contains more than one telephone number. When SideKick finds more than one number, it highlights the first number and waits for your next command. If you press the right-arrow key, the Dialer highlights the next telephone number on the display and offers you the same choices again.

You also can use the Dialer in conjunction with other SideKick utilities. For instance, you could dial a number that appears in the Notepad display automatically. To do this with the Notepad window displayed, you have two options: you can press ALT-D, or you can hold down ALT for a second until the main menu appears and then press F5, D, or ALT-D. In each case, if the Dialer finds a telephone number in the Notepad window, it highlights it and waits for your command. Pressing ESC returns you to the Notepad. If the Dialer doesn't find a telephone number in the Notepad window, or if it does but you press SPACE BAR, the Telephone Directory window appears on top of the Notepad.

Telephone Directory Window

The Telephone Directory is almost like a utility within the Dialer utility. It can be used as a storehouse of phone numbers that the Dialer can dial, and it also can function almost on its own as a small database for phone numbers and addresses. If the Dialer isn't installed for a COM port, SideKick automatically opens the Telephone Directory window (Figure 7-2) when you open the Dialer. Also, if you open the Dialer on a display without a recognizable telephone number, or if you press SPACE BAR instead of dialing a recognized number, the Telephone Directory window appears.

Moving the Telephone Directory Window

Once your Telephone Directory window is displayed, remember that you can move it to any vertical position on the screen. To do this, press SCROLL LOCK and use the up- and down-arrow keys. When you have the Telephone Directory window where you want it, press SCROLL LOCK again. Unlike the Notepad window, the window cannot be enlarged or contracted.

If you want SideKick to remember the new Dialer window position and use it automatically the next time you run SideKick, press ALT-S to open the Setup window and then press F3 or F4 to save your new window setup.

Leaving the Telephone Directory

You can exit the Telephone Directory window, and therefore the Dialer utility, by pressing ALT-CTRL, SHIFT-SHIFT, or ESC. If you leave the Telephone Directory window via ALT-CTRL (rather than ESC), you later can return directly to the Telephone Directory window by pressing either ALT-CTRL or SHIFT-SHIFT. It is only if you exit the Telephone Directory via ESC that SideKick routes you through the main menu the next time you want to use the Dialer.

Opening the Telephone Directory Window on Top of Other Utilities

There are two options to call up the Telephone Directory window on top of another application or SideKick window, such as the Notepad. First, you can press ALT-D, and the Dialer appears on top of the other application or SideKick window. Second, you can hold down ALT for a second until the main menu appears on top of the other application or SideKick window. Then you can press F5, D, or ALT-D to open the Dialer window on top of the other SideKick window. In either case, the Dialer is now the active window.

You can return to your previous application or utility by pressing ALT-CTRL or ESC or by calling the other application or utility's window to the front. To do that, press any of the commands that normally would open that window, such as ALT-N for the Notepad window.

Telephone Directory Command Menu

The Telephone Directory presents its own menu on the command line. These commands are listed:

F1	As always in SideKick, this is the Help key. If you press it while using the Dialer, you receive descriptions of commands and options specific to the Dialer. (You also can press ALT-H.)
ESC	Pressing ESC gets you out of the current operation or utility; in this case, it gets you out of the Telephone Directory window. Repeatedly pressing

ESC returns you to the previous application or utility you're running.

F3

Pressing F3 allows you to load a different or "new" telephone directory file into the Telephone Directory window.

UP ARROW, DOWN ARROW

Pressing the up- and down-arrow keys lets you scroll, one line at a time, through the telephone directory.

RETURN

Pressing RETURN dials the phone number in the highlight line of the Telephone Directory window.

F5

INIT. Pressing F5 lets you search through the telephone directory for an entry with particular initials. After pressing F5, you are prompted to enter the initials you want to search for. The search commands, including F5, are described in more detail in a later section of this chapter.

F6

All. Pressing F6 lets you search through the telephone directory for an entry containing any given series or characters. After pressing F6, you are prompted to enter the series or characters you want to search for. The search commands, including F6, are described in more detail in a later section of this chapter.

F7

Stop. Pressing F7 stops any search you started with F5 or F6. The search commands, including F7, are described in more detail in a later section of this chapter.

Using the Currently Displayed Telephone Directory

If you want to use the telephone directory that is already in the Telephone Directory window, use the up- and down-arrow keys to move the highlight bar to the phone number you wish to dial automatically. Then press RETURN, wait for the number to be dialed, pick up your telephone receiver, press SPACE BAR, and talk. If this procedure doesn't work, check through this chapter a little more thoroughly, particularly the section on installation, and if that still doesn't help, contact your dealer or Borland.

Loading a New Telephone Directory File

You can keep a number of different phone directory files on disk under different names. F3 lets you call up a different phone directory file into the Telephone Directory window. PHONE.DIR is the name of the file that is loaded automatically when you first open the Telephone Directory window. (You can change the name of the default file and the default file directory itself by using the Setup window, as described in the next section.)

The New File command works much the same as the New File

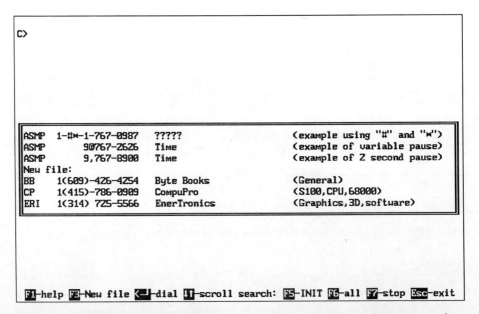

Figure 7-4.   Prompts for the New File command in the Telephone Directory window

command in the Notepad. After you press F3, you answer the prompts on the status line in the middle of the display (Figure 7-4). If you answer with a name that SideKick can find on the disk, that new file is loaded into the window and the old file disappears. If no such file is found, you are asked to choose another name.

You can use wildcards in response to the name prompt. As described in Chapter 3, wildcard characters can stand for any other character, and they allow you to select a range of possible files designated by the parameters you set. For instance, if you answer

phone?.*

in response to the name prompt, a File Directory window appears at the top of the screen (Figure 7-5). You can choose a file from the File Directory window by moving the highlight bar with the arrow cursor keys to the file name you want. Then press RETURN, and that file is loaded into the Telephone Directory window.

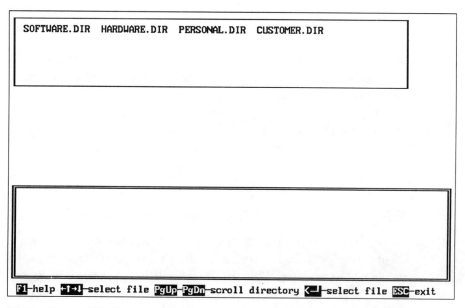

Figure 7-5. File Directory window for Telephone Directory wildcard search

Using the Setup Window to Change
the Default Phone Directory File

You can use the Setup window to change the file that is selected
automatically when you first open the Dialer's Telephone Directory
window. To do this, return to the SideKick main menu or to another
SideKick utility and press ALT-S to call up the Setup window. Then press
the up cursor arrow twice or the down cursor arrow six times. You'll be in
the bottom section of the Setup window, the section devoted to the
Dialer's phone directory. The default filename is PHONE.DIR, and the
default file directory is the root file directory. You can select a new
default filename and a directory for that file. Enter whatever values you
desire on these two lines and press RETURN each time you're finished on
a given line. If you don't press RETURN after each line, the new value will
disappear when you leave the line.

You can use wildcard characters on the name line. If you do, a File
Directory window appears at the top of the screen when you first open
the Dialer's Telephone Directory window (Figure 7-5). From this File
Directory window, you can select the phone directory you want to load.

The directory comments can be confusing. Just remember that the
Dialer utility has an associated Telephone Directory window that can
hold a file of phone numbers, names, and addresses. At the same time,
SideKick sometimes lets you choose which files to load into the Dialer or
Notepad by offering you a File Directory window of files on the disk. This
file directory and the telephone directory are quite different, although
the telephone directory is listed in the disk file directory.

When you are finished with the Setup window, press F2 or F4 to save
the changed files setup (F4 also saves your current window position).
Your changes appear automatically the next time you start SideKick and
open the Dialer's Telephone Directory window.

Telephone Directory Window Anatomy

As Figure 7-6 illustrates, a SideKick Telephone Directory window is a
list of entries, with each entry having three major parts: initials, phone
number, and comment. What you put in each of these areas is up to you,
but you should be sensitive to the Dialer's commands. For the computer
technophiles, the entire file must be text only, the fields must be comma

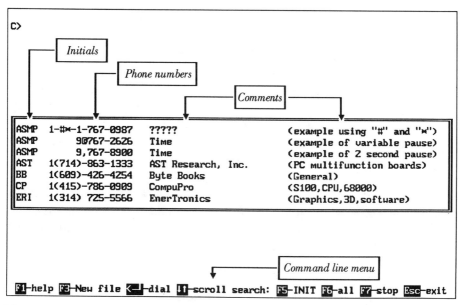

Figure 7-6.   Telephone Directory anatomy

delimited or position delimited, and the lines should be separated by a carriage return and line feed. If you don't know what that means, don't worry about it. You don't need to know.

For the initial section, it is typical to use a company abbreviation or an individual's nickname or initials. It is important that the initials begin in column one on the screen, because a "Search Initials" command can look for a specified name among the entries that begin in the first column. The reason that this first section is abbreviated is that the Dialer only displays 78 characters on each line. A directory file may have entries longer than that, but only the first 78 characters will be shown, and if the entire phone number isn't within that portion of the line, you won't be able to automatically dial it.

The second portion of the line is for the phone number. This number must contain the minimum number of digits and at least one of the special characters defined in the Installation program (as discussed earlier in this chapter). If a phone number meets both of these requirements, the Dialer is able to recognize it as a phone number.

Three characters have distinctive meanings in the phone number part of the line. A "T" in the number instructs the modem to use tone dialing for that number. A "P" instructs the modem to use pulse dialing. You can even mix the two methods within a single number; the special character affects the digits that come after it. An @ sign in a phone number creates a pause in the dialing at that point, which is sometimes necessary for long-distance or credit card dialing.

The comment portion of the line can be used for anything, such as names, addresses, key words, and so on.

Because a phone directory file is a text file, you can put whatever other text you want into the file, including such things as an introduction and section explanations. Other text merely disrupts the visual organization of the file, but it doesn't hamper the phone directory's searching or dialing.

Creating or Modifying a Telephone Directory File

Where do all these directories come from? You make them. This is also known as *compiling* a phone directory. An example phone directory is included with the original SideKick files. But you'll want to make your own, and there is no command within the Dialer for adding new information. However, there are several ways inside and outside of SideKick to make or change telephone directories.

Using the Notepad to Create a Telephone Directory File

Probably the easiest way to create or modify a phone directory is to use SideKick's own Notepad. You can load a phone directory file into the Notepad window and then treat it as a notefile. Put different phone directory entries on different lines, and separate the initials, phone number, and comment sections with commas or by at least one space. You can even make these changes to a telephone directory file while the Telephone Directory window is on the screen. Just press ALT-N to call up the Notepad, open the phone directory file by pressing F3, then type the name of that file, press RETURN, and make your changes.

When you're finished, press F2 to save the file, press ESC to exit the Notepad, and then load the new version of the file into the Telephone Directory window by pressing F3 from within that window, typing in the same filename, and then pressing RETURN. In the newest version of SideKick, you don't have to type the same file name: it appears as the default in the New File prompt line. All you have to do is press RETURN to reestablish the link to the full phone directory file on disk. This last step is important, because the phone directory file you changed with the Notepad is the file that is on disk. The copy of it in the Telephone Directory window is mainly in memory and doesn't reflect your modifications.

(*A technical note:* short phone directory files are kept completely in memory. Long phone directory files are kept only partially in memory. For long files, the extra data that is kept on disk only is read into memory when you search beyond the section in memory. A phone directory file can be as big as about 62K, or about 30 pages. The impact of the fact that only part of long files are kept in memory is that some programs can interrupt SideKick's access to that extra information. If you are using the Telephone Directory window, exit it to use another program, and return to the window, you may find that the file is strangely "cut off" part way through. You must use the New File command to reload it again from memory. Regardless of the length of your file, if you modify a file using the Notepad and save it to disk, you still must load the new version into memory to see the changes.)

The Notepad Block Sort function can be used to organize a phone directory alphabetically, by area code, or in many other ways. This can make phone directory use more efficient, and is discussed further in the section "Sorting a Phone Directory."

Using Other Programs to Create or Modify a Phone Directory File

You also can employ any other word processor, database manager, or programming language to create a phone directory for the Dialer as long as it meets certain criteria. The program must be able to turn out a file that contains only text characters (no special control characters, for example), must have the three portions of the line delimited by commas or spaces, must have the important information within the first 78 columns of the line, must have each entry separated by a carriage return and line feed, and must have phone numbers in the form that Dialer can recognize. To find out if a program meets the required criteria, ask your dealer or call Borland for technical support.

Finding Numbers in the Phone Directory

Several commands allow you to find a specific number in the Telephone Directory window (see the previous section "Telephone Directory Command Menu"). The simplest way to do this is to use the up- and down-arrow keys to scroll through the phone directory file until you find the line with the phone number you want to dial. When you find it, use the arrow keys to place the highlight bar on that line, press RETURN to dial the number, pick up your telephone receiver, press SPACE BAR, and get ready to speak.

There are also some *search* commands, which are discussed in the following sections. (The keys used for some search commands have been changed in more recent versions of SideKick. If you have version 1.56, the commands you need match those described here. If you have a previous version, you must contact your dealer or Borland to get the precise commands.)

Searching by Initials   If you press F5, the following prompt is displayed:

Search for INITials:

You can answer this prompt with any characters you wish, then press RETURN or either of the up or down cursor arrow keys. A SEARCH ACTIVE status signal will remain on while SideKick searches through the Telephone Directory window for the first entry that has your search characters beginning in the first column of the window. This is why initials must begin in the first column and why leading spaces or blanks in an initial are important: they change what the Search for Initials command finds.

If you press either UP ARROW or DOWN ARROW, SideKick searches in the direction of the key you use. If there is more than one entry with those initials, it stops on the first match it finds.

When a match is found, SideKick highlights it. If the entry is the one you want to use, press RETURN to dial the number, wait for the dialing, pick up the receiver, press SPACE BAR, and get ready to speak.

If the number is not the one you want to use, then press UP ARROW or DOWN ARROW again to search for any other entry with the same beginning initials. If an entry is found, SideKick highlights it, and you can then dial that number. If no other entry is found, either the last or the first entry of the Telephone Directory is highlighted (depending on whether you are searching with UP ARROW or DOWN ARROW), and the SEARCH ACTIVE status signal remains on at the top of the directory window. You then can press the up- or down-arrow key again to start another search. A search only can end when you press F7.

You can begin a new search for a new set of initials at any time: just press F5 again to start the process over.

Search Through All   You can perform a different type of search by pressing F6 instead of F5. F6 searches through all of the characters in the phone directory file, not just through the initials. F6 can be made more useful if you put *key words* in the comment area of phone directory entries. Key words are words associated with an entry, words that can help you find it later. For instance, if you have the phone number for Hayes Corporation, you might use the key word modem. If you have a Borland phone number, you might add the key word Turbo. And if you have a pizza-delivery service whose initials are something nondescript such as DP, you might want to put the words pizza and food in the comment area.

When you press F6, the following prompt appears:

Search for:

Enter any characters, words, or numbers you think might lead to the phone directory entry you want, then press RETURN or either of the cursor arrow keys. SideKick searches through the Telephone Directory window for the first entry that has your search characters anywhere on the line. The characters can be in the middle of a word and do not have to be capitalized. When F6 finds a match, it highlights the line that contains the match.

The procedure works the same as that discussed in the previous section on searching by initials.

Ending a Search   As mentioned, a search can only be completely ended by pressing F7. Until you do so, any time you press UP ARROW or DOWN ARROW, you continue the search for the same characters. If they can't be found, you keep zipping back and forth between the beginning and end of the file. If you want to use the cursor arrow keys to scroll through the file one line at a time, you must end the search by using F7.

Sorting a Phone Directory

You can use the Block Sort function of Notepad to alphabetize your directories. Searching through a phone directory file, especially searching by initials, is quicker if the phone directory is in alphabetical order.

To organize a phone directory alphabetically, open the Notepad, read in the phone directory file using the New File command, mark the beginning and end of the entries with CTRL-K-B and CTRL-K-K, and then use the sort command CTRL-K-S. As described in the section on sorting in Chapter 4, you'll be asked which columns you want to sort on. To sort alphabetically by initials, use columns 1 through 4 or 5. To sort phone numbers, start with the first column and end with the last.

To see the column numbers, you can move the cursor within the Notepad and check the column status information at the top of the window on the status line. You can even sort sections within sections by repeatedly applying CTRL-K-S.

When you're finished sorting, save the file by pressing F2, and then reopen the Telephone Directory window and load the changed file, even though it has the same name, with the F3 (New File) command.

Traveling SideKick

If you want to make even more use of the Dialer than is discussed in this chapter, you may appreciate the extra power of Traveling SideKick, a separate program available from Borland. Traveling SideKick is not just another version of SideKick; it is an independent program made for people who handle complicated schedules, telephone lists, and address lists.

It offers a wide range of features that let you work with the phone directories. It also adds muscle to the Calendar and comes with a special binder and paper for printing and carrying long and complex appointment files and phone directories. Chapter 10 describes Traveling Side-Kick in more detail.

8

The ASCII Table

The ASCII Table is the most specialized utility in the SideKick repertoire. It was originally included because SideKick was seen as a programmer's toolkit, a collection of little programs that the software developers at Borland needed when writing programs on their own computers. (This programming emphasis still can be seen in the logical operations and different number modes of the Calculator utility, as described in Chapter 7.)

Computers work with digital information — 1s and 0s — that is used to represent all other forms of information including text, numbers, graphics, and so on. One of the most common ways to convert the 1s and 0s into human-readable information is to assign a code to each character. The most popular code is called ASCII, which stands for American Standard Code for Information Interchange. With codes like ASCII, it is possible to convert information from the form a computer wants — numbers — to the form a human can use directly — letters, numbers, graphics, and so on.

Programmers work with ASCII all the time. When a program sorts a series of characters, it most often sorts them by comparing their ASCII values. When a printer is told to print certain characters, it often looks for ASCII information both to tell it which characters to print and to tell it how to print them.

But you don't have to be a programmer to be interested in ASCII. For instance, it is useful to be able to look up ASCII values for making small print control changes. With your printer reference manual and an ASCII table, you probably can adapt your printer to print in different fonts, sizes, and styles.

For another example of ASCII use, look at SideKick's own Notepad. The Notepad's Graphics mode allows you to write all of the ASCII characters, and so lets you build and print a variety of graphics.

Standard and Extended ASCII

The complete ASCII code consists of 256 characters. There are two parts to the code: the first part assigns a character to every number from 0 to 127. The second part, sometimes called Extended ASCII, assigns other characters to the numbers from 128 to 255. There's a mathematical reason for this division. Numbers from 0 to 127 can be represented by seven binary digits. Numbers after 127 require eight binary digits, or a full byte. (Some early systems saved memory space and simplified display processing by only working with seven bits.)

The standard ASCII code includes the ten decimal numerals (0 through 9), the complete 26-letter English alphabet, in both uppercase and lowercase, the standard punctuation marks, and some graphics characters. The Extended ASCII codes include many foreign language (to English speakers) characters, scientific and mathematics symbols, and graphics characters.

Control Characters

Some ASCII characters also are pressed into a second service, having computer or printer control meanings associated with them, in addition to their character meanings. If preceded by the proper signals, they are interpreted as commands for certain actions instead of simple descriptions of a character to be displayed on the screen, saved in memory, or printed on paper.

SideKick's ASCII Table utility displays on the screen all of the ASCII characters and their standard control definitions, and the utility shows them exactly as they appear when used by a program.

Opening the ASCII Table

To choose the ASCII Table from the main menu —to open the ASCII Table window —you may use any of the following four methods:

1. Press F6.

2. Press A, which is the highlight option for the ASCII Table in the main menu. (You don't have to use the capital form of the letter.)

3. Press ALT-A.

4. Use the up- and down-arrow keys to move the highlight line of the main menu to the ASCII Table option, then press RETURN.

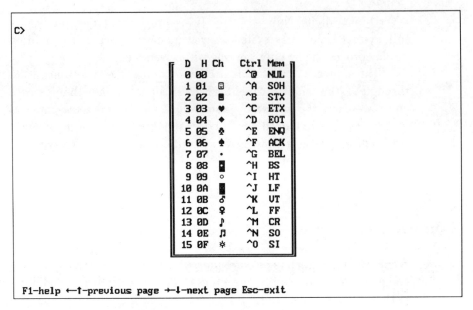

Figure 8-1. ASCII Table window: first page

The quickest methods to open the utility are to press F6, A, or ALT-A. But after instigating any one of the preceding commands, the ASCII Table window appears, similar to that shown in Figure 8-1. This initial window is only the first page of the window; the other seven pages can be called up by using the cursor arrow keys, as discussed in "ASCII Table Commands."

To exit the ASCII Table you can press ALT-CTRL, SHIFT-SHIFT, or ESC. If you already have used the ASCII Table during the current computer session (without turning off the system or removing SideKick from memory) and left the ASCII Table via ALT-CTRL (rather than ESC), you can return to the ASCII Table directly by pressing either of the SideKick activation commands, ALT-CTRL or SHIFT-SHIFT. It is only if you exit the ASCII Table window by pressing ESC that SideKick routes you back through the main menu the next time you want to open the ASCII Table.

Opening the ASCII Table on Top
of Another SideKick Utility

You have two options if you want to open the ASCII Table when you have another SideKick window or application on the screen: first, you can press ALT-A, and the ASCII Table appears on top of the other window or application. Second, you can hold down ALT for a second to call up the main menu on top of the other SideKick window or application. Then you can press F6, A, or ALT-A to open the ASCII Table window on top of the other window or application. When on top, the ASCII Table is the active window — the one that responds to keyboard commands. Figure 8-2 illustrates the ASCII Table open on top of other SideKick windows and applications.

You can return to using the other displayed SideKick utility by removing the ASCII Table (press ALT-CTRL or ESC) or by bringing the

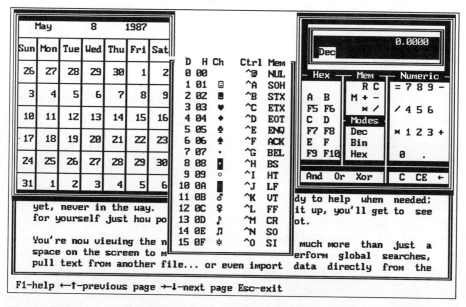

Figure 8-2. Multiple SideKick windows open, ASCII Table on top

other utility's window to the front. To do that, press any of the commands that would normally open that window, such as ALT-N for the Notepad window.

Moving the ASCII Table Window

Once the ASCII Table window becomes active, you can move it to any position on the screen. To move the window, press SCROLL LOCK and use the cursor arrow keys to move the window to your desired position. When you have the ASCII Table where you want it, both vertically and horizontally, press SCROLL LOCK again. Unlike the Notepad window, the ASCII Table window cannot be enlarged or contracted. If you want SideKick to remember the new position of the ASCII Table window so that it appears automatically the next time you run SideKick, you can press ALT-S to open the Setup window and then press F3 to save the new window setup.

ASCII Table Anatomy

When you first open the ASCII Table, a single page of ASCII codes and their character equivalents appears (Figure 8-1). At the bottom of the display is a command line with a menu of available commands. At the top of the first page of the ASCII Table window are five labels, which represent five columns of information on the display. These columns are listed and defined as follows:

D   decimal number value
H   hexadecimal number value
Ch   character
Ctrl   control character
Mem   mnemonic for a control character

The first two columns represent the decimal (base ten) and hexadecimal (base sixteen) numbers in proper sequence. Numbers side by side in these two columns have the same value; they are written differently because they are in different number systems. (See Chapter 5 for further discussion of decimal and hexadecimal systems.)

The "Ch" column illustrates how the number in the first and second columns appears on an IBM PC screen. Systems other than the PC may display different characters for the same numeric values: not all systems use the absolute standard ASCII. The number "0" that is at the top of this first screen is not unassigned: the blank space indicates the zero in ASCII is translated as the space character. In many computer systems, blank space is not a void but is instead an *all-white* character, treated just like any other character.

The fourth column, labeled "Ctrl," lists the control character equivalents of the numbers in columns 1 and 2, and therefore of the characters in column 3. If the information preceding a character tells the computer to interpret that character as a control character, this column lists the translation the value is given. The caret symbol ($^\wedge$) is used widely to mean *control* and is part and parcel of the letter that follows it. It may seem odd that a single numeric value has a display character translation and a control character translation, and that these are different characters. A lot is due to tradition. Don't worry if you are confused. This material is quite technical and oriented to those who want to dig into their software or printers.

The fifth column, "Mem," lists the *mnemonic* (memorable) or commonly used name for the control characters listed in column 4. For example, the decimal number 7 can be translated into the ASCII control character $^\wedge$G, which is called BEL. In many systems, $^\wedge$G rings a bell or sounds a buzzer. The decimal number 8 is translated as $^\wedge$H, which is called BS, and causes a BACKSPACE.

You should note that only the first two pages of the ASCII Table window, which represent numeric values 0 through 31, have all five columns. Only the first 32 ASCII codes have standard control character meanings. Many systems use ASCII codes after that point to represent control characters, but the meanings are not standardized. Therefore, the remaining seven pages of the ASCII Table display only three columns: decimal, hexadecimal, and character. To save space, two sets of these three columns are presented side by side on each page.

ASCII Table Commands

The command line across the bottom of the computer display lists a menu of commands that refer to the ASCII Table window (Figure 8-1). These commands are listed:

F1
: As always in SideKick, F1 is the "Help" key. If you press F1 while using the ASCII Table, you'll receive descriptions of commands and options specific to the ASCII Table.

ESC
: Pressing ESC exits you from the current operation or utility. Repeatedly pressing ESC returns you to DOS or whatever application you're running.

DOWN ARROW, RIGHT ARROW
: The down- and right-arrow keys let you change the page of the ASCII Table. Either of these keys moves you downward through the decimal number values of the code. If you're already on the last page of the code, pressing either key returns you to the beginning of the list.

UP ARROW, LEFT ARROW
: The up- and left-arrow keys also let you change the page of the ASCII Table. Either of these keys moves you upward through the decimal number values of the code. If you're already on the first page, pressing either key returns you to the end of the list.

Touring the Characters

A quick tour of the ASCII Table shows where the most-used characters are located. The first 32 characters are used mainly as control characters, and they have some odd display character graphics translations. Decimal numbers 32 to 47 translate into punctuation and arithmetic symbols. Decimal numbers 48 to 57 (hexadecimal numbers 30 to 39) represent the standard ten numerals: 0, 1, 2, 3, 4, 5, 6, 7, 8, 9, and 10. Interestingly

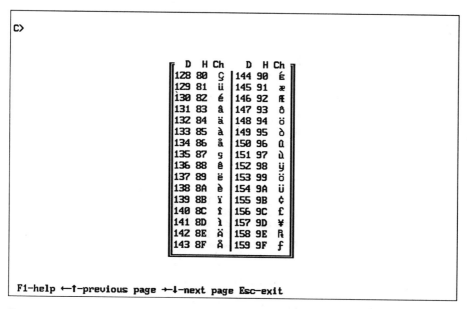

Figure 8-3.   European-language characters in Extended ASCII

enough, these do not correspond directly to the ASCII values of 0 through 9. Decimal numbers in the fifties and sixties continue with more mathematics symbols and punctuation. Decimal numbers 65 through 90 represent the uppercase English alphabet; decimal numbers 97 through 122 represent the lowercase English alphabet. Decimal numbers 91 through 96 represent additional punctuation marks.

The Extended ASCII character set begins (decimal numbers 128 through 168) with many European-language characters, some of which are illustrated in Figure 8-3. Here are many accent marks, tildes, umlauts, monetary signs, and the like. After a few more punctuation marks, decimal numbers 176 to 223 present a host of graphics characters: lines, angles, shapes, and so on that can be combined into all manner of graphics displays (Figure 8-4). Although some computer systems now present graphics as bit-maps, building images a single dot at a time, many have and continue to present graphic images as combinations of graphic characters such as these. Decimal numbers 224 to 239 translate into most of the Greek alphabet letters. Decimal numbers 240 to 255 represent a variety of mathematical symbols (Figure 8-5).

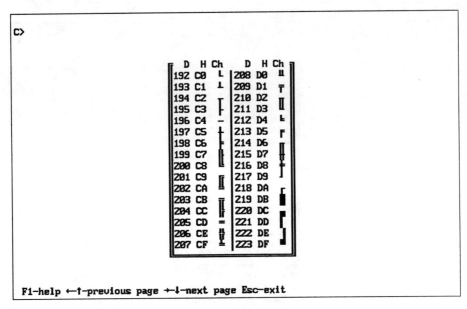

Figure 8-4.   Graphics symbols in Extended ASCII

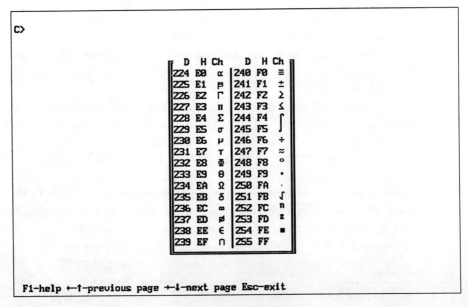

Figure 8-5.   Mathematical symbols in Extended ASCII

Using the Characters

Chapters 3 and 4 on the Notepad contain some references to uses of the ASCII Table. For instance, Chapter 3 describes how you can set the Notepad into the Graphics mode and then type some of the Extended ASCII characters into the notefile. Chapter 4 mentions how some ASCII characters can be used for their control character values to format printer output.

9

The
Setup Utility

The SideKick Setup utility is not meant to be a practical program in its own right. Rather, it is a tool for customizing the default file choices and window positions of three SideKick utilities: the Notepad, the Calendar, and the Dialer. (The SideKick Installation program — SKINST — offers many other customizing controls and is discussed in Chapter 2.) All of the necessary information on how to customize these three utilities using the Setup window is described in Chapters 3, 4, 6, and 7 respectively. This chapter briefly restates that information and adds some explanation of the Setup window's own commands.

Opening the Setup Window

To call up the Setup window from SideKick's main menu, use any of the following four methods:

1. Press F7.

2. Press S, which is the highlight for the Setup option of the menu. (You don't have to use the capital form of the letter.)

3. Press ALT-S.

4. Use the up- and down-arrow keys to move the highlight line of the main menu to the Setup option, then press RETURN.

The quickest methods are to press F7, S, or ALT-S. But after using any one of these four commands, the Setup window appears, similar to that shown in Figure 9-1.

To exit the Setup window, press either ALT-CTRL or ESC. If you already have used the Setup window during the current computer session (without turning off the system or removing SideKick from memory) and exited the Setup window via either ALT-CTRL or SHIFT-SHIFT (rather than ESC), you can return directly to the Setup window by pressing either of the SideKick activation commands, ALT-CTRL or SHIFT-SHIFT. It is only if you leave the Setup window by pressing ESC that SideKick routes you back through the main menu the next time you want to use the Setup window.

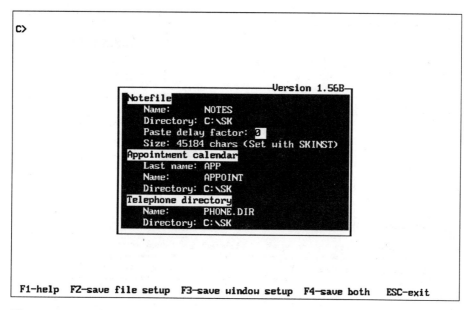

Figure 9-1.   The Setup window

Opening the Setup Window on Top of Another SideKick Utility

You have two options if you want to call up the Setup window when you have another SideKick window or application on the screen: first, you can press ALT-S, and the Setup window appears on top of the other SideKick window or application. Second, you can hold down ALT for a second to call up the main menu on top of the other window or application. Then you can press F7, S, or ALT-S to open the Setup window on top of the other SideKick window or application. Using either option makes the Setup window the active window —the one that responds to keyboard commands. Figure 9-2 shows the Setup window on top of other utility windows.

You can return to other displayed SideKick utilities or applications by removing the Setup window (press ALT-CTRL or ESC) or by calling up the other utility or application's window to the front by pressing any of

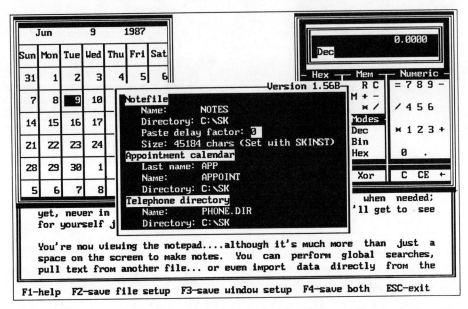

Figure 9-2.   Multiple SideKick utility windows open, Setup window on top

the commands that normally open that window. For example, press ALT-N to call up the Notepad window.

Moving the Setup Window

Once your Setup window becomes active, remember that you can move the window to any position on the screen by pressing SCROLL LOCK and then using the cursor arrow keys. When you have positioned the Setup window where you want it, press SCROLL LOCK again. Unlike the Notepad window, the Setup window cannot be enlarged or contracted. If you want SideKick to remember the new position so that it appears automatically the next time you run SideKick, press F3 to save the new window setup. This procedure is explained in more detail in the following section.

The Setup Window's Anatomy

The SideKick version number you're using appears at the top left of the Setup window display (Figure 9-1). Within the window are three sections: notefile, appointment calendar, and telephone directory. Within each section are lines listing the present settings. You can move between these lines either by pressing RETURN or by using the up- and down-arrow keys.

Setup Window Commands

The command line across the bottom of the computer display lists a menu of commands that refer to the Setup window. These commands and others that you can use when working in the Setup window are listed:

F1   Help. Pressing F1 calls up descriptions of commands and options specific to Setup.

ESC   Escape. Pressing ESC exits you from the current operation or utility. Here it removes the Setup window from the display and returns you to a previous SideKick utility (if any) or (if no previous utility) to DOS or whatever application program you are running.

F2   Save file setup. Pressing F2 saves any changes you make to the default file and directory settings.

F3   Save window setup. Pressing F3 saves any changes you make to the window positions of any of the SideKick utility windows (including the main menu) and to the size of the Notepad.

F4   Save both. Pressing F4 saves any changes you make to the window positions of any of the SideKick utility windows (including the main menu) and to the size of the Notepad window as well. Pressing F4 saves any default file and directory changes you make within the Setup window. Pressing F4 has the same effect as pressing both F2 and F3.

BACKSPACE   This is the only function key you can use to edit an entry on a line of the Setup window. BACKSPACE moves the cursor one position to the left and erases the character found in that position.

Let's look at the Setup window's save commands, F2, F3, and F4, in greater detail. Before pressing F2, F3, or F4, you should make sure that the SK.COM file you used to load SideKick into RAM is in the same disk drive and directory from where you loaded the program. (If you used one of the limited versions of SideKick, such as SKM.COM, then that file should be in the disk drive and directory from where you loaded the program.) The save commands save changes to that file. The changes also are available for immediate use in the version of SideKick that is already in memory. (Unlike with the Installation program, you don't have to reload SideKick into RAM to see the changes.)

F2 saves any changes you make to the file and directory settings within the Setup window. These changes are saved in both the main SideKick file on disk and in the version of SideKick that is in memory. In other words, if in the Setup window you change the directory file name for the Dialer, that new file is loaded into the directory both when you exit the Setup window to use the Dialer and when you later reload SideKick into RAM and call up the Dialer.

F3 saves the present window setup. Each time you move or resize a window, that window automatically maintains the new position and shape during a single computing session. (For example, make the Notepad window very tiny and move it to the top right corner of the screen. It will remain the same size and in the same position no matter how many times or for how long you exit Notepad to call up another SideKick utility or application.) But if you reboot your system, the position and shape are lost; they return to the default shape and placement. However, if you open the Setup window, you can press F3 to save on disk all your new positions and placements, although you must save *all* of the SideKick utilities, positions and placements at the same time. F3 even saves the Notepad's right margin value. Like F2, F3 saves changes both in the main SideKick file on disk and in the SideKick version in memory. In other words, you can view your changes immediately (unlike the Installation program mentioned previously).

F4 saves both the file setup and the window setups. It is the equivalent of pressing F2 and then F3.

The Notefile Section

This notefile section of the Setup window consists of four lines (Figure 9-1), even though only three of them can be changed through the Setup commands. The notefile size (described as a certain number of characters) is only a status report: it can be changed only by using the Installation program, SKINST, as described in Chapters 2 and 3. The default size is 4000 characters, although this is not the maximum notefile size (as some versions of the SideKick manual claim). The maximum is actually closer to 50,000 characters.

The name and directory lines let you enter a new notefile default file name and disk drive directory that will be loaded automatically when you first open the Notepad. You can enter information on these lines by moving to the lines with the up- and down-arrow keys and then typing in your desired file information. Press BACKSPACE if you make a mistake — it moves the cursor one character position to the left and erases any character found there. Be sure to press RETURN, which records your new information, before leaving any line. If you don't press RETURN, the new value vanishes, and the old one reappears as soon as you move to another line. When you're done with the Setup window, press F2 or F4 to save all of your file name and directory changes to memory and to disk.

You can use wildcards in the default file name listings. Just type **?** for a single wildcard letter or an ***** for one or more wildcard letters in a row. Follow the rest of the instructions as described in the preceding paragraph. When you later open the Notepad utility, a small file directory window displays all of the files that fit within your wildcard description. You can choose which file to load by pressing the arrow keys to move the highlight area to that file name and then pressing RETURN.

The Paste delay line is described in some detail in Chapter 4. The Notepad has a "Paste" function that lets you mark blocks of text and then send them to another application program. Some programs can't accept characters as quickly as can other programs, so sometimes there is a need to delay between each sent character. The *Paste delay* can be set anywhere from 0 to 99, with a higher number indicating a longer delay. The 0 default means no delay, which is approximately 1000 characters per second on an IBM PC. The actual delay factor introduced by any given number larger than 0 depends on the program pasted to.

Appointment Calendar Section

The second and central section of the Setup window is dedicated to the Calendar utility. There are three lines —last name, name, and directory — that let you see the name and location of the default Calendar file that will be loaded into the Calendar window. You can change the default setting by entering new information onto these lines. Use the same procedure as discussed in the previous section to enter the new information. When you are done making changes, press F2 or F4 to save your changes both to the currently loaded SideKick memory and to the SideKick disk.

You can use wildcards in the default file name listings. Follow the same procedure as discussed in the previous section to enter wildcard letters. Then press F2 or F4 to save the changes. When you later open the Calendar utility, a small file directory window displays all of the files that fit within your wildcard description. You can choose which file to load by pressing the arrow keys to move the highlight area to that file name and then pressing RETURN.

Telephone Directory Section

The final and bottom section of the Setup window is dedicated to the Telephone Directory of the Dialer utility. There are two lines —name and directory —that let you see the name and location of the default directory file that will be loaded into the Dialer's Directory window. You can change the default setting by entering new information on these lines, as discussed previously. When you are done making changes to Dialer's Directory defaults, press F2 or F4 to save your changes both to the currently loaded SideKick memory and to the SideKick disk.

You can use wildcards in the default file name listings, as discussed previously. Then press F2 or F4 to save the changes. When you later open the Dialer utility's Directory, a small file directory window displays all of the files that fit within your wildcard description. You can choose which file to load by pressing the arrow keys to move the highlight area to that file name and then pressing RETURN.

II

SideKick in a Team

10

Traveling SideKick

If you're a confirmed user of the SideKick Calendar or Dialer utilities, you should consider adding Traveling SideKick to your program library. If you use some sort of special calendar booklet or binder to keep track of appointments, you should consider adding both Traveling SideKick and SideKick to streamline and computerize your organizational tasks.

Traveling SideKick is a separate program from SideKick, and it can be used with or without SideKick. It lets you record and manipulate addresses (with phone numbers) and a schedule, and it provides a special binder for holding printouts of those records. Traveling SideKick runs as a standard application program — it isn't RAM-resident or TSR (terminate and stay resident) as is SideKick (these terms are explained in Chapter 2). You run Traveling SideKick any time you want to add new addresses or appointments to the lists, look up old ones, delete addresses or appointments, or print the lists.

As mentioned, you don't have to have SideKick to use Traveling SideKick, but the two certainly fit together well, each as an extension of the other. SideKick allows you instant access to schedule and address information through its Calendar and Dialer directories. Traveling SideKick allows you to build larger and more informative appointment and address lists and to print those lists on paper to carry around when you're away from a computer. And, of course, you can exchange files between the two programs.

Meeting the Traveler

Traveling SideKick is packaged in a three-ring binder that looks and functions a lot like a standard business "day scheduler" binder. There are some differences, however. The first difference is that the binder has room for the Traveling SideKick floppy disk that contains its programs and files. As mentioned previously, these programs let you work more intimately with the Calendar and Dialer directory files you may have built into SideKick. They let you bring in information from other databases to add to those lists, directly add, modify, and delete entries from those lists, and print the lists so that they can be inserted into the binder.

Within the binder there is a wealth of additional reference materials to help you when you travel or work. These materials include an instruction booklet for Traveling SideKick, alphabetical dividers for your address list, and other dividers for your Calendar and "Pending," "Financial," "Information," and "Miscellaneous" notes. There are also maps, currency conversion charts, area code lists, command cards for other Borland programs such as SideKick and SuperKey, blank note pages, a pen, and even a solar-powered hand calculator. Finally, there is a variety of pre-printed forms for writing down appointments, addresses, expenses, and similar information.

First Things First: Make Backups

Traveling SideKick is not copy protected. You can make a backup copy of the single Traveling SideKick disk using the procedure outlined in Chapter 2 for backing up non-copy-protected versions of SideKick. You should make your program backup before going any further with the program. If you have a hard disk, you also should copy the Traveling SideKick files onto the hard disk, again using the procedure given in Chapter 2 for copying SideKick files onto a hard disk. You even should copy the Traveling SideKick files onto your SideKick directory.

The README File

Next, you should check the README file information. The Traveling SideKick disk contains two README files: one is a text file, and one is a program that makes reading the text file easy. Just type **readme** with the Traveling SideKick disk in the drive and directory appropriate for your system (which will be A> for most floppy-disk users and C> \sk for most hard-disk users) and press RETURN. The first page of the README text file then appears (Figure 10-1). This file contains the latest information about Traveling SideKick, material that was too recent to be included in the manual. You should read this file before using Traveling SideKick for the first time. Use the up- and down-arrow cursor keys to scroll through

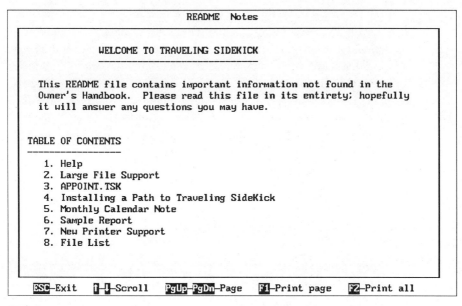

```
                            README  Notes

                   WELCOME TO TRAVELING SIDEKICK
                   -----------------------------

    This README file contains important information not found in the
    Owner's Handbook.  Please read this file in its entirety; hopefully
    it will answer any questions you may have.


    TABLE OF CONTENTS
    -----------------
        1. Help
        2. Large File Support
        3. APPOINT.TSK
        4. Installing a Path to Traveling SideKick
        5. Monthly Calendar Note
        6. Sample Report
        7. New Printer Support
        8. File List




   ESC-Exit    ↑-↓-Scroll   PgUp-PgDn-Page   F1-Print page   F2-Print all
```

Figure 10-1. First page of Traveling SideKick README file

the file, or use PGUP and PGDN to move an entire page at a time. You even
can use F1 and F2 to print out either a single page or the full README
text file, if you find it easier to read that way.

Installation

Traveling SideKick is easier to install than is SideKick, because it offers
fewer installation options. There is a TSKINST program on the Traveling
SideKick disk that allows you to change the screen colors and display. If
you're using an IBM PC or a computer that is completely compatible
with an IBM PC, you don't even need to use TSKINST. But if you're not
sure how compatible your system is, or if you want to make sure the
colors in the display are right for you, run the Installation program by
typing **tskinst** and then pressing RETURN. A series of displays along with
instructions for using them appears on the screen. Work through these
displays to select the screen type and colors that are best for your system,

and then exit the Installation program by pressing ESC. The changes you made will be implemented when you start the Traveling SideKick program.

Starting Traveling SideKick

Starting Traveling SideKick is simpler than starting SideKick, because Traveling SideKick is not a TSR program — you don't have to load it into memory before activating it. Place the Traveling SideKick program disk in the drive and directory appropriate for your system (as discussed in the section "The README File"), type **tsk**, and press RETURN. The Traveling SideKick main menu then appears (Figure 10-2). This menu resembles the main menu of SuperKey or Turbo Lightning, with a menu line across the top of the screen. At the bottom of the screen are some descriptions of the commands for manipulating the menu.

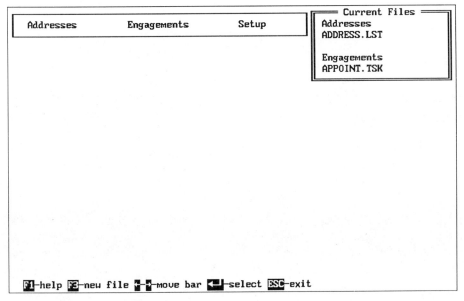

Figure 10-2.   Traveling SideKick's main menu

Note: although you are now running Traveling SideKick, you can activate and use SuperKey, SideKick, Turbo Lightning, or any other RAM-resident program at any time. Just treat Traveling SideKick as you would any application program. But if you use SideKick to alter your calendar or address files, those changes are not included in the Traveling SideKick files until you reload the program and reopen the files.

Menu Commands

This section describes how to work with the Traveling SideKick main menu, what commands control it, and how to move about within the menu.

Getting Help

Just as in SideKick, you can press F1 at any point to call up helpful information in Traveling SideKick. Use PGUP and PGDN to move around in the Help window, and then use ESC to exit the Help window and return to Traveling SideKick. (There is more Help information in Appendix D of the Traveling SideKick instruction booklet.)

Menu Sections

There are three sections to the Traveling SideKick menu: Addresses, Engagements, and Setup. The Addresses section deals with the address-listing files. These files are made up from SideKick's Dialer utility directory. The Engagements section deals with appointments. The files from this section are made up from SideKick's Calendar utility schedules. The Setup section allows you to customize some of the default file settings and formats, just as does the SideKick Setup window.

To choose one of the three sections on the main menu line, you either can press the first letter of that section's name or you can use the right- and left-arrow cursor keys to move the highlight bar to that section's name and then press RETURN. When you select a section, a

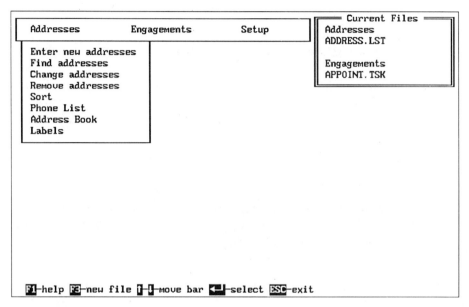

Figure 10-3.   The Addresses menu

menu for that section extends down from the main menu line. Figure
10-3 shows the menu for the Addresses section. If you then want to exit
the specific menu to return to the main menu line, just press ESC. As in
SideKick, ESC extricates you from your present position in the program.
(Addresses, Engagements, and Setup all are described in detail later in
the chapter.)

Loading Files

When you first start Traveling SideKick, a window, called the Current
Files box, appears to the right of the main menu line. This window tells
you which address and engagement files have been loaded by default.
You can change these defaults as described in the section called "Setup
Menu" later in this chapter, or you can simply load a new file by pressing
F3. But first you should select the Addresses or the Engagements section
from the main menu, so let's discuss these sections now.

Addresses

From the Traveling SideKick main menu you can select the Addresses section by pressing A or by moving the highlight bar to the Addresses title and pressing RETURN. The Addresses menu then appears (Figure 10-3). Using the commands and options listed on the menu, you can print or display phone and address information as a phone list, an address book, or mailing labels. You can sort the listings by name, company, or ZIP code, and you can add, erase, or change individual address records in many different address files.

To choose any of the options (Enter new addresses, Find addresses, Change addresses, Remove addresses, Sort, Phone List, Address Book, Labels), just press the first letter of that option or move the highlight bar to that option and press RETURN.

A New Address File

If you want to work with a different address file than is shown in the Addresses line of the Current Files box, press F3 and then type in the name of the file you wish to work on. If that name cannot be found on the disk, Traveling SideKick opens a new file for you. If you use wildcard characters (such as ? for any single letter or * for any group of letters), Traveling SideKick opens a file directory window of all files that meet your wildcard specifications. To choose one of these files, move the highlight bar to the file name and press RETURN. If you don't want any of these files, press ESC.

Converting Address Files

You can load Traveling SideKick with files from programs other than Traveling SideKick, including the phone directory files from SideKick. But to do so, you first have to convert the files to the Traveling SideKick format. The CONVERT program that comes with Traveling SideKick can convert any ASCII files (that is, files that don't have any special codes and consist entirely of standard ASCII characters as described in Chapter 8) into Traveling SideKick files. The CONVERT program can work on files from editors or files that have character delimiters, such as

ASCII output files from database managers. You can convert an entire file at a time, or you can convert single address records from a file. To convert an entire file at a time, every record in the file must have the same format, the fields must be in the same order, and each record or listing must have the same number of lines. This process is described in detail in the Traveling SideKick instruction booklet, Appendix B.

Converting SideKick Files　　If you're going to convert SideKick files to Traveling SideKick format, you should take some special steps before you open CONVERT. Load the SideKick phone directory file into the Notepad and edit it to make all of the entries follow the same format: same number of lines, same length of fields (such as initials, phone number, comments, and so on). Taking these preliminary steps makes converting an entire file faster and easier.

Running CONVERT　　To run CONVERT, you have to exit Traveling SideKick. CONVERT is a separate program. Place the program in the appropriate disk drive and directory to call up the DOS prompt for the Traveling SideKick files (typically A> for floppy-disk systems or C> \sk for hard-disk systems), then type **convert** and press RETURN. The initial CONVERT display window then appears (Figure 10-4).

　　The two choices in this initial display are "Character delimited" or "Fixed length." The options tell CONVERT how to divide the fields within a record. A field is a single chunk of information, such as a phone number or a name. A record is one entire set of organized fields for one entry, such as a single, full address. Character-delimited fields are set apart by some character, such as a comma. Fixed-length fields are a set number of characters long: anything after that length is considered part of the next field. SideKick produces fixed length fields, so you should make that choice if you are converting SideKick files for use in Traveling SideKick. Press the first letter of your choice. For example, press F for fixed length. (If you choose C because your file uses character delimiters, you must specify which character is to be used as the delimiter.) You then must specify the name of the file you want to convert and the name you want to give to the converted results file. You should give the new file a new name, so you don't overwrite the old file, unless you are sure you want to delete the old file. Press RETURN after each file name, and then press Y to confirm your choices. (Note: do *not* press RETURN again.)

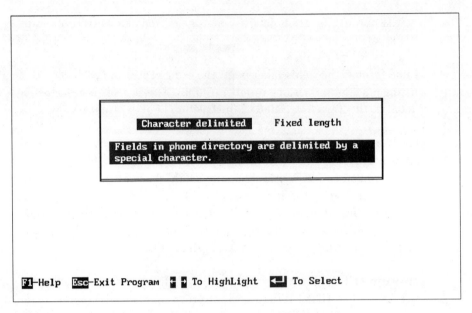

Figure 10-4.   The initial display for the CONVERT program

At this point, the Convert Address File display appears (Figure 10-5). The top portion of the display shows the format for Traveling SideKick records, the format that your file information will be converted to. At the bottom of that section, on the right, is a request from the program for some more information:

Number of Lines per Entry:

An entry is the same as a record.

The bottom portion of the screen shows the beginning of the address file you are going to convert. From looking at that section, count the number of lines in a record and enter that number. Then press RETURN.

Defining Fields   The next step is to set the beginnings and endings of the fields you are going to convert. The commands are listed in two lines at the bottom of the screen. Press F1 if you need help in understanding the commands.

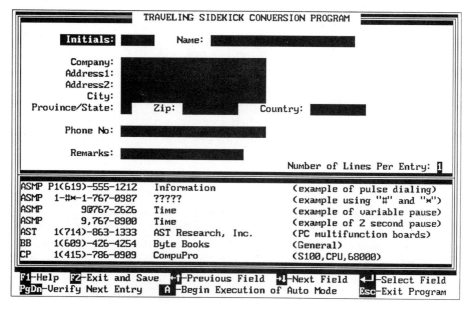

Figure 10-5.   CONVERT's Convert Address File display

Use the cursor arrow keys to move the cursor to a specific field within the top portion of the window. For example, if you place the cursor after the

Initials

title, that title will be highlighted. Press RETURN to select that field. The cursor then moves to the bottom portion of the display. There you can use the cursor arrow keys or CTRL-A (to move one word to the left) and CTRL-F (to move one word to the right) to manipulate the cursor. Move the cursor to the beginning of the file-to-be-converted section that has the information for the Initials field.

When the cursor is on the first letter of the section, press B. Then move the cursor to the end of the section. The characters and spaces of that section become highlighted. When you hear a beep, you have gone as far as you can go: the Initials field, for instance, cannot hold more than six characters. Choose a field length that can contain the longest entry in the file you are converting. If you're not happy with your field selection or its length, press ESC. When you come to the end of the field you want to use, press RETURN. The cursor then returns to the top portion of the display and moves to a new field. In this manner, you can define any or all of the fields of the file you are converting.

Manual or Automatic Conversion   Once you have defined the fields to be converted for the first entry or record, you either can choose to convert other records automatically or to convert them manually a single record at a time. If your records differ in the lengths of their fields, you may want to choose the manual method. To do so, press PGDN to convert the record you have defined and to change the display to the next record in the file you are converting.

If you press A instead, you begin automatic conversion of all of the records, following the format you defined for the first record. You can watch the bottom portion of the display to monitor this conversion. If you want to stop the conversion at any point, just press any key. Then you can return to manual field definition and conversion, or you can switch back to automatic conversion again by pressing A. You also can select a new field-length definition and then press A to use that definition automatically to convert the remaining addresses. Finally, you can press any of the numbered keys 1 through 9 to choose the speed of conversion (1 for slowest, 9 for fastest). When the automatic conversion is complete, the CONVERT program returns you to a DOS prompt. The converted file thus is on disk with the name you specified at the beginning of the process.

Entering New Addresses

Once you have converted an address file, opened a current Traveling SideKick file, or started a new file, you can use the Addresses section of the main menu to manipulate that file. The first option in that menu is to Enter New Addresses (see Figure 10-3). From the Addresses menu, press E to call up the Enter or Change Addresses display (Figure 10-6). The top portion of the display is the empty page for a new address. The bottom portion lists the addresses in the current address file (the name of that file is in the bottom right corner of the display). Finally, the bottom line of the display is a command line that lists the options and commands you can use to manipulate addresses in this file.

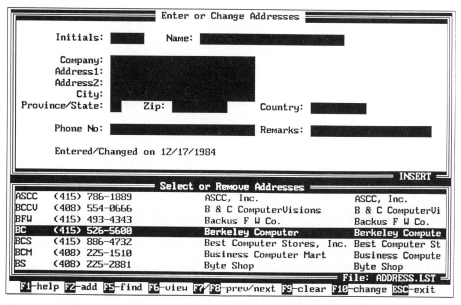

Figure 10-6. The form view of the Enter or Change Addresses display

To enter a new address, type the information into the appropriate blanks on the top portion of the display. Use TAB, SHIFT-TAB, and the cursor arrow keys to move around the display, and use BACKSPACE to correct any mistakes. Press F1 if you need help. When you have entered all the information you want, press F2 to add this new address record to the list. It then appears at the end of the list in the bottom portion of the display. Only fields that can be displayed in a SideKick directory appear on the screen, but other information still is recorded and can be called up and viewed with Traveling SideKick. If you're not happy with your entries, you can clear the entire top portion of the display by pressing F9.

In the bottom portion of the display, you can see one highlight line. You can move the highlight bar up or down in the list, and whatever entry it falls on then is displayed in the upper portion of the screen. One way to move the highlight bar is to press F7 or F8, which moves you up or down one listing at a time. Another way to move the highlight bar is to press F5 to "find" a specific entry. Pressing F5 immediately moves you to the Find display, which is described in detail in the section "Finding Addresses."

You also have a third option: pressing F6. Pressing F6 changes the display to the list view of the Enter or Change Addresses display. In this view, the bottom section of the display takes precedence over the top, and you can use the up- and down-arrow cursor keys as well as PGDN, PGUP, HOME, and END to scroll through the list. You can affect the highlight entry directly by using the commands listed at the bottom of the screen. For example, pressing DEL deletes the highlight entry, and pressing RETURN returns you to the form view of the display.

To exit either the form view or the list view of this display, just press ESC, and you return to the Addresses menu.

Find Addresses

To find an address in a list, you can use the Find Addresses display, which you can reach by pressing F from the Addresses menu or by pressing F5 from within the Enter or Change Addresses display, as mentioned previously.

The Find Addresses display is shown in Figure 10-7. The top portion of the display is an empty address form, and the bottom portion presents the instructions for using that form. You move about the form with the same TAB, SHIFT-TAB, and cursor arrow key commands used in the Enter or Change Addresses display, and you put in the information you want to use for an address search. Only enter as much information as to specify the address or addresses you want to find. You can use information from any or all of the fields. Once you have entered that information, press F4 to find exact matches (where the entered letters or numbers are in the same positions and fields as you entered) or F5 to find any matches (where the entered letters or numbers are anywhere in the specified field). For example, if you enter **Alex** in the Name field and then press F4, a list of addresses with the name "Alex" or "Alexandra" is displayed. But the name "Tom Alexander" is not displayed, because that "Alex" is not at the beginning of the line. Pressing F5, though, would list all three addresses. You also can search for groups of addresses. For instance, if you typed in **Borland** in the Company field, a list of all of the addresses for people who work at Borland is displayed.

As mentioned in the instructions at the bottom portion of the display, you can use spaces as wildcards for the Find operation. If the information you entered isn't correct for what you want to do, you can

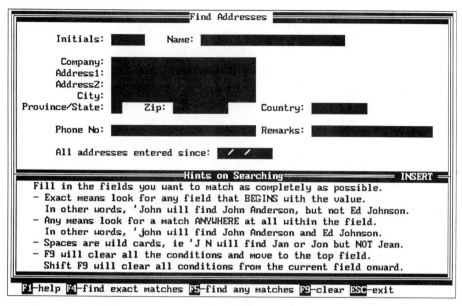

Figure 10-7. The Find Addresses display

press F9 to clear it from the display. If you search with the form blank, you receive a list of all of the records in that file.

When the Find operation is complete, the screen moves to the list view of the Enter or Change Addresses display. You can use this display to modify the found entry or just to read it. If more than one entry met your conditions, you can move to the next entry by pressing DOWN ARROW.

Changing an Address

To change an address record that is already in the file, you first must use the Find Addresses display as previously described to find that address record, and then you must display it in the list view of the Enter and Change Addresses display. To call up that display, press C from the Addresses menu or press F6 or F10 from the form view of the Enter or Change Addresses display. When you have done so, use the cursor arrow keys along with PGUP and PGDN to scroll through the list of addresses until you reach (highlight) the one you want to change.

When you have highlighted an address, you can delete it altogether by pressing DEL, as is described in the next section, or you can press F6, edit the information about it in the top portion of the display, and then press F10. The new version of the record replaces the old version and is highlighted in the lower portion of the display. Press ESC to exit this display and return to the Addresses menu.

Removing an Address

If you select R from the Addresses menu, you call up the list view of the Enter or Change Addresses display. Use the up- and down-arrow cursor keys and PGDN, PGUP, HOME, and END to move the highlight bar to the record you want to remove. You also can use F5 to start a Find operation as previously described and then press DEL to delete that record.

Sorting Address Files

The address files are displayed in four sections in the bottom portion of the Enter and Change Addresses display (see Figure 10-6): initials, phone number, person's name, and company name. Normally, they are sorted alphabetically by the person's name. If you want to sort by last name, you must enter the addresses with last names preceding first names on the Name line in the upper portion of the display; otherwise, your names are sorted by first name.

You also can sort by ZIP code or by company name. To do so, press S from the Addresses menu to open a small menu window (Figure 10-8). Choose the type of sort you want by pressing the first letter of that option, such as pressing Z for a ZIP code sort. The computer then performs the sort — you can hear the disks whirring — and saves the file to disk in the new order. The file entries in the Enter or Change Addresses display now are listed in that new order.

Printing Address Files

The last three options on the Addresses menu — Phone List, Address Book, and Labels — are "printing" options. If you press the first letter of any of these options, you can print your address list in the specified

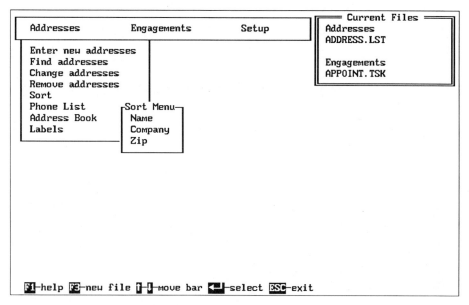

```
┌──────────────────────────────────────┐┌══ Current Files ══┐
│ Addresses        Engagements    Setup ││ Addresses         │
│┌─────────────────────────┐            ││ ADDRESS.LST       │
││Enter new addresses       │            ││                   │
││Find addresses            │            ││ Engagements       │
││Change addresses          │            ││ APPOINT.TSK       │
││Remove addresses          │            │└───────────────────┘
││Sort                      │
││Phone List   ┌Sort Menu─┐ │
││Address Book │Name      │ │
││Labels       │Company   │ │
│└─────────────│Zip       │ │
│              └──────────┘
│
│
│
│
│
│
│
│
│
│ F1-help  F3-new file  ↑↓-move bar  ↵-select  ESC-exit
└──────────────────────────────────────────────────────────┘
```

Figure 10-8. The Sort display for address files

format. The Phone List "prints out" only one line of information, in the style of the SideKick phone directory. The Address Book "prints out" six addresses on a page. The Labels option "prints out" only the address information that would be printed on a mailing label. By default, these labels are printed in a single column, but you can use the Setup menu to print multiple columns, which is described in the section called "Labels Across and Height of Label."

The so-called "print" can be to the screen (so you can see the complete list without the special displays for modifying the list), to a printer (so you can carry them around in your Traveling SideKick binder), or to another disk file (so you can use them with other programs). Also, you don't have to print an entire address file: you can print any part of one. Note: you may want to use the Sorting procedure before you follow the printing instructions.

No matter which of the three print options you select, a Print menu then appears (Figure 10-9). If you select Printer, Screen, or File from this menu, you "print" the entire address file, named in the Current Files box, to that particular device.

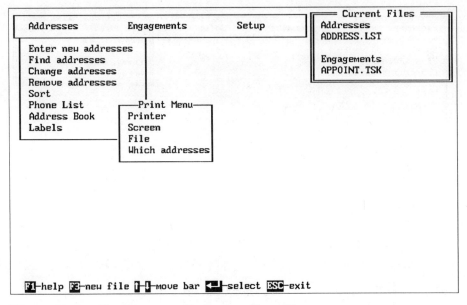

Figure 10-9.   The Print menu display for address files

Printing Part of a File   If you only want to print a portion of a file, you first must press W before you select which addresses to print. Pressing W calls up the Enter Address Selection Conditions display (Figure 10-10). Here you enter the specifications that instruct the computer as to which addresses to print. Use this display as you might use the Find Addresses display, explained previously. You can use wildcards to print only exact matches to the information you enter into any number of fields, or to print records that match anywhere within a field. Press F1 if you need help in understanding how to enter the conditions. When you are satisfied with your selection, press F4 or F5 (F4 to find exact matches, F5 to find any matches), and the display returns to the Print menu. A selected list of addresses is now ready for printing.

     If you change your mind about what you want to print, press F9 to clear the display or press ESC to return to the Print menu.

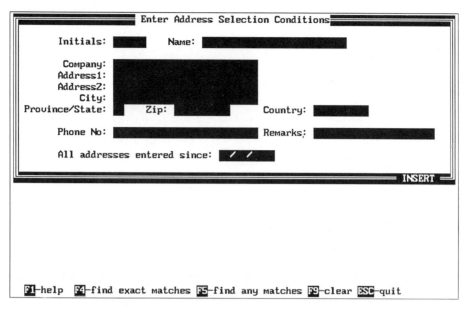

Figure 10-10. The selection display for choosing which addresses to print

Printer Setup   You can send special commands to your printer to control the style of printing. To do so, you need to input some of the control characters specific to your printer. Selecting control characters is discussed more thoroughly in the section on the Setup menu called "Printer Setup."

Printer Direction   To start printing, just press the first letter of the device you want the print to go to. If you press S for Screen, the entries scroll by. You can press SPACE BAR to pause the scrolling or ESC to quit the display and return to the Addresses menu. If you press P for Printer, a message is displayed that tells you that the file is printing. If you have any printing problems, you can stop the printing by pressing ESC. If you press F for File, you then are asked to specify the name of the file that you want to hold the printed information. Figures 10-11, 10-12, and 10-13

```
                        Quick Reference Report


┌─────────────────────────────────────────────────────────────────────────┐
│                                   - A -                                   │
├─────────────────────────────────────────────────────────────────────────┤
│   AVS     A V S Computer Systems      (408) 262-9134    computer time rental
│   AKC     A&K Computers               (408) 224-4811    Televideo systems
│   AS      Aardvark Systems            (408) 996-3070    software supplies
│   AC      Access Computers            (408) 973-0111    personal computers
│   ACP     ACP Technology Center       (408) 946-7010    computers, accessories
│   AES     AES Computer Systems        (408) 738-2800    Turnkey solutions
│   AEC     Alamo Electronic Comp.      (408) 227-0891    personal computers
│   AMT     Applied Microcomputer       (408) 438-1608
│   ASCC    ASCC, Inc.                  (415) 786-1889    hardware/software
│
│                                   - B -
│
│
│   BCCV    B & C ComputerVisions       (408) 554-0666    printers, modems, etc.
│   BFW     Backus F W Co.              (415) 493-4343    word processing
│   BC      Berkeley Computer           (415) 526-5600
│   BCS     Best Computer S
├─────────────────────────────────────────────────────────────────────────┤
│ SPACE-to continue  ESC-exit                                               │
└─────────────────────────────────────────────────────────────────────────┘
```

Figure 10-11.   An example of a Phone List screen printout

```
                          Address Book Report
┌─────────────────────────────────────────────────────────────────────────┐
│                                   - A -                                   │
├───────────────────────────────────────┬───────────────────────────────────┤
│ A V S Computer Systems       AVS       │ A&K Computers              AKC     │
│ A V S Computer Systems                 │ A&K Computers                      │
│ 105 Serra Way                          │ 375 Saratoga Ave.                  │
│                                        │                                    │
│ Milpitas                               │ San Jose                           │
│ CA            USA                      │ CA            USA                  │
│ (408) 262-9134                         │ (408) 224-4811                     │
│ 12/17/1984     computer time rental    │  2/ 7/1986     Televideo systems   │
├────────────────────────────────────────┼──────────────────────────────────┤
│ Aardvark Systems             AS        │ Access Computers           AC      │
│ Aardvark Systems                       │ Access Computers                   │
│ 1514 S. Saratoga-Sunnyvale             │ 5357 Prospect Rd.                  │
│                                        │                                    │
│ San Jose                               │ San Jose                           │
│ CA            USA                      │ CA            USA                  │
│ (408) 996-3070                         │ (408) 973-0111                     │
│ 12/17/1984     software supplies       │ 12/17/1984     personal computers  │
├────────────────────────────────────────┴──────────────────────────────────┤
│ ACP Technology Cen                                                         │
├─────────────────────────────────────────────────────────────────────────┤
│ SPACE-to continue  ESC-exit                                               │
└─────────────────────────────────────────────────────────────────────────┘
```

Figure 10-12.   An example of an Address Book screen printout

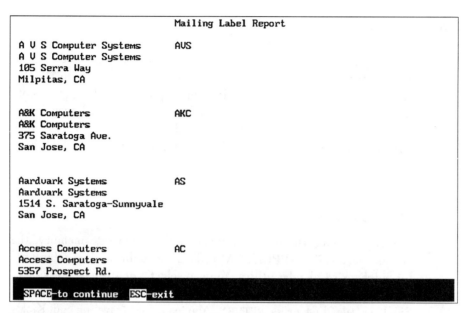

Figure 10-13.   An example of a Mailing Labels screen printout

show examples of Phone List, Address Book, and Labels options. Once you print a phone list or an address book, you should use a hole-punch so that you can insert the lists into your Traveling SideKick binder.

Using Traveling SideKick
Address Files with SideKick

As you can see, you can build more detailed and larger address lists with Traveling SideKick than you can with SideKick's Dialer directory. And you can build those lists around a SideKick directory file by using CONVERT to convert that file into Traveling SideKick format and then by manipulating it with Traveling SideKick. You also can return the list to SideKick, where you instantly can access its basic information about phone numbers, names, and initials. To return a phone list to SideKick, for example, press P from the Addresses menu to call up the Print menu, and then press F from the Print menu and type the name of the file you want your printing to convert to in SideKick, such as PHONE.DIR.

Engagements

The second section of Traveling SideKick's main menu is titled Engagements. Press E or move the highlight bar to that title and press RETURN to open a menu that deals exclusively with keeping a list of appointments and dates (Figure 10-14). Like the Addresses menu, the Engagements menu lets you enter, delete, change, find, and print a schedule. It is directly compatible with the SideKick Calendar utility: you don't have to convert the file as you would do for an address file.

Choosing a File

The engagements file that is automatically loaded into memory, the default file, is called APPOINT.APP. This is also the original default file for SideKick's Calendar utility. You can select a new file by pressing F3 and then typing in the name of the file. If you want to work with the SideKick file, just press RETURN. You can use Traveling SideKick's

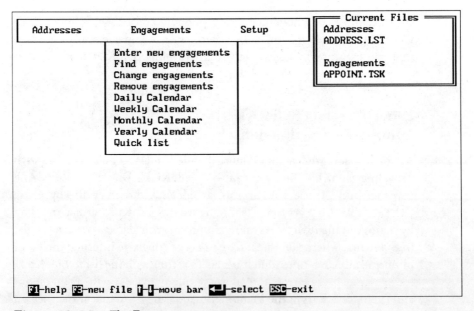

Figure 10-14. The Engagements menu

Setup menu to change the default engagements file, as is described in the section called "Addresses File and Engagements File."

Entering Engagements

The first option on the Engagements menu allows you to enter new appointments into the schedule file. To choose this option, press E. The form view of the Enter or Change Engagements display then appears (Figure 10-15). The top portion of the display shows a form where you can enter a new engagement. The bottom portion shows the engagements already in the file. To enter an engagement, just type in the date, time, and a comment on the appropriate lines. Use the cursor arrow keys, RETURN, and SHIFT-TAB to move between the lines. Use the BACKSPACE to erase any mistakes. Press F1 if you need further help information.

In the Date field, you must enter information in the form *mm/dd/yyyy*, using numerals to specify the month and the day. You can change this date format in the Setup menu, as described in the section

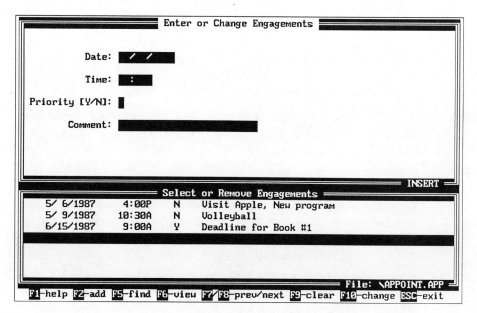

Figure 10-15. The form view of the Enter or Change Engagements display

called "Date Format." If you press TAB on this line, you enter the current date, taken from the PC's internal calendar/clock. In the Time field, you can enter times rounded to any half-hour, but you only can enter times from 8:00 A.M. to 8:30 P.M. Any other times cause the computer to issue a warning beep. If you press T while in the Time field, you are assigning a "title" to that day. If you press Y while in the Priority field, you are telling Traveling SideKick that this engagement is important enough to be printed on weekly, monthly, and yearly calendars. Nonpriority engagements (activated by pressing N) only appear on daily calendar printouts. Finally, while in the Comment field you can type in anything that fits into the allocated space. Comments are typically information about the actual engagement.

When you have finished entering information and are pleased with it, press F2 to add the results to the engagement file. You can have only one engagement per half-hour time period.

If you don't like what you have typed into the form, you can use the cursor arrow keys to move around and edit the information, or you can press F9 to clear the information from the display. You also can press ESC to exit this display and return to the Engagements menu. If you press F5, you move to the Find Engagements display, and if you press F6 you move to the list view of the Enter or Change Engagements display. (Both the Find Engagements display and the list view of the Enter or Change Engagements display are described in the following sections.)

Finding an Engagement

To find a specific engagement, you must use the Find Engagement display (Figure 10-16). You can call up this display by pressing F5 from the Enter or Change Engagements display or by pressing F from the Engagements menu. The top portion of the display is a form you fill in with the specifications for the search. The bottom portion contains information about how to enter your specifications. Use TAB, SHIFT-TAB, and the cursor arrow keys to type the search conditions into the top portion of the display. If you want to find an appointment on a specific day, enter the date in the Date field. If you want to find an appointment with a specific person, enter that person's name in the Comment field. You can use whatever fields you wish to search for a single engagement or for a set of engagements that meet broader conditions. For instance, you could search for all appointments at a certain time by entering that time

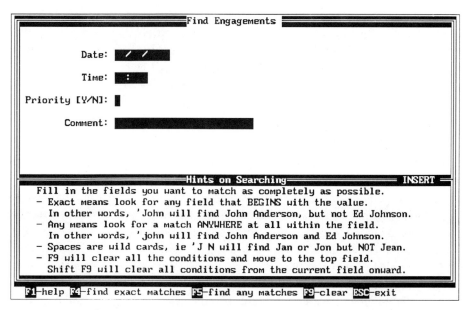

Figure 10-16.   The Find Engagements display

in the Time field and not entering any other conditions. Or you could search for all of the schedule meetings with people from Borland by typing in Borland in the Comment field and not entering any other conditions.

Then press either F4 or F5 to find engagements in the file that match the conditions given. F4 looks for exact matches (where the times and words you specify are in the exact positions you typed them). F5 is more general and searches for any matches. For instance, if you enter **phil** in the Comment field and then press F4, a list of engagements with the comment "phil" or "phillip" is displayed. But a comment that says "meet with phil" is not displayed, because "phil" wasn't at the beginning of the line. Pressing F5 , though, would list all three appointments. You also can search for groups of appointments. For instance, if you type **01/01/88** into the Date field, a list of all appointments on that day is displayed. Also, you can use spaces as wildcards for the Find operation — the procedure is the same as that described in the previous section "Find Addresses."

When a match is found, the screen shows the list view of the Enter or Change Engagements display, and the "found" appointment appears at the top of the display and is also in highlight in the list at the bottom of the screen. If more than one appointment met the conditions, you can find the next appointment in the list by pressing DOWN ARROW.

Changing Engagements

You can alter engagements by using the list view of Enter or Change Engagements display. To call up that display, press C from the Engagements menu or press F6 or F10 from the form view of the Enter or Change Engagements display. To change an engagement, you first must use the Find operation as previously described to find that engagement, and then you must display it in the list view of the Enter or Change Engagements display. When you have done so, use the cursor arrow keys along with PGUP and PGDN to scroll through the list of appointments until you reach (highlight) the one you want to change. The procedure for editing appointments is the same as the procedure for editing addresses, which is described in the previous section "Changing an Address." The altered engagement then appears in the list at the bottom of the screen, sorted by time.

Removing Engagements

If you select R from the Engagements menu, you call up the list view of the Enter or Change Engagements display. The procedure is the same as that described in the previous section "Removing an Address."

Printing Engagement Calendars

The last five choices on the Engagement menu all refer to "printing." You can print a Daily, Weekly, Monthly, Yearly, or Quick Calendar by pressing the first letter of any of these options. As discussed in the previous section "Printing Address Files," "printing" can be to the screen, to a printer, or to another disk file; you can review this section if you need further information.

The Daily Calendar prints out all engagements for a selected day or days (Figure 10-17). The Weekly Calendar prints out up to seven priority engagements for each day, tacking a "more" at the end if this doesn't complete the day's list (Figure 10-18). The Monthly Calendar prints out up to three priority engagements (and no nonpriority engagements) per day, but it allots only nine characters for each engagement (Figure 10-19). The Yearly Calendar places asterisks on days that have priority engagements (Figure 10-20). The Quick List Calendar prints out a simple list of selected engagements showing the date, time, and comment only (Figure 10-21).

No matter which option you select, a Print menu then appears (Figure 10-22). Option selection and printer setup follow the same procedures as those described in the previous sections "Printer Direction" and "Printer Setup."

```
                         Daily Calendar Report


   Name: APPOINT.APP    Title:                          Tue   6/23/1987

   08:00a  _____
   08:30a  _____
   09:00a  Finsh Laser review_____
   09:30a  _____
   10:00a  _____
   10:30a  _____
   11:00a  _____
   11:30a  _____
   12:00p  Deliver chapter 11_____
   12:30p  _____
   01:00p  _____
   01:30p  _____
   02:00p  *Call Fred, re:Miami___
   02:30p  _____
   03:00p  _____
   03:30p  _____
   04:00p  _____

   SPACE-to continue  ESC-exit
```

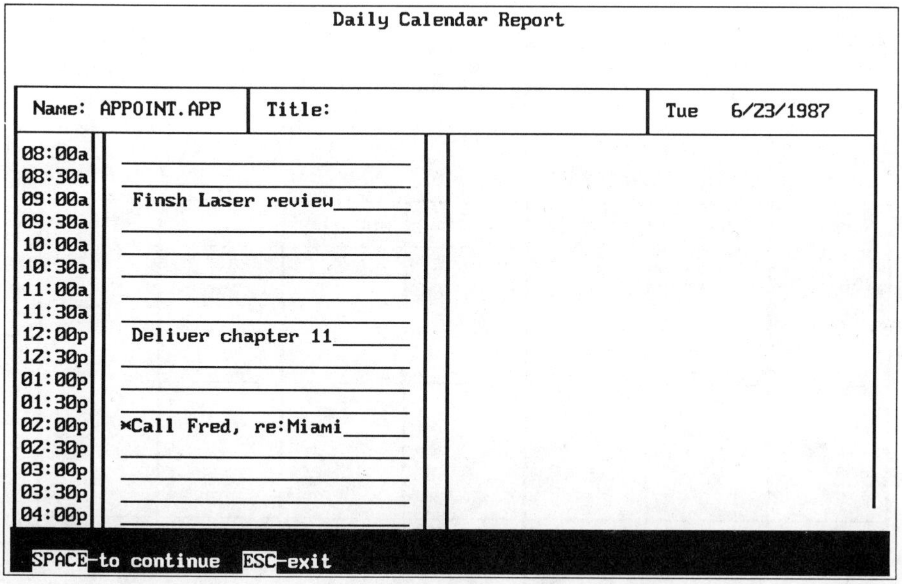

Figure 10-17.   An example of a Daily Calendar screen printout

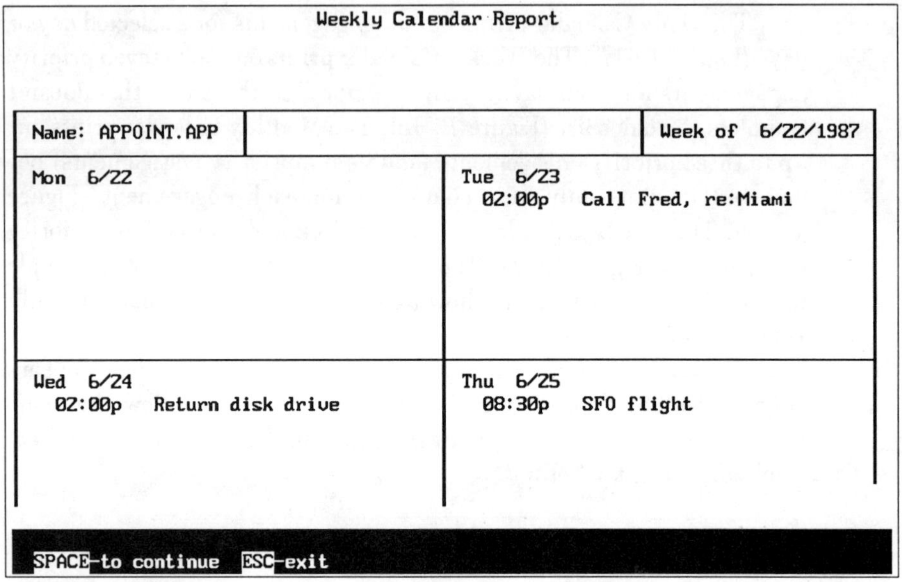

```
                       Weekly Calendar Report


  ┌─────────────────────────┬───────────────────┬──────────────────────┐
  │ Name: APPOINT.APP        │                   │ Week of  6/22/1987   │
  ├─────────────────────────┴──────────┬────────┴──────────────────────┤
  │ Mon  6/22                           │ Tue  6/23                     │
  │                                     │    02:00p   Call Fred, re:Miami│
  │                                     │                               │
  │                                     │                               │
  │                                     │                               │
  │                                     │                               │
  ├─────────────────────────────────────┼───────────────────────────────┤
  │ Wed  6/24                           │ Thu  6/25                     │
  │    02:00p   Return disk drive       │    08:30p   SFO flight        │
  │                                     │                               │
  │                                     │                               │
  │                                     │                               │
  └─────────────────────────────────────┴───────────────────────────────┘
   SPACE-to continue  ESC-exit
```

Figure 10-18.   An example of a Weekly Calendar screen printout

```
                       Monthly Calendar Report


                                                        May 1987
  ┌────────┬────────┬────────┬──────────┬─────────┬────────┬─────────┐
  │ Sunday │ Monday │ Tuesday│ Wednesday│ Thursday│ Friday │ Saturday│
  ├────────┼────────┼────────┼──────────┼─────────┼────────┼─────────┤
  │        │        │        │          │         │       1│        2│
  │        │        │        │          │         │        │         │
  ├────────┼────────┼────────┼──────────┼─────────┼────────┼─────────┤
  │       3│       4│       5│         6│        7│       8│        9│
  │        │        │        │          │         │        │         │
  └────────┴────────┴────────┴──────────┴─────────┴────────┴─────────┘
   SPACE-to continue  ESC-exit
```

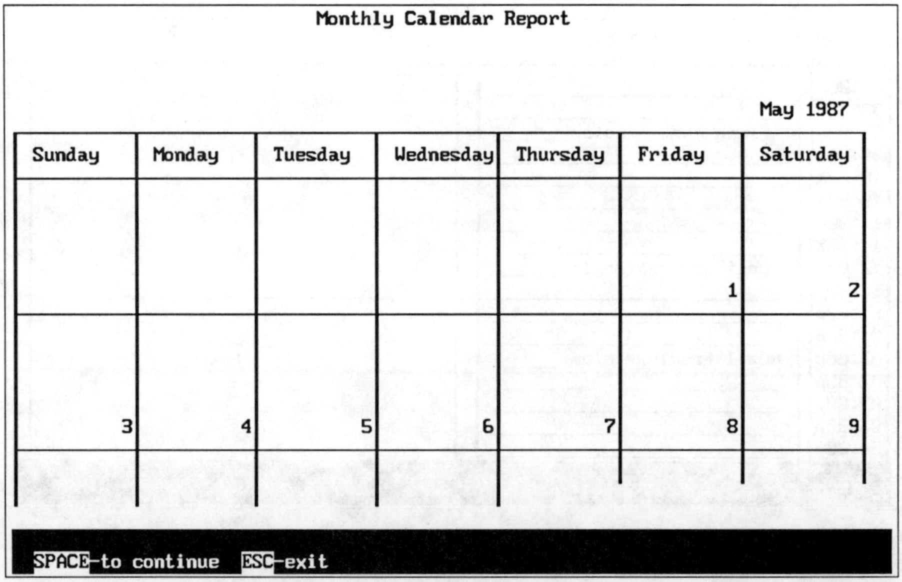

Figure 10-19.   An example of a Monthly Calendar screen printout

```
                        Yearly Calendar Report

            Apr                      May                      Jun

 Su Mo Tu We Th Fr Sa     Su Mo Tu We Th Fr Sa     Su Mo Tu We Th Fr Sa
            ⋈                              ⋈
            1  2  3  4                     1  2     31  1  2  3  4  5  6
                                 ⋈  ⋈              ⋈
  5  6  7  8  9 10 11      3  4  5  6  7  8  9      7  8  9 10 11 12 13
                                                      ⋈
 12 13 14 15 16 17 18     10 11 12 13 14 15 16     14 15 16 17 18 19 20
                                                      ⋈  ⋈  ⋈  ⋈
 19 20 21 22 23 24 25     17 18 19 20 21 22 23     21 22 23 24 25 26 27

 26 27 28 29 30           24 25 26 27 28 29 30     28 29 30
```

SPACE-to continue **ESC**-exit

Figure 10-20.   An example of a Yearly Calendar screen printout

```
                        Daily Calendar Report



            6/23/1987        Tue
         ─────────────────────────────
         09:00a      Finsh Laser review
         12:00p      Deliver chapter 11
         02:00p     ⋈Call Fred, re:Miami
```

SPACE-to continue **ESC**-exit

Figure 10-21.   An example of a Quick List Calendar screen printout

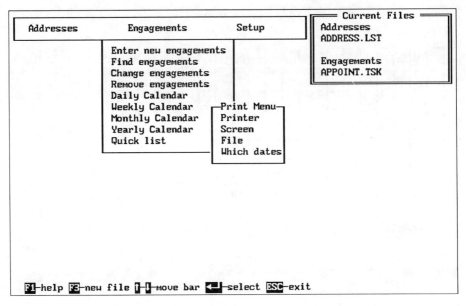

Figure 10-22.   The Print menu display for engagement printing

Printing Part of a File   If you want to print only part of an engagement file, you must press W before you select any of the print directions (printer, screen, or file). Pressing W calls up a Select Date Range window similar to that shown in Figure 10-23. This window lets you specify which dates to print. The window is a little different for each of the five calendars you can print, but it basically works in the same way.

You fill in the information in the fields, using the cursor arrow keys and TAB to move around the window. In most cases, you don't have to fill in all of the fields: the program can infer some information from other information. For instance, if you enter the first day and last day of a period to print, the program automatically can deduce how many days are in that period. You also can use wildcards to select for printing only exact matches to the information you enter (by pressing F4) or to select records that match anywhere in the field (by pressing F5). If you need further clarification, press F1 for help information; also, refer to the previous section on addresses called "Printing Part of a File" for further details on the use of wildcards and F4 and F5. The last field —Current Week —lets you simply enter a Y if you want to print the current week's

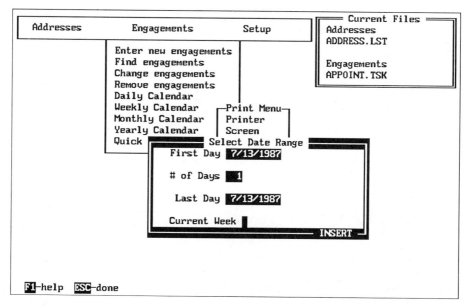

Figure 10-23. The Select Date Range window for printing partial engagement files

engagements without further specification of dates.

If you change your mind about what you want to print, press F9 to clear the display. But when you are satisfied with your dates, press ESC. You then are returned to the Print menu, where you can choose a print direction and start printing. Once you have printed a calendar, you should use a hole-punch to insert the calendars into your Traveling SideKick binder.

Using Engagement Calendars with SideKick

Unlike the address files described earlier in this chapter, Traveling SideKick Engagement files do not have a different structure from Side-Kick Calendar files: you can use Traveling SideKick directly to manipulate Calendar files you made in SideKick; and you can use Traveling SideKick Engagement files as input files for SideKick's Calendar utility. No conversion is necessary.

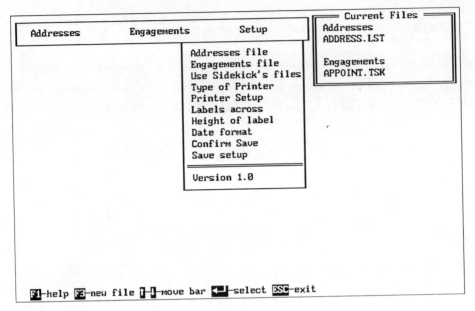

Figure 10-24.   The Traveling SideKick Setup menu

Setup Menu

Like SideKick, Traveling SideKick has a Setup menu for setting defaults and for customizing printouts and other aspects of the program. The Setup menu can be opened directly from the main menu by pressing S or by moving the highlight bar to that option and pressing RETURN (Figure 10-24).

At the bottom of the menu is a notice about which version of Traveling SideKick you're using. This information is important if you ever need to call Borland for help with your program. Above that version number are 10 setup options. You can select any one of these options by pressing the first letter in its title. To choose an option, use the cursor arrow keys to move around in the Setup menu. Press F1 if you need any helpful information concerning the options or the menu itself. If you want to exit the Setup menu or any of its options, just press ESC.

Addresses File and Engagements File

The first two options simply let you enter the drive, directory, and file name of the files you want to use as default files for addresses and engagements in Traveling SideKick. You also can work with other files by pressing F3 to call up a new file.

Use SideKick's Files

If you choose the Use SideKick's files option, a line appears on which you can type a file name. The default on this line is SK.COM. If you press RETURN at this point, you return to the Setup menu, and Traveling SideKick automatically uses the default directory and calendar files from the SideKick file SK.COM, no matter what you put on the Setup menu's Addresses file and Engagements file options. (These SideKick default files are the ones you specified in the SideKick Setup window.) If you use one of the other forms of SideKick (such as SKM.COM), and you want to use the default files belonging to that program, type in that program's file name on the option line. If your SideKick defaults contain wildcards, Traveling SideKick won't be able to work properly. If the keyboard seems to freeze, probably because Traveling SideKick can't find the SideKick file, just press ESC to free the keyboard.

If you call up the Use SideKick's files option, and you decide not to use its files, just press ESC. If you already have pressed RETURN, and you don't want to use SideKick's files, return to the Addresses file and Engagements file lines and enter or reenter information there. This action nullifies the Use SideKick's files input.

Printer Type

The Type of Printer option calls up a new menu that lists several types of printers: Epson FX-80, IBM, Generic, or HP Laserjet. Choose the printer that is closest to what you're using by pressing the first letter of that printer's type. If you have questions about which printer to choose, you can ask an expert or call Borland.

Printer Setup

You can instruct the printer to use special formatting by sending it special control characters before sending the file to be printed. These controls can regulate the margins, type style, spacing, and so on. This Printer Setup option gives you two lines to record the control characters you want to send to your printer whenever you print Traveling SideKick files. The control characters you use depend on the printer you have. Some examples of control characters for the Epson FX-80 are listed in Figure 8-1.

Labels Across and
Height of Label

The Labels Across and Height of Label options regulate the printing of mailing labels from the address files. You can choose to print one, two, three, or four labels across and to have each label be six, nine, or twelve lines tall.

Date Format

By default, Traveling SideKick expects you to enter dates in the form *mm/dd/yyyy*. You can use the Date format option to change to either dd-mmm-yy, in which the month is represented by the first three letters of its name, or to month dd, yyyy, where the name of the month is written out in full.

Confirm Save

Traveling SideKick automatically saves the current address or engagement file to disk whenever you leave the Addresses or Engagements menu. If you don't want this to happen automatically but want to choose when to save and when not to save, you can use the Confirm Save option to choose "yes" for Confirm Save. Then, Traveling SideKick will ask before it saves.

Save Setup

You can save to disk any changes you make in the Setup menu by choosing the Save setup option. Those changes then become the new defaults the next time you use Traveling SideKick.

11

SuperKey

SuperKey is another Borland program that, like SideKick, is a TSR (terminate and stay resident) utility: a program that loads into memory and then is available even while other application programs are running. SuperKey offers many handy functions —including screen protection, a large key buffer, keyboard redefinition, a command stack, a cut-and-paste ability, and data encryption —but its foundation is its macro capability. Macros let you avoid repetitive typing, thereby allowing you to do more work in less time. Macros have the capability to remember complex actions, freeing you the user to get on to other tasks.

If you like SideKick —with its frequently useful utilities always at hand —you'll also like SuperKey. But where SideKick works alongside other programs, streamlining your computing so you don't have to stop and start other application programs so often, SuperKey gets right into your applications and makes them more powerful. Where SideKick lives easily with other programs and even helps you transfer information between them, SuperKey practically becomes part of other programs and makes them easier and faster to use.

Because SuperKey's macros are so versatile, it would be easy to write an entire book on them. This chapter can give you only a brief look at the SuperKey macros. It describes the SuperKey features and briefly illustrates how to make, save, and use macros and how to employ the practical macros that Borland includes on the SuperKey disk. With this information, you should be able to take SuperKey and apply it to your favorite programs, including SideKick, effectively enhancing them as if you suddenly had new versions with more power and speed.

Hardware Requirements

If your system is powerful enough for SideKick, it's also powerful enough for SuperKey. Like SideKick, SuperKey requires an IBM PC, XT, AT, PCjr, or compatible computer with at least 128K RAM, one disk drive, and DOS 2.0 or greater.

Note: loading both SuperKey and SideKick into memory at once uses up a fair amount of RAM, so even though each program only requires a minimum of 128K, realistically, you should use a system that has at least 512K or even 640K.

Making a Backup

The first step in using SuperKey, of course, is to make a backup copy of the original disk. SuperKey is not copy protected. Use the procedure outlined in Chapter 2 for backing up non-copy-protected versions of SideKick. If you have a hard disk, you also should make a copy of SuperKey to that disk —this too is described in Chapter 2—putting all of the files into a directory called key.

Installation

SuperKey has its own installation program, just as does SideKick. To run it, type **keyinst** and then press RETURN. The initial Installation program display allows you to choose which SuperKey program to customize for your system (Figure 11-1). The only difference between the two options

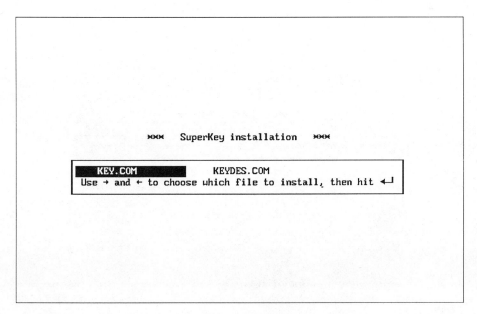

Figure 11-1.   The SuperKey initial Installation program display

listed is that KEY.COM uses a Borland technique for encoding files (in the SuperKey encryption features), and KEYDES.COM uses the more secret DES method for encryption. This difference also means that KEYDES.COM codes and decodes files more slowly than KEY.COM does. (The encryption feature is explained in more detail in the section called "Encryption.") Use the cursor arrow keys to move the highlight bar to the program you want to install (which in almost all cases is KEY.COM) and press RETURN to call up the main Installation menu (Figure 11-2).

Here you can choose your own settings for three factors listed in a central box: screen type, display colors, and the size of memory for holding macros. The second line of the box describes in more detail the option highlighted on the first line. You select one of the three factors by moving the highlight bar to your chosen option and then pressing RETURN or by pressing S for screen or C for colors. After you make one of those selections, you are presented with more displays and menus that list specific options for the screen and for color. To make selections from

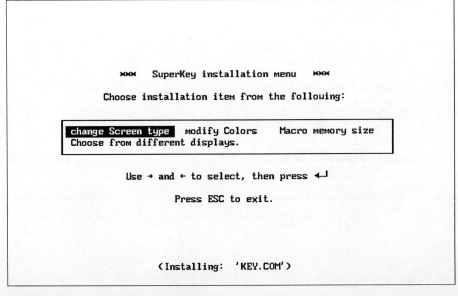

Figure 11-2.   The SuperKey Installation menu

these menus, follow the instructions at the bottom of the screen and use the cursor arrow keys to move about within the menus.

The Macro memory size choice lets you decide how much RAM to set aside for holding macros that you create. Your size can range from 128 bytes to 64K bytes. The original default is 8000 bytes. The less memory you use, the more there is for other programs to use — but if you run out of memory in the middle of some operation, you must stop the operation, remove SuperKey from memory (and remove any programs loaded after it such as SideKick), use KEYINST to change the macro memory size, reload SuperKey (and the other programs) into memory, resume the operation, and try again to save the macro. For now, if you don't know what setting to use, you should maintain the default value.

The README File

Before you begin working with SuperKey you should open the README file. This file contains information about SuperKey that was too recent to be included in the manual. The easiest way to read this file is to use the special program that accompanies it — README.COM. Just type **readme** and press RETURN to call up the README window (Figure 11-3). To scroll through this file, use UP ARROW, DOWN ARROW, PGUP, and PGDN. If you want to print out a single page of the file, press F1. Pressing F2 prints out the entire file. When you're finished with README, press ESC to return to the DOS prompt.

Loading SuperKey into Memory

After you have made backups and have stored the original disk away in a safe place, you need to know how to load SuperKey into your computer's memory. That procedure is much the same as for loading SideKick. Keep in mind that you should load SuperKey before you load SideKick, and you should load SuperKey *after* you load any other non-Borland TSR programs. If you're not using SideKick, then SuperKey should be the last TSR program you load into memory. This rule, like the rule about

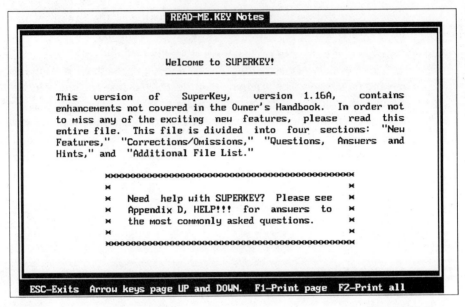

Figure 11-3. The README window showing the first page of the README file

loading SideKick last of any TSR programs, helps ensure that your programs all work together smoothly.

From the DOS prompt (which is typically A: \> for a floppy-disk version of SuperKey or C: \key> for a hard-disk directory version), type **key** and then press RETURN to call up the SuperKey loading display (Figure 11-4). (If you want secure file encoding and choose the DES algorithm, as explained in the "Encryption" section, type **keydes** instead of **key**.) This display shows how much RAM is free, how much SuperKey has taken, and how much is reserved for macros.

Removing SuperKey from Memory

If you want to free memory for use by other programs, or if you want to reload SuperKey from disk because you used KEYINST to change the SuperKey installation after SuperKey was loaded into memory, then you

```
┌──────────────────────────────────────────────┐
│ Superkey              Version 1.16A            │
│                   IBM-PC/XT/AT/PCjr            │
│                                                │
│ Copyright (C) 1984,85 BORLAND Inc.             │
└──────────────────────────────────────────────┘



    524288 bytes total memory
    413968 bytes were free
    355920 bytes free
      8000 bytes macro memory


 C>
```

Figure 11-4.   The SuperKey loading display, showing memory usage

need to remove SuperKey from memory. To do so, first remove any program loaded after SuperKey, such as SideKick. (Chapter 2 explains how to remove SideKick from RAM.) Press ALT-/ and then CTRL-ALT-DEL.

Suspending SuperKey — Turning It Off Without Unloading It

You also can "suspend" SuperKey temporarily —put it in limbo without removing it entirely from memory. This feature is helpful when you temporarily want to reestablish normal key definitions, but you don't want to lose your macros entirely from memory. Press ALT-/ to call up the SuperKey main menu (as explained in the next section), then press O and U. To return SuperKey to action, type **key /ou**, and press RETURN after you see the DOS prompt. Remember that you must be in the directory that contains the SuperKey files.

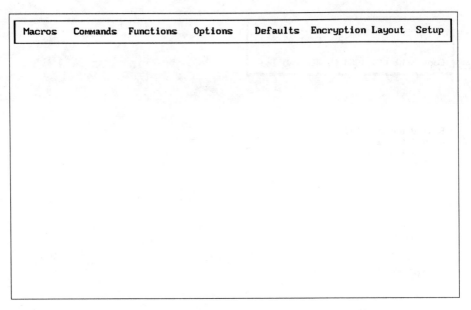

Macros   Commands Functions   Options   Defaults Encryption Layout   Setup

Figure 11-5.   The SuperKey main menu

Activating SuperKey

Once SuperKey is in RAM, you can activate it by pressing two keys simultaneously: ALT-/. Notice that this is the regular "slash" mark, not the backslash (\ ). The SuperKey main menu then appears (Figure 11-5). The eight options at the top of the screen each harbor a "pull-down" menu of more specific commands and options. You can select an option either by moving the highlight bar to your choice and pressing RETURN or by simply pressing the first letter of your chosen option. For example, Figure 11-6 shows the Options menu that is selected when you press O.

Getting Help

As with most of the Borland programs described in this book, you can press F1 any time SuperKey is activated to call up helpful information on

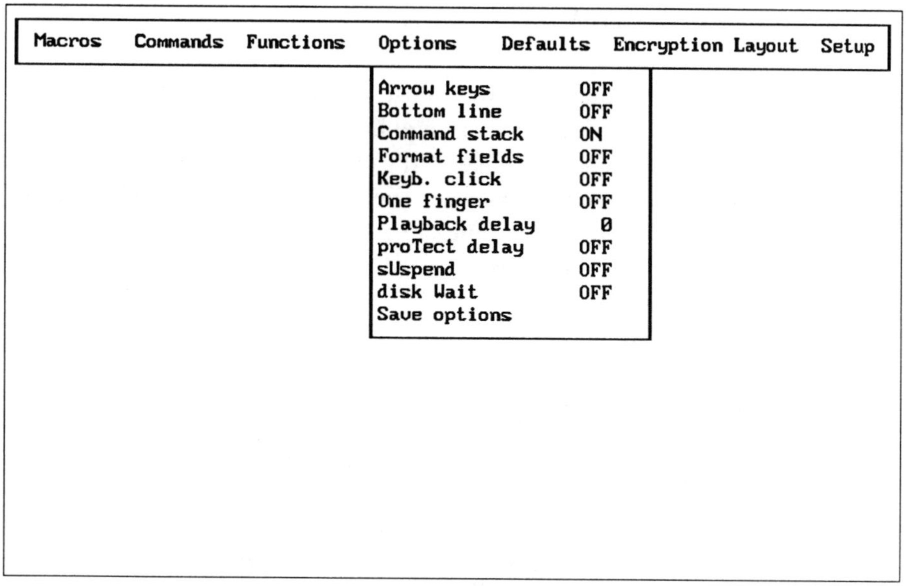

```
┌─────────────────────────────────────────────────────────────────┐
│ Macros   Commands  Functions   Options   Defaults  Encryption Layout  Setup │
│                              ┌─────────────────────────────┐      │
│                              │ Arrow keys        OFF       │      │
│                              │ Bottom line       OFF       │      │
│                              │ Command stack     ON        │      │
│                              │ Format fields     OFF       │      │
│                              │ Keyb. click       OFF       │      │
│                              │ One finger        OFF       │      │
│                              │ Playback delay      0       │      │
│                              │ proTect delay     OFF       │      │
│                              │ sUspend           OFF       │      │
│                              │ disk Wait         OFF       │      │
│                              │ Save options                │      │
│                              └─────────────────────────────┘      │
│                                                                   │
│                                                                   │
└─────────────────────────────────────────────────────────────────┘
```

Figure 11-6.   The Options pull-down menu

commands and options. Also, if you're lost in the menus of SuperKey, pressing ESC moves you back up one level each time you press it, eventually moving you out of SuperKey and back to your current application program or to DOS.

Keyboard Type-Ahead Buffer

The simplest feature of SuperKey is one you don't have to learn anything about to use: the type-ahead buffer. Normally, the IBM PC has a 16-key buffer. That is, if the computer is busy processing or saving some information to disk, for example, but you're typing anyway, the keyboard can save up to 16 keystrokes. This buffer then presents these keystrokes to the computer as soon as it is ready to take them. If you type more than 16 strokes, you may lose some of them and you may hear a warning beep. SuperKey has a 128-key buffer, so you can type quite a bit ahead of what the computer is doing and not lose any of those strokes.

DOS Command Stack

DOS always lets you review your most recent command: if you press F3, that command appears on the prompt line. But SuperKey remembers far more than just a single command. It can store the last 256 characters of DOS commands you have used and then present them to you in a special window for reuse or inspection later. This feature can be handy if you either want to see what you just did or if you want to reuse long commands that are tedious to retype.

Command Stack Window

The commands for manipulating the command stack are spread throughout several of the portions of the SuperKey main menu. There are two commands that let you view the Command Stack window. You can press ALT-/ (to call up the SuperKey main menu), then press C (for the Commands menu), and finally press C for the command stack. Or you can press just ALT- \ (note the backslash). Using either method, the Command Stack window appears (Figure 11-7).

Each line in this window has a separate DOS command. One line is highlighted at any time. You can move the highlight bar up and down using the cursor arrow keys, and you can scroll through more pages within the same window by pressing PGUP or PGDN. At any point, you can execute the highlight DOS command by pressing RETURN. That command then appears on the screen, as well as the RETURN that followed it. Note: if you don't have DOS behind the SuperKey Command Stack window (if you are using some other application), the command may not have any effect.

Editing the Command Stack

You also can edit commands that are saved in the Command Stack window. Just use the right- and left-arrow cursor keys to move to the portion of the highlight line you want to change, and then use the alphanumeric keys to enter information, DEL to delete characters, and INS to insert blank spaces.

Turning the Command Stack On and Off

The Command Stack feature is turned on automatically when you first activate SuperKey, but at times you may wish to turn it off. For instance, if it has captured a series of complex DOS commands that you want to reuse, but you first have to execute some other, less important commands, you can stop it from recording commands by using the Options menu. To call up the Options menu from the SuperKey main menu, press ALT-/ to call up the main menu, then press O to call up the Options menu, then press C to choose the Command Stack option. This procedure toggles the command stack to the opposite state from which it was in: since it was turned on, it now is turned off. To turn it back on, go through the same procedure, and the toggling then turns the command stack on again. From the Options menu, you also can move the highlight bar to the Command Stack option and then press + to turn the command

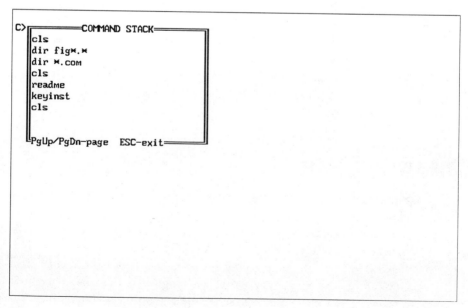

Figure 11-7. The Command Stack window

stack on or − to turn it off. This method is sometimes easier to understand than the previous method; since the toggling also immediately changes the display, it doesn't leave the menu visible so you can see the changed state of the stack.

Keyboard Lock and Unlock

As another security feature, SuperKey allows you to "lock" your keyboard so that none of the keys can work. That is, after you give the command to lock it, the keys still can move if pressed, but they can't allow the computer to receive any input or instruct the computer to perform any function until you enter the *key word* (Borland's term for a password) again to "unlock" the keyboard. This can be handy if your computer is out in the open at home where children can get at the keyboard or insecure at work where other people can try the keyboard while you're away from the desk or office.

To lock the keyboard, activate SuperKey by pressing ALT-/, from the main menu press F to call up the Functions menu, and then press K to initiate the Keyboard Lock function. The display then prompts you for your key word. When you press RETURN, the keyboard locks and can't become active again until you type in the same key word and press RETURN.

Screen Off and On

SuperKey also lets you turn your screen display on or off. This feature allows you to blank the screen out if you don't want someone else to see what you are working on. Just press ALT-/ to activate SuperKey, from the main menu press F to open the Functions menu, and then press S to toggle the screen off. To turn your screen display back on, you must press ALT-/, F, and S again to toggle. You can assign all of these keystrokes to a single key, so you can turn the screen on and off more simply. Read the sections on macros later in this chapter to see how to perform this function.

Screen Protect

You don't have to use the Screen Off function to blank the screen: you also can instruct it to blank automatically after a certain period of time. This option is actually included in SuperKey to protect the physical screen, not your information. Some screens can have images *burned* into them if one image remains on the screen for too long. To call up this option, activate the main menu by pressing ALT-/, then press O to call up the Options menu, and finally press T for "proTect delay." You also can move the highlight bar down the Options menu to the proTect delay line and then press RETURN. You then are prompted as to how long you want the delay to be, and you answer with a number of minutes (the default is 5). Then press RETURN. Whenever that number of minutes passes without the program sending any new information to the screen or without any key being pressed, the screen image blanks. This option protects the screen from image burning and also obscures what you are working on (although touching a key will call up the former display).

Running Options Automatically

In the latest versions of SuperKey, any of the Options menu commands or features can be invoked automatically when you initially load Super-Key from disk into RAM. Just press O to call up the Options menu, and then the selection letter of the option you want to invoke or toggle. For instance, although typing **key** simply loads SuperKey into RAM, typing **key /oc** loads SuperKey and turns the command stack off. Typing **key /ok** loads SuperKey and turns the keyboard click sound on.

If you want to invoke several functions automatically, use commands in sequence, such as

    key /ok
    key /oc

This method of loading configurations when loading SuperKey also applies to loading keyboard layout files and macro files. Keyboard layout files are discussed in the section "Automatically Loading a Layout File When You Open SuperKey." Macro files are discussed in the section "Loading Macro Files Automatically."

Cut and Paste

SideKick's Notepad contains a Paste feature that lets you assign any block of notefile text to a key that you then can use to "paste" the text into any other application's display. SuperKey has an even more powerful Paste feature: it combines the SideKick Paste feature with the ability to "cut" text from one application and then "paste" it into another. This feature is essentially a specialized type of macro, and so is contained in the Macros menu. First display the block of text you want to cut from. Then, press ALT-/ to call up the main menu, press M to call up the Macros menu, and then press U to choose "cut and paste." A small window appears that says

CUT AND PASTE
Press Key to Use

You should press the key or key combination you wish to use. This key will have the macro of the cut text assigned to it. Try pressing, for instance, ALT-F1. You'll be asked if you really want to redefine that key. If you haven't chosen a key that might become troublesome when redefined (for instance, if you redefined ESC , you couldn't use its normal exiting function), then press Y. (If you decide you don't like the key or key combination you have chosen, press N, and you can start the procedure over.) The SuperKey display will be replaced by the text you have chosen to cut a block from.

Use the cursor arrow keys to move the cursor to the top left corner of the block of text you wish cut, then press B. Now use the cursor arrow keys to move the cursor to the bottom right corner of the block, which becomes highlighted as you move the cursor. When you reach that bottom corner, press RETURN. The text block now is assigned as a macro to the key you chose. Any time you press that key, the entire block is written to the display, to no matter what application program you have active at that time. You should try this feature with SideKick's Notepad.

Playback Delay

Occasionally, you may have problems writing the text to another program. When you press the Cut-and-Paste macro key, the text may begin to write, but then a warning beeps or the text won't appear fully in the other program's display. This can happen if SuperKey is sending the text too fast for the other program to insert. It also can happen, temporarily, if programs just aren't fast enough to display the new text immediately, although they are inserting it. WordStar, for instance, may display exclamation points while accepting the text and then show the real text after the macro is finished its sending.

SuperKey normally sends or "pastes" at around 1000 characters per second, but you can slow down this rate by using the Playback delay option from the Options menu: press O from the main menu and then press P for Playback delay. This delay factor affects all macros and sets the time that SuperKey waits between sending succeeding characters. The default is 0; and you can set the delay as high as 999. Normally a small value such as 5 is enough to allow most programs to accept macros. Type in such a number, press RETURN, and then try using the Cut-and-Paste macro key again. If it works, you may want to save your playback delay value for the next time you load SuperKey. To do so, call up the main menu, press S to call up the Setup menu, and then S again for "Save Setup." Any changes in your options specified in the Options menu then are saved to the SuperKey file on disk.

Changing the Keyboard Layout

Because SuperKey can assign new meanings to keys on the keyboard, you can use it literally to change the keyboard around, placing the key commands you are familiar with where you want them. Of course, you can't change the markings on top of the keys, but you can change the function of the keys, which sometimes can help if you are working with an awkward or unfamiliar keyboard.

To change the keys, you must load a new keyboard *layout*: call up the main menu, press L to call up the Layout menu, and then press L again for "Load Layout." You are prompted for the name of a layout file. There is only one other layout file on the original SuperKey disk:

DVORAK.LAY. (Layout files always end with .LAY.) You can type in this file name and press RETURN to change to the Dvorak-style keyboard, which scientifically rearranges all of the letter keys to allow faster typing than on a standard keyboard. Or you can press ESC to exit the loading step until you create your own layout file.

Making a New Keyboard Layout File

To create a layout file, you must use a separate program that is on the SuperKey disk: LAYOUT.COM. To call up LAYOUT.COM, call up a DOS prompt, type **layout**, and press RETURN. You then are asked for the name of a layout file. If you choose a name that already has been used by one of the files on the disk, that file is opened for modification. If you choose a new name, a new file is opened. (You don't have to type the .LAY extension to the name: SuperKey does that for you automatically.) You then must make a choice about display readability. If your display is easy to read at this point, press any key. If you cannot see the display well, press F10 to call up a set of instructions that can help you increase the screen's readability. After you have decided that your screen display is readable, a display similar to that shown in Figure 11-8 appears.

This display contains the images of two keyboards. The cursor first appears as a highlight on the top keyboard. You can use the cursor arrow keys to move that highlight to any key on the top keyboard. When you find a key whose function you want to put in a different place on your working keyboard, press SPACE BAR. The cursor then moves to the bottom keyboard. Use the cursor arrow keys again to move the highlight on the bottom keyboard to the key you want to insert the previously chosen function, then press SPACE BAR again. For instance, if you want to make the right-side SHIFT (labeled "Shr" on the screen) into BACKSPACE, you would move the cursor to BACKSPACE (labeled "Bsp") on the top image, press SPACE BAR, move the cursor on the bottom keyboard image to SHR, and press SPACE BAR again. You can see the change reflected in the bottom keyboard titles. The cursor then moves back to the top keyboard image to allow you to make more changes. When you have made all the key changes you wish, press F2 to save your changes to the layout file. If you want to exit LAYOUT.COM without saving your changes, press ESC.

Loading or Clearing a Layout
File in SuperKey

Once you have created a layout file you want to use, activate SuperKey again and load that layout file using the instructions mentioned previously in "Changing the Keyboard Layout" (ALT-/, L, L, *file name*, RETURN). If your changes don't work as you intended, or if you want to alter a definition for a task, you can clear the changes and revert to the original meanings of the keys by using the Clear function of the Layout menu: call up the main menu, press L to call up the layout menu, then press C for "Clear."

Automatically Loading a Layout
File When You Open SuperKey

In the latest versions of SuperKey, you have the option of automatically loading a new keyboard layout when you load SuperKey into RAM. If

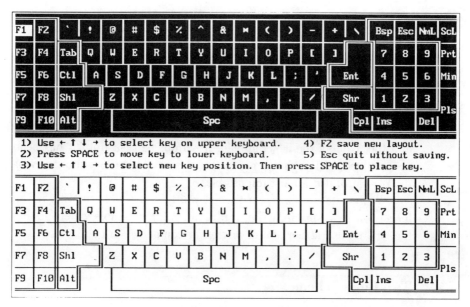

Figure 11-8.   The LAYOUT.COM program display for redefining keys

you choose to load a new keyboard layout automatically, do not type **key** (or **keydes**) and press RETURN to load SuperKey into RAM. Instead, use the command

    key *filename*/ll

where *filename* is the name of your layout file without the .LAY extension, and then press RETURN to load SuperKey. The *ll* stands for layout menu and the load command. If you want to use the DES encryption scheme, as explained in the next section, use the command

    keydes *filename*/ ll

You also can use the command

    key *filename*/lc

to clear a layout and return the keys to their default state.

Encryption

The encryption feature stands apart from the other SuperKey features. This option allows you to change files into code and then later to decode them again. It offers you some information security, making it far more difficult for others to use your disks and read your files. The Encryption routine uses mathematical formulas to scramble the bits of information in a file. Once a file is scrambled, it cannot be read until it has been descrambled. Although it is possible to descramble a file without having the key word, it is almost impossible.

You create your key word when you first scramble the file. If you forget your key word for a file, you're not going to be able to decode that file, and no one at Borland or any other company can help!

Two Code Schemes

SuperKey offers two different scrambling formulas, each in a different SuperKey program file. You only can use the program in the SuperKey file you loaded into memory (refer to the previous section "Installation" for more details). These files and formulas are listed:

KEY.COM   This is the standard SuperKey file. It contains a scrambling formula from Borland. Its code is quite secure, but it is not as secure as the DES code in the other version of SuperKey. Still, it works faster than the DES version and is therefore the one most people use unless they have good reason to fear someone may want to read their files.

KEYDES.COM   This is the more advanced scrambling formula. It is a DES scheme, meaning it follows the Data Encryption Standard of the United States National Bureau of Standards. It should be secure against even fairly determined code breakers armed with computers, but it functions more slowly than the simpler KEY.-COM formula.

If you use KEY.COM to load SuperKey into memory (you type **key** when starting), then you automatically are using the first, simpler, and faster scrambling scheme when you choose encryption. If you use KEYDES.COM to load SuperKey into memory (you type **keydes** when starting), then you automatically are using the second, more complex, and slower scrambling scheme when you choose encryption. The rest of SuperKey functions the same, no matter which of the two files you choose to use.

Of course, if you have some files that absolutely require the higher level of security, but most of the time you don't want its slower speed, you may be tempted to alternate which version you use when you load SuperKey into memory. This probably isn't a good idea, because it is so easy to forget which was used to encrypt which file.

Encrypting a File

You can choose the Encryption command by working through the menus: press ALT-/ to call up the main menu, press E to call up the Encryption menu, and then press E again or press RETURN (if the highlight is already on "Encrypt") to select the Encrypt function. A small window then appears that asks you to specify which file to encrypt and what key word to assign to it (Figure 11-9).

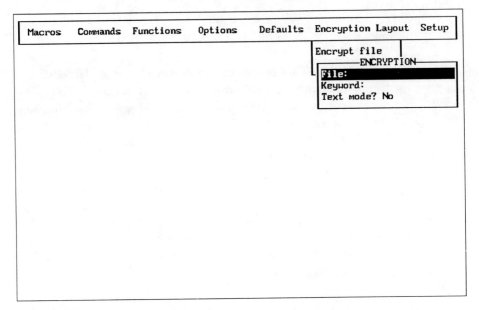

Figure 11-9. The Encryption file name and key word window

File Name

Type in the name of a file that you wish to encode and then press
RETURN. As soon as you enter a key word and answer a question about
Text mode (both of which are discussed in the next two sections), your
file is encrypted.

You can include wildcard symbols (such as ? for any single character and * for any sequence of characters) in the file name; if you do, you
are instructing SuperKey to encrypt all files that meet your wildcard-
conditioned file name and to use the same key word for each file. If you
use wildcards, you then are asked if you want to verify your order to
encrypt a file as each file name is presented to you. If you answer yes, you
must press Y before each valid file name. If you answer no, all the file
names that match the wildcard-conditioned file name are encrypted as
soon as you enter a key word and answer the question about Text mode.

Key Words (Passwords)

Next assign a key word to your file — a key word you're sure you can remember. It sometimes makes sense to use one key word for all of your encrypted files, if you think it is a good key word and you don't need rigid security. The higher the security level you want, the larger the variety of key words you should use; but of course, more key words also means a greater chance of forgetting them or of having to write them down somewhere, which nullifies part of their value.

Type in your key word and press RETURN. Only a plus sign (+) appears on the screen, in case anyone is looking over your shoulder. The program then asks you to type in your key word again, on the same line. Type it in again, and press RETURN. If you don't type in the same word both times, the program beeps at you and you must start the procedure for entering a key word again. If you do type in the same word, it is accepted as the key word for your file, and you move on to the last line on the Encryption menu, which asks you about Text mode (which is discussed in the next section).

Text Mode

You can encrypt files in the Text mode or the Nontext mode. When a file is encrypted in the Nontext mode, the new file is made up of all sorts of jumbled characters and is written right on top of the old file, leaving no part of the old file that still can be read. Figure 11-10 shows an example of what this encryption looks like. When a file is encrypted in the Text mode, the new, encrypted version is made up entirely of capital letters from A to Z and does not replace the old file. The new file also is larger than the old, uncoded file, so you need plenty of disk space to use this mode. Figure 11-11 shows an example of what this encryption scheme produces.

The advantage of the Nontext mode is that it immediately protects what is on your disks: no part of the old file hangs around for potential reading. The advantage of the Text mode is that you can send text-mode encrypted files over a modem to another computer. Some communications programs cannot send characters other than the simple ones used in text-mode encrypted files.

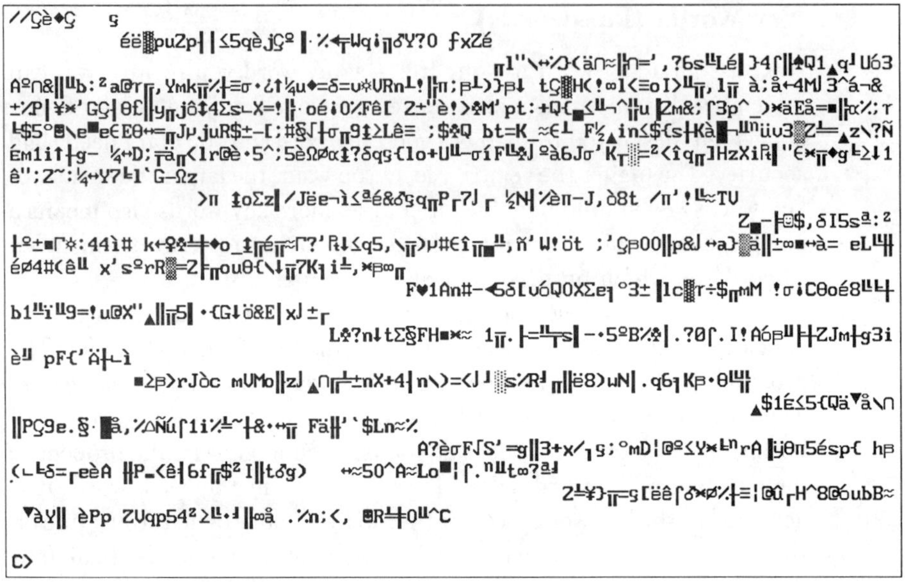

Figure 11-10. An example of file encrypted in the Nontext mode

```
HCGIEGGEHDBFDHLPGCOKMPPMOLNOCGICDHCDHCCDCMHCKCCIIAOENDHDPLCPMLHD
DLBBJBJJJKLPLBNBHAIEGLJFFKMLKCEMEDONLLJCIPEFMJNKADNBFNFOEMNGJAIE
ODOMCEDOMMOIOMNECCODEIDAIJCDLIIGCPBFNAAIFADEHGEHFDBHDFPONLPMPPIO
BBEPMKCHADCPKAMPKFNOJDKOHALLDEKMPDDFNCHFIJAOOPECKJJIHMABBENBEBFI
CPDMCHHDCCGGDCOCFHEMAFMMANENGDIFDOLCLPKDCMCCFCMKMOMOMDPHEMDAMIDH
CMFPFGOCNPGKGFJBAABDGLFEGIDGBOMAIBPOOEBPKKKPEAIALDFEFFFOJGOHOHDN
AFGNGGPFENAFNEIOGDAGCEDCFECGLOMLONOPIPPNKBDDCCCDDEEHGBEMAEMMFIFM
EOHPCHLHPIJOPBKEJKMPIMIEGOKOEFNNKCEANBELLCACLGMEEMLOOLOAOBFENKCF
GGDMDDPOHNJNBHLIPDHADKIIKJKNCDNOHEMCBINCDNDDGPFAJFBMFDEHCFDDEBCD
FHLCAPLOPOIGJEEDEFILHNBHPPHFFJPEPHHGDCHJBIAHOEHOFOCOEFHHOMLEJJDH
OCEMLOMOOIOPMOKCDHGCCDDHCGCDLGMAMEANMEIFMBDHDLODPPLHDBGEDKNMOMNM
BEGLKEFBGDLGIJAKCFFGNALGCJHLPCCEGFJFIFBBBDNECCOFDMPGFHAEAODOCKKL
DLGMODFICBIICFJGKHCGPBENFAMEDCMEHGBGCFFHGMCOKMOOMLPMOCCCCGCDCCHG
MFPIEFPCMLOKKNLGNPCAEHABCDBIGNJNEDJOIGEKMCAEHGGBAKEKCFGCHCJFEOFL
AAMNAMFEMIEMFMNOFFDHLPDKPPHDKEMHEDOMJKIKNADKGEJDBINCDBDGPFFNBANE
DMEDOAJOAPMNEGDKNIKCEMILKBKPNMFNBANELCKAFDFGAKOGOMOJJDDOADFNGNFD
GCDNEHGEHCFBCGPMGFJKILOMPPNOGHMDGHCCDCCDGNCAIHEMMEMEMHHDPLCLPLDH
IDBOMKKNALNJOJNIMPEEFNKBLEEKLECHICDKKODBLOMOLJJHCOPAILALLJKNNAIL
PDPNGAGLMILMOMNEEFKDAIDAINCDLNMCHLBFMBBMEBDEGGEGDFEDHBLNMOKMPPIO
BAPHJFLNELCGEBDHNIOAJHDFDHODJBKBEFOBFKMADGLGMPKGEHIEMDAMAKEGFCAE
DODMCDDCCDCDHDPCEFCIAAMMEIEMDHIGCPPCPOLGCIDGFCLIMOIOMHPHEIHAIICH
GNPHMKBLOPJDBBEIFFBEFFKKKNIKBCOPCJNIFMPIIGKLKCBDHKKMBFFONHPEBCKL
FEGMGCMBENBBMEKJCHAGCFHCEBCHKKNPKMPPMLPIOADCCHCCHDCCDBEMEAMMFMA^C

C>
```

Figure 11-11. An example of file encrypted in the Text mode

So unless you need to use the Text mode to send your files over a modem, you can answer N to the final question —that is, "No, don't use the Text mode." Now press RETURN to start the encryption. A notice is displayed that tells you the encryption is in progress, and you can hear the disk work as the file is read and then is rewritten.

Rules for Code Safety   You can avoid some potential problems by not encrypting files that already are encrypted, and by only decoding files that are encrypted.

Macros

Macros are saved sequences of keyboard actions. By saving things that are typed on the keyboard and then assigning those things to a single key or a simple combination of keys, you can repeat computer activities with less typing. SuperKey can make and save macros that can improve almost any application you use on a computer, including SideKick.

Text Macros

The simplest macros are just sequences of characters. Recording these with SuperKey is like having your computer perform shorthand. For instance, you may be typing a long manuscript that constantly refers to the German Democratic Republic. You can save that phrase as a macro, and then it would appear each time you pressed the macro's assigned key or key combination.

Recording a Macro

The easiest way to create a macro is to turn on SuperKey's recorder, type in the series of keys that you want to save, and then turn off the recorder. To begin recording, press ALT-/ to call up the main menu. Then press M to call up the Macros menu (Figure 11-12). Finally, press B to begin to record your macro. A small window opens and asks you to choose a key for the macro. This assigned key, or combination of keys, is what you press to recall and use your macro. Most of the time, it's a good idea to

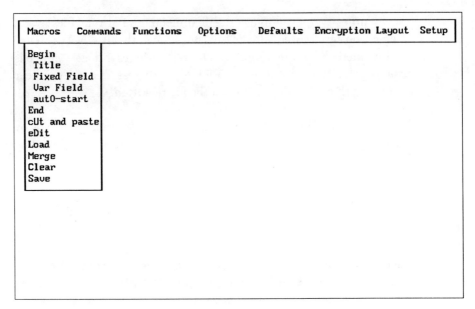

Figure 11-12. SuperKey's Macro menu

use ALT, CTRL, or SHIFT in combination with some other key: this sort of combination is least likely to conflict with other key definitions.

Key Assignment

You must be careful when choosing a key assignment, because you temporarily lose the normal function of the key. For instance, if you redefine J by assigning your macro to it, you won't be able to type in the letter "J." Each time you press J, SuperKey inserts the text you assigned to J. You can avoid this sequence by inserting a special *skip* command. If you want to use the normal function of a key that has had a macro assigned to it, press ALT-/, C, K, and finally the assigned key to invoke the skip command from the Commands menu (Figure 11-13). This procedure "skips" the macro just the one time: you must use the command again if you want to skip the macro again.

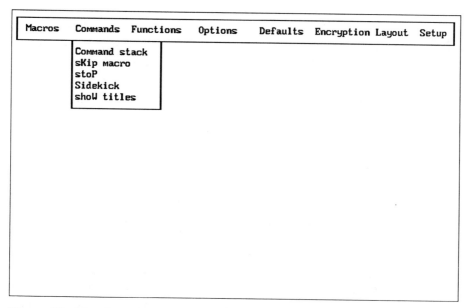

| Macros | Commands | Functions | Options | Defaults | Encryption | Layout | Setup |

Command stack
sKip macro
stoP
Sidekick
shoW titles

Figure 11-13.   SuperKey's Command menu

After you decide which key combination to assign the macro to, press that key or keys. A small notice appears at the top of the display that tells you that SuperKey is recording your keystrokes and assigning them to your chosen key. Each key or key combination can hold only a single macro, but there are many possible key combinations.

Typing the Macro

Once the recorder is turned on, you can type in any keys, and they are stored in memory as a single macro. You can type letters and numbers, and you can type special function keys and even key combinations. As noted on the top line of the display, SuperKey stops recording only when you press ALT- (ALT and -) or return to the Macros menu with ALT-/ and press M, E for "End." The macro will then be ready for use; you just have to press the assigned key.

Macros as Commands

You can record not only words and phrases in a macro, but also program commands for any program. When you execute a macro by pressing its assigned key, the keystrokes that you recorded are played back from RAM in place of the macro key. In some cases, those characters appear on the screen as text, but you can also record commands. The commands will be executed in whatever program you have recorded to.

For example, you can record **dir *.com Return** in a macro (where "Return" is a press of the RETURN or the ENTER key, not the letters r-e-t-u-r-n). If you press the assigned macro key while you are using SideKick's Notepad, you simply would be typing the sequence dir *.com into the notefile and then advancing to the next line. But if you press the assigned macro key while you have a DOS prompt on the screen you soon would see a directory of all the files that end with .COM.

Similarly, you can record ESC , DEL , or any of the special function keys (such as F2) in a macro. In fact, you can record the macro's own assigned key, which would instruct the macro to call itself. This situation probably would lead to trouble, with no way out, except that there is a command — CTRL-ESC — that halts the macro recording as if you never started it.

Saving Macros

You don't have to create new macros every time you use SuperKey, because you can save all of the macros to a disk file: press ALT-/ to call up the main menu, press M to call up the Macros menu, then press S to save your macro, and finally, enter a name for the macro file. You don't have to add an extension to the name: SuperKey automatically adds the .MAC extension. You can't save just some macros to the disk, you must save them all at once.

Loading Macros Manually

You also can load macros from a disk file. Once the Macros menu appears on the screen, press L for "load." Then you must specify the name of the macros file and press RETURN. All of the macros in the file are thus loaded into RAM and are active. (You can set the amount of memory set aside for holding macros in the Installation program, as described in the previous "Installation" section.) Unfortunately, they also erase any other macros that were already in memory. Merging files, instead of loading a new file, can solve this problem.

Loading Macro Files
Automatically

The latest versions of SuperKey also let you load macro files when you load SuperKey itself into memory. This feature allows you to automate your installation completely, including the macro file names in an AUTOEXEC.BAT file as explained in Chapter 12.

To load a macro file automatically, type in the following loading command in place of typing **key** or **keydes**:

key *filename*/ml

where *filename* is the name of your macros file without the .MAC extension. The *ml* stands for the "macros" menu and the "load" command. If you want to use the DES encryption scheme, use the command

keydes *filename*/ml

You also can use the command

key *filename*/mc

to clear the macros from memory.

Merging Macro Files

If you have some macros in memory that you want to keep using and some others in a disk file that you want to load into memory for use, you can use the *merge* command of the Macros menu. After calling up the Macros menu, press M and then name the file you want to merge into memory. Although, if two macros have the same assigned key, the old macro (the one already in memory) is deleted and is replaced by the new macro.

Clearing All Macros or
Deleting One Macro

You can clear all macros from memory, returning the keys to their original functions, by choosing the *clear* command from the Macros menu. You can clear or delete a single macro by recording a new, "blank" macro (no keys pressed at all) for the macro's assigned key. The original key definition then is returned.

Editing Macros

You can create or modify macros without using the recorder. Choose the command for eDit from the Macros menu by pressing D. Then press the macro's assigned key. An instruction line appears at the top of the display, and your macro begins on the next line. Use the keys listed on the top line to enter and delete portions of your macro. A macro can be as long as 64K bytes, although the macro memory must be set large enough to hold such a quantity; the default macro memory is only 8000 bytes.

To edit a long macro, you must use a separate text editor such as SideKick's Notepad. When you're finished with the editor, press ALT-ESC to exit the editor.

Titles, Auto-Start,
Fields, and More

When you use the Macros menu to record a macro, you also can add some special effects to that macro. If you press B to begin recording a macro, then press ALT-/ to return to the SuperKey main menu, and M to return to the Macros menu, the commands Auto-Start, Fixed Field, Title, and so on become available. If you choose Auto-Start, you are instructing SuperKey that whenever this macro is loaded from disk, it should be executed automatically, without you even pressing the assigned key. The Fields options, both Fixed and Variable, let you create macros that can pause part way through execution and look to the keyboard for input. This option allows you to customize a macro to work in any situation, offering you the chance to input specific information such as a file name. If you choose Title, you may assign your macro a title of up to 30 characters, a title that can explain the purpose of the macro.

Listing the Macros

If you want to see what macros are in memory, you can use the *show titles* command from the Commands menu: press C from the SuperKey main menu to call up the Commands menu, then press W (for "shoW titles") to display a small window (similar to that in Figure 11-14) that lists the macros, along with any titles assigned to them. The bottom line of this window shows which commands you can use to browse through succeeding pages, if there are too many active macros to fit on a single page.

Prerecorded Macros

Borland includes a number of different macro files on the SuperKey disk. These are tailored to a variety of popular applications. Table 11-1 lists these macro files.

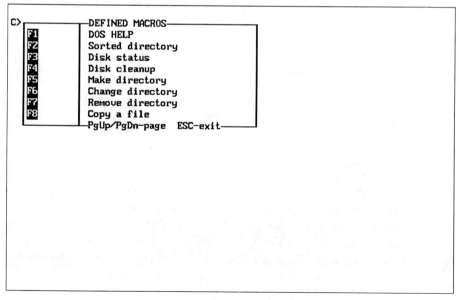

Figure 11-14.   Listing the active macros and their titles

Table 11-1. Some Prerecorded Macro Files that Come with SuperKey

123.MAC	Macros for LOTUS 1-2-3
BASICA.MAC	Macros for BASICA
DOS.MAC	Macros for common DOS commands
EDIX.MAC	Macros for EDIX
FOREIGN.MAC	Macros for using letters most commonly found in foreign languages
GRAPH.MAC	Macros for using extended ASCII characters for graphics
GRAPH2.MAC	More Macros for using extended ASCII characters for graphics
INVENT4.MAC	Macros to demonstrate sound making
LUNCH.MAC	Macros to demonstrate keyboard lockout
REFLEX.MAC	Macros for Reflex
SUPCALC3.MAC	Macros for SuperCalc3
TAPE.MAC	Macros for SideKick's calculator, allows you to use the Notepad as a tape
TAPEOFF.MAC	File that allows you to turn TAPE on and off
TURBO.MAC	Macros for Turbo Pascal
VOLKSWTR.MAC	Macros for Volkswriter
WORDIX.MAC	Macros for Wordix
WORDPER.MAC	Macros for WordPerfect 4.0
WS.MAC	Macros for WordStar

Quick Keys

Although there is a "menu" route to each SuperKey command, you also can invoke many of the commands without working through the menus. Figure 11-15 shows the Defaults menu that lists a number of key combinations (Quick Keys) that directly can invoke or execute Super-Key commands. You don't have to use the Defaults menu to employ these commands; it's just a handy place to read their definitions.

```
┌─────────────────────────────────────────────────────────────────────────┐
│  Macros   Commands  Functions   Options    Defaults  Encryption Layout   Setup │
│                                 ┌──────────────────────────┐               │
│                                 │ Begin macro       Alt=   │               │
│                                 │ Title             Alt'   │               │
│                                 │ autO-start        Alt`   │               │
│                                 │ End macro         Alt-   │               │
│                                 │ Menu              Alt/   │               │
│                                 │ Fixed field       Ctrl]  │               │
│                                 │ Var field         Ctrl-  │               │
│                                 │ cUt and paste     Alt]   │               │
│                                 │ beGin block       B      │               │
│                                 │ sKip macro        `      │               │
│                                 │ stoP              CtrlESC │               │
│                                 │ shoW titles       AltPRT  │               │
│                                 │ Command stack     Alt\    │               │
│                                 │ Decimal point     .      │               │
│                                 │ deLimiter         ,      │               │
│                                 │ fill cHaracter  <SPACE>  │               │
│                                 │ help sYstem       F1     │               │
│                                 │ Arrow keys               │               │
│                                 │ Save defaults            │               │
│                                 └──────────────────────────┘               │
│                                                                           │
└─────────────────────────────────────────────────────────────────────────┘
```

Figure 11-15.   The Defaults menu with Quick Key commands

Other Macro Features

SuperKey deserves an entire book — it contains far more features than can be described in any one chapter. For instance, you can assign key combinations to a single key, which works well for people who can press only one key at a time but want to use ALT and CTRL key combinations. You can create display macros that can place text anywhere on the screen, not just at the cursor's position. You can add delays to your macros to make them wait a certain amount of time. And you even can record macros within macros in certain circumstances.

Many of these possibilities are contained within the Options menu. Mastering some of these features allows you to customize your application programs, so they fit your needs more closely. The following chapters in this book (Chapters 12 through 17) give some simple examples of how SuperKey might be used with some chosen applications.

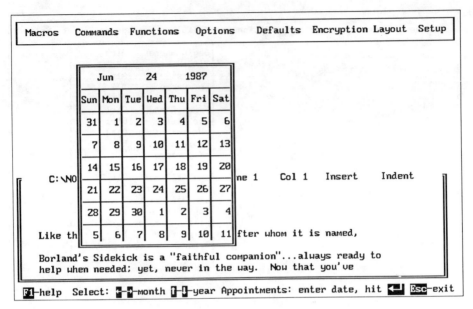

Figure 11-16.   SideKick and SuperKey on screen simultaneously

Using SuperKey with SideKick

As mentioned at the beginning of this chapter, SideKick and SuperKey work well together, as long as you have enough memory (which you will in any 640K machine and in most 512K machines) and you load Super-Key just before SideKick. Once both programs are in memory, you can call both to the screen at the same time, although only the top screen can be active (Figure 11-16). You even can jump directly from SuperKey to SideKick by pressing S from the Commands menu. If SideKick isn't active, this command calls up the SideKick main menu.

You also can use SuperKey macros to control SideKick's utilities, just as you can use them with any application. There are even two prerecorded macro files that are specifically intended for SideKick: TAPE.MAC and GRAPH.MAC. If you load TAPE.MAC first, you can use SideKick's Notepad as a paper tape (on screen) to record SideKick's Calculator's work. If you load GRAPH.MAC first and press CTRL-Q-G from the Notepad to enter the Graphics mode, you can use a variety of keys to draw graphics characters with SideKick's Notepad.

12

DOS

DOS tops the list of software to team with SideKick. You use DOS every time you turn on your computer, and the program has serious weaknesses, such as a clumsy text editor and some complex, cryptic commands. It also lacks a full macro facility to let you nest or telescope phrases and commands into smaller, more easily remembered operations. SideKick can help alleviate all of these problems.

SideKick can act almost as a part of DOS, and especially if SuperKey is added, the combination can make you think you've entered the next generation of operating systems. The three elements that lend the most advantage to DOS are SideKick's Notepad and SuperKey's command stack and macros. The following sections show how these elements can be used to simplify some common DOS operations.

SideKick's Notepad

The text editor that comes with DOS—EDLIN—is a "line editor," which means it can work on only a single line of text at a time. EDLIN also relies on a group of cryptic, single-letter keys to execute editing commands, and it is difficult to see what you're doing as you edit. Because of these problems, most people have opted to use a word processor for even simple editing: inspecting DOS files, creating and modifying DOS command files, and so on. Unfortunately, starting up a word processor just for a few simple editing tasks is like calling a taxi to get to a store one block away: it takes too long and is expensive. In addition, some word processors don't output pure ASCII text easily, a necessity if you are creating and modifying DOS files. SideKick automatically outputs ASCII, and if you have SideKick loaded into memory, you can call up the Notepad at any time and use it as your DOS editor. In sum: learn how to use the Notepad, and you can forget about EDLIN.

Batch Files

The DOS editor often is used to create and modify special, small files such as batch files and configuration files. These files help instruct DOS as to how to configure and start running the system when you turn on the computer. Any file with the extension name ".BAT" is a batch file, a sort of command-list file. If you type in the name of that file (without typing the .BAT), and then press RETURN, DOS will look into the file and try to execute the commands within it, and DOS will assume that each line contains a command. For instance, with DOS and the SideKick Notepad, you can create a simple batch file that can load SideKick and SuperKey into memory with a single command:

1.   First, put SideKick and SuperKey onto a hard disk (as described in Chapters 2 and 11). But instead of putting them both into a directory entitled \sk, put SideKick into \sidekick and SuperKey into \superkey.

2.   Next, change DOS to the SideKick directory by pressing **c:** and RETURN and then **cd \sidekick** and RETURN.

3.   Then load SideKick into RAM, because you must use the Notepad editor. To load SideKick, type in **sk** and then RETURN.

4.   Next, activate the SideKick editor by pressing SHIFT-SHIFT or ALT-CTRL.

5.   Then press F3 and tell the system that a new file is to be called, for example, loadem.bat. You can use any file name, as long as it ends in the .BAT extension.

6.   When the Notepad window indicates that you are working on the new file, type the following:

```
c:
cd \superkey
key
cd \sidekick
sk
cd \
cls
```

on separate lines as shown and press RETURN at the end of each line, including the last line. Figure 12-1 illustrates your work thus far.

7.   Then press F2 to save the new batch file and CTRL-ALT-DEL (all three simultaneously) to reset the computer. After all, even though SideKick is already in memory, you want to make sure the batch file works.

8.   After the computer is restarted, and you have answered the date and time prompts, type in **loadem** and press RETURN.

9.   The commands now appear on the screen, one line at a time, and are executed. The drive and directory are thus set; Super-Key's and then SideKick's loading displays appear.

This rather small example is handy, but really only saves you a bit of typing trouble. Imagine, however, if you are loading five different TSR programs into RAM, and each program is in a different directory. In that case, a batch file can save you lots of time and effort every time you start your system. If, for instance, you also wanted to load Turbo Lightning and Traveling SideKick along with SideKick and SuperKey, you can create a notefile like that shown in Figure 12-2.

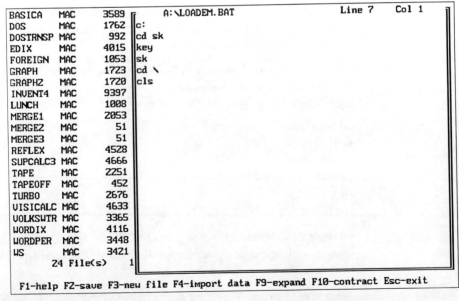

Figure 12-1.   A simple batch file created in SideKick's Notepad

```
READNE     COM     17867  ┌New note file: BORLAND.BAT
TSK        COM     54016  │c:
TSK        000     59904  │cd utils
TSK        HLP     43248  │cd lightnin
TSKINST    COM     33761  │light
CONVERT    COM     64731  │cd \utils\superkey
APPOINT    TSK       434  │key
ADDRESS    LST      7982  │cd \utils
READNE     TSK      8302  │cd sidekick
APPOINT    APP         0  │sk
TSKCOMM    NTS        54  │cd \
INSTANT    EXE     47104  │cls
INSTANT    NXT     37398  │cd travsk
INSTANT    NEW      9296  │tsk
CUTFLOP    BAT       521  │
CUT163     EXE     48128  │
CUTHARD    BAT       594  │
COMMAND    COM     23612  │
GRID       EXE     36864  │
FORMAT     EXE     11160  │
MODE       EXE      6016  │
LABEL      EXE      2750  │
      23 File(s)      ^C│

F1-help F2-save F3-new file F4-import data F9-expand F10-contract Esc-exit
```

Figure 12-2. A more complex batch file created in the Notepad

AUTOEXEC.BAT

A special batch file in DOS is called AUTOEXEC.BAT. Whenever you restart your computer, either by a "warm boot" pressing ALT-CTR-DEL simultaneously or a "cold boot" (turning the power switch off and then on again), DOS automatically runs the AUTOEXEC file as if you had typed it in as a command and then pressed RETURN. Thus, if you want SideKick and SuperKey to be placed in memory automatically every time you use your computer, just put them into this file. Remember, though, to load SuperKey next to last and SideKick last of any TSR programs.

CONFIG.SYS

Some programs ask you to add special lines to the CONFIG.SYS file. This is a file that DOS automatically reads when you first start your computer.

The information in it tells DOS how to structure certain parts of memory: how much to set aside for special uses such as "buffering" data from the disk. A buffer is a section of memory that holds information you may not immediately need. A disk buffer lets information be transferred from the disk to RAM. When the CPU — the main processor — needs the information, it can get it much faster from RAM than from disk. Thus, in some cases, more buffers can improve your computer's operating speed. However, buffers can eat up a lot of memory, leaving less for the program and for TSR utilities. Some programs run slower when they have less memory to use; others may not run at all. So the challenge when setting up the memory configuration is to choose the maximum number of buffers and similar constructs that won't impinge on needed memory space.

You may find that a program you want to run asks for certain lines, such as these

Files = 20
Buffers = 40

to be added to the CONFIG.SYS file. These lines will configure memory in the optimum layout for that particular program. SideKick's Notepad provides a quick and easy tool for adding such lines. Just open the Notepad, press F3 to read a new file, type **CONFIG.SYS** in response to the file name question, and press RETURN. The CONFIG.SYS file appears in the Notepad window, and you can use the editing commands to move within it and add the necessary lines. The order of the lines is not important. When you're done, save the changed file by pressing F2. For this new configuration to make its mark, you must either turn the computer off and then on again, or reboot.

Printing

SideKick's Notepad also can be handy for printing DOS files. The Notepad offers a simple way to employ control characters to manipulate the printer. Control characters can signal a boldfacing or italicizing of type, line spacing and character size, and many other aspects of printing. To add control characters (which are described in more detail in Chapters 3 and 8), first call up the DOS file into the Notepad, move the cursor to the position in the file where you want such a character. Then press

```
┌──────────────────────────────────────────────────────────────────────────┐
│     A:\BORLAND.BAT                    Line 14   Col 1    Insert    Indent   │
│ c:                                                                         │
│ cd utils                                                                   │
│ cd lightnin                                                                │
│ light                                                                      │
│ cd \utils\superkey      ┌ D  H Ch     Ctrl Mem ┐                           │
│ key                       0  00         ^@  NUL                            │
│ cd \utils                 1  01  ☺      ^A  SOH                            │
│ cd sidekick               2  02  ■      ^B  STX                            │
│ sk                        3  03  ♥      ^C  ETX                            │
│ cd \                      4  04  ♦      ^D  EOT                            │
│ cls                       5  05  ♣      ^E  ENQ                            │
│ cd travsk                 6  06  ♠      ^F  ACK                            │
│ tsk                       7  07  ·      ^G  BEL                            │
│                           8  08  ▯      ^H  BS                             │
│                           9  09  ○      ^I  HT                             │
│                          10  0A  ◙      ^J  LF                             │
│                          11  0B  ♂      ^K  VT                             │
│                          12  0C  ♀      ^L  FF                             │
│                          13  0D  ♪      ^M  CR                             │
│                          14  0E  ♫      ^N  SO                             │
│                          15  0F  ☼      ^O  SI                             │
│                                                                            │
│                                                                            │
│ F1-help ←↑-previous page →↓-next page Esc-exit                             │
└──────────────────────────────────────────────────────────────────────────┘
```

Figure 12-3.   Page one of the ASCII Table showing control characters for printing

CTRL-P and the character you wish to use. The ASCII Table, which you can view when you press ALT-A from the Notepad, lists some common control characters on its first two pages. The first page of the ASCII table is shown in Figure 12-3.

SuperKey's Command Stack

DOS commands are sometimes hard to remember and to type. They can be long and filled with lots of options, and you may find yourself typing some commands over and over. Imagine if you were copying certain files from one disk to another and had to type

        copy c:\ws\text\wildlife a:\text\toprint

even a couple of times. That's a lot of typing and a lot of chances to make mistakes. Even a single letter out of place can cause this command to

perform the wrong action or not to work at all. Why should computing be
that tedious? It doesn't have to be. SuperKey lets you eliminate the work
of repetitive keystrokes and reused commands in two different ways: by
using the command stack and by using macros. The Command Stack
option records the last 255 keystrokes of DOS commands and can display
them in a little window. It is activated automatically as soon as you load
SuperKey into memory. (You can turn off the recording, as explained
shortly.) To view the Command Stack window, make sure SuperKey is in
memory and then press ALT-\ (ALT and backslash, not the regular
forward slash you press to call up the SuperKey main menu). Figure
12-4 shows the Command Stack window on top of a DOS display. You
don't have to use the SuperKey main menu to call up the Command
Stack window; it is a separate operation entirely.

Once the Command Stack window is on the screen, you can execute
any of the commands it has recorded just by moving the highlight to the
line of that command (use UP ARROW and DOWN ARROW) and then

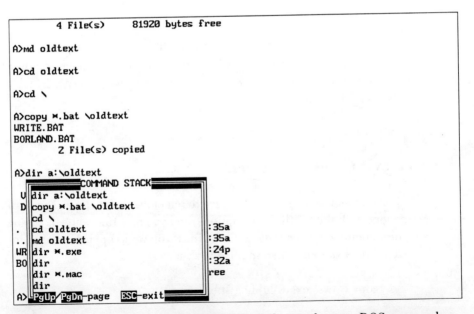

Figure 12-4.   SuperKey's Command Stack window used to save DOS commands

pressing RETURN. To make this function work, you must activate the Command Stack window on top of a DOS display, as shown in Figure 12-4. If it is activated on top of something else, such as on top of the Notepad window, the DOS command you choose is printed in that window or application and isn't executed as you want it to be. If the command you want to use is further down in the "stack," you can use PGDN and PGUP to scroll in search of it. You cannot change the size of the Command Stack window. If you want to exit the window and return to DOS, just press ESC.

Since there is limited room in the stack, as you execute new DOS commands, they are recorded (up to 255 keystrokes worth), and the oldest ones are pushed off the end of the stack and erased. If you have recorded a stretch of commands that you want to use again and again, you can turn off the recording, so that the command stack retains your chosen commands. To turn off the recording, open the SuperKey main menu by pressing ALT-/, choose the Options menu by pressing O, and then press C for command stack (or move the highlight bar to that menu option and press RETURN). The status of the command stack then toggles off. Later, to turn the command stack back on, repeat the same process, and the status then toggles on.

You might be tempted to import some of the command stack commands into the Notepad window for longer term saving. You then could paste one of these commands to the DOS line and press RETURN whenever you wanted to use it. This method is not very efficient, however. If you want to reuse a command often, you should create a SuperKey macro.

SuperKey's Macros

As explained in detail in Chapter 11, SuperKey lets you record and save strings of characters or commands and then play them back by pressing a single keystroke or key combination. If you find yourself typing a lot of DOS commands, it is only natural to want to streamline that typing by creating some macros. You can use SuperKey to create and modify macros that consolidate these operations into a few simple keystrokes. SuperKey also comes equipped with a file of ready-to-use DOS macros.

Prerecorded DOS Macros

To load the SuperKey DOS macros, you first must activate SuperKey
using the procedure discussed in Chapter 11. Then press ALT-/ to call up
the SuperKey main menu, press M for macros, and then L to load a
macros file into RAM. A prompt asks you for the name of the file you
wish to load: you should type in **dos** and press RETURN. The program
automatically assumes that the "dos" name is followed by the ".mac"
extension (the standard extension for macros files) and loads DOS.MAC
into memory. A menu of prerecorded DOS macros then appears (Figure
12-5). These macros all are assigned to the programmable function keys
F1 through F10. By pressing one of these keys, you can instruct DOS to
execute a complete operation such as printing a sorted directory of disk
files or backing up those files from one disk to another. Try pressing
some of the function keys and see how they cause complete command
strings to appear on the screen with a single keystroke.

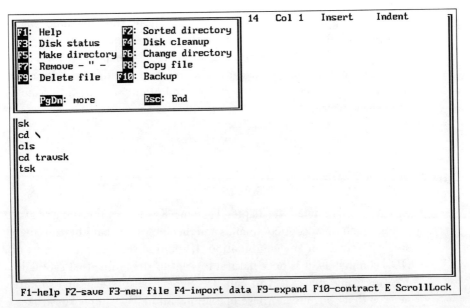

Figure 12-5.   SuperKey's prerecorded DOS macros

Recording Your Own

Of course, you can use SuperKey's macro facility to record and save your own DOS macros. You can use this capability to record those operations you execute most frequently. You can assign them to combinations of keys, such as ALT-F1 and so on. To record a macro, you can call up the SuperKey main menu by pressing ALT-/ and then pressing M to call up the Macros menu, or you can use SuperKey's Quick Key combinations (where you press ALT = to start recording a macro). After you answer the question about which key you want to assign the macro to (choose something that you can remember relatively easily but that doesn't interfere with other key definitions you want to use), just start typing in the characters that make up your DOS command. When you're done entering that command, including any cursor movements or anything else you normally would use, stop to consider whether you want to add RETURN to the macro. If you add a RETURN, the macro will execute automatically as soon as you press its assigned key. If you don't add a RETURN, you'll have to press RETURN after pressing your macro key each time you want to input the command. Make your decision, and then stop recording the macro by pressing ALT− or by working through the Macros menu again. To save your macros to disk, call up the SuperKey main menu, press M to call up the Macros menu, and then press S to save your macros.

Caution on Redefining Keys

Unfortunately, there is one drawback when using keys that are redefined by macro files: you lose the old meanings of the keys. In the case of the DOS.MAC definitions, for example, the special function keys are all redefined. And those definitions carry across program boundaries. Even if you load DOS.MAC while using DOS, they remain activated if you open another application, such as the Notepad. If you're using the Notepad, you'll soon notice that pressing F2 doesn't save your file and that pressing F4 no longer has any power to import data. These keys now sort the DOS directory and clean up your disk. In fact, pressing F1 calls up SuperKey help and not Notepad help. The situation is the same when using your own specially designed macros: if you press the key or key combination assigned to your macro, you can only use your macro function; any previous meaning of the key or key combination is superseded.

     If this becomes a problem, you can rid yourself of the DOS macro meanings by pressing ALT-/ to call up the SuperKey menu, M to call up the Macros menu, and C to clear the macro functions from memory (or type in **key /mc** at the DOS prompt). The original meanings of the keys then return. DOS.MAC remains saved on your disk, although any specially designed macros are deleted.

SuperKey's Layout Program

Sometimes the keyboard layout isn't what you want it to be: for example, CAPS LOCK might not be where you expected it to be, ESC might have been moved from its position on your previous keyboard, and CTRL could have been shifted out of easy reach. Don't worry. You always can use the SuperKey Layout program to redefine the keyboard to your own uses. In fact, you can keep several keyboard definition files for different tasks.

     Just type **layout** and press RETURN after the SuperKey DOS prompt (using the correct drive and directory for the SuperKey files). Then follow the instructions, as described in Chapter 11, to move the definitions you want to where you want them. After you have created a new layout file, you can use SuperKey's main menu to load the new keyboard definitions into the computer. To do so, press ALT-/ to call up the main menu, L for layout, and L again for loading. (Recent versions of Super-Key offer the shortcut command **key filename /ll** to load the layout file automatically.) Then type in the name of your layout file and press RETURN. Your keyboard now is arranged for your benefit.

13

Using SideKick with Lotus 1-2-3 and Other Spreadsheet Packages

Lotus 1-2-3 is adept at handling rows and columns of numbers, at producing simple charts and graphs from those numbers, and even has some ability to organize and sort its rows and columns. Because it combines these three capabilities in a single program, it is more versatile than most software. However, it can still benefit from the addition of SideKick's utilities. (Note: there have been some minor incompatibilities between certain versions of SideKick and certain versions of 1-2-3. Appendix B discusses these incompatibilities and shows you how to avoid any related problems.)

Although most modern spreadsheet programs and even some "integrated" programs that combine spreadsheets with other types of program functions often can duplicate some of SideKick's features, rarely are they so easy to start up or use as is SideKick. For instance, a word processor module in a large program may offer more features and options than does SideKick's Notepad, but it almost certainly isn't as simple to learn and use as the Notepad. If you learn how to write your memos, letters, and personal notes in the Notepad, you'll receive a word processing education that you can put to use in any other program. If you learn how to use the word processor module of some large, integrated package, you can't use its features, or even your knowledge of the program, in another program.

What's more, SideKick is a champion at moving information between different programs and between different sections of the same program. The Notepad's import and paste capabilities let you move text and numbers. Even the Calculator can paste numbers to an application such as 1-2-3. For additional power, you can team SuperKey with SideKick and use SuperKey's cut-and-paste capability.

Although the SuperKey macros aren't as vital to 1-2-3 as to other application programs, because 1-2-3 has its own macro facility, SuperKey macros can add to and extend the Lotus macros. The SuperKey disk even contains a file of macros tailored specifically for 1-2-3.

The Notepad

The key feature of SideKick desired by most 1-2-3 users is the Notepad. Lotus 1-2-3 combines spreadsheet, graphics, and simple database functions, but it lacks any text-processing ability. In fact, for a long time

SideKick was the only word processor that you *could* use with 1-2-3, and for many 1-2-3 users, the SideKick Notepad became their main word processing program.

For such avid spreadsheet users, the only practical note writer or word processor is a TSR program such as SideKick. A few other TSR word processors work specifically with 1-2-3, but these programs lose the SideKick advantage of being able to work with and transfer information between different application programs.

Writing About 1-2-3

Notepad serves three main functions when used with Lotus 1-2-3. The first function it serves is to write notes, memos, and even reports about or relating to the spreadsheet on the screen. Figure 13-1 shows a Notepad window that has been reduced to work conveniently with an underlying spreadsheet. By pressing F10 and then using the cursor arrow keys, you can reduce the Notepad window size. (Remember to change the right

```
A3: [W25] 'Title                                                    READY


                    A            B         C        D        E
 1  VIDEO CASSETTE DATABASE
 2
 3  Title                   Director      Format   Length   Year
 4  Black Orpheus           Camus         BETA        106   1958
 5  It Happened One Night   Capra         BETA        105   1934
 6  Magnificent Ambersons   Welles        BETA         88   1942
 7  Ninotchka               Lubisch       BETA        110   1939
 8  North by Northwest      Hitchcock     BETA        136   1959
 9  Annie Hall              Allen         UHS          93   1977
10  Auntie Mame             da Costa      UHS         144   1958
11  Citizen Kane            Welles        UHS         119   1941
       C:\NOTES.                          UHS         110   1939
                                          UHS         136   1959
                                          UHS         112   1940
                                          UHS         119   1962
                                          UHS          93   1934
                                          UHS         120   1959
                                          UHS          98   1968
                                          UHS         125   1968

    F1-help  F2-save  F3-new file  F4-import data  F9-expand  F10-contract  Esc-exit
```

Figure 13-1.   The Notepad window sized to work with a spreadsheet

margin to a bit less than the width of your window. Otherwise, when you type in information you won't be able to see all of your work on the far right of the screen. Press CTRL-O-R and then type in a number to set the margin.)

Once you have the window sized as you want it, press SCROLL LOCK and use the cursor arrow keys to move the window so that it doesn't obscure the portion of the spreadsheet that you want to write about. Press SCROLL LOCK again when you have finished moving the window. At any time, you can move the window again or change its size without affecting the text in the window. Of course, if the window really is in the way, you can press ALT-CTRL or SHIFT-SHIFT to remove it from the screen altogether. Then you can study your spreadsheet and even move around within it. When you wish, you can call up the Notepad window, with the cursor in its same place, by pressing CTRL-ALT or SHIFT-SHIFT again.

You also can include sections from a 1-2-3 display in your notefile by using the Notepad's F4 Import function or the SuperKey Cut-and-Paste function to move some of the Lotus information across to the Notepad window. Moving part of the spreadsheet in this way lets you add text to your Lotus 1-2-3 numbers to create quick reports and letters.

To perform this function using the Notepad, open the Notepad window on top of the spreadsheet and move the cursor in the Notepad window to the place where you want your spreadsheet section to start, which thus is the top left corner of the rectangle you copy or "cut" from the spreadsheet. Now press F4. The spreadsheet then becomes completely visible. Use the cursor arrow keys or the Notepad's WordStar-style cursor commands to move the cursor to the top left corner of the section you want to copy and press CTRL-K-B. Then use the cursor commands to move the cursor to the bottom right corner of the section and press CTRL-K-K. The Notepad now reappears. Make sure the cursor is in the location where you want the material to copy to and then press CTRL-K-C. For a moment or two the Notepad disappears, and you can see the cursor flashing over the spreadsheet. The Notepad then reappears, with the copied section in place. Figure 13-2 shows an example of 1-2-3 data imported to a notefile.

If you want to use a section of your spreadsheet in a report, but you want to write that report with a more powerful word processor than the Notepad, you can import the spreadsheet section into the Notepad, save it there, exit the Notepad, open and input your report text into the other word processor, and then reactivate the Notepad and paste the spreadsheet section into the other word processor.

```
E8: (C0) [W10] 15099                                                    READY


          B          C          D          E          F          G          H
1
2       Tokyo
3
4       Annual
5       Quota    October   November  December    Total
6       ---------------------------------------------------------
7       $140,000  $15,200   $15,700   $15,000   $45,900
8       $123,000  $23,000   $21,000   $15,099   $59,099
9       $120,000  $13,000   $14,500   $21,000   $48,500
10      $125,000  $10,900   $21,000   $16,500   $48,400
11      $134,000  $14,000   $17,000   $14,200   $45,200
12      $135,000  $11,000   $12,000   $22,000   $45,000
        C:\NOTES.                        Line 1    Col 1    Insert     Indent
        Annual
        Quota    October   November  December    Total

       $140,000  $15,200   $15,700   $15,000   $45,900
       $123,000  $23,000   $21,000   $15,099   $59,099



 F1-help F2-save F3-new file F4-import data F9-expand F10-contract Esc-exit
```

Figure 13-2. An example of importing Lotus 1-2-3 data to a notefile

If you want to move a spreadsheet block from Lotus 1-2-3 to another word processor, do the following: mark the spreadsheet section you wish to import (using the procedure described previously), and when you have started up your word processor, use the Notepad command CTRL-K-E. Choose a Paste key (such as CTRL-F1), and then type **b** to make a "block" paste. Exit the Notepad, move the cursor to the proper position in the word processor, and then press the Paste key.

It's a good idea to give your notefile a name similar to that of your spreadsheet file. For instance, if your spreadsheet is called acctsrec.wks, then you might call your memo acctsrec.txt or acctsrec.nte. The extension you choose becomes your own key that this is a "notepad" file.

Using the Notepad as an Organizer

The second function the Notepad serves when used with 1-2-3 is as an organizer. Figure 13-3 shows an example. As you create or modify a spreadsheet, you probably can think of formulas you want to check, sections you want to alter, and formatting that you want to add. Why

```
E8: (C0) [W10] 15099                                                    READY

            B        C        D        E        F        G        H
1
2     Tokyo
3
4     Annual
5     Quota    October  November December  Total
6     ─────────────────────────────────────────────
7     $140,000 $15,200  $15,700  $15,000  $45,900
8     $123,000 $23,000  $21,000  $15,099  $59,099
9     $120,000 $13,000  $14,500  $21,000  $48,500
10    $125,000 $10,900  $21,000  $16,500  $48,400
11    $134,000 $14,000  $17,000  $14,200  $45,200
12    $135,000 $11,000  $12,000  $22,000  $45,000
   ┌─ C:\NOTES.                        Line 1    Col 1   Insert    Indent ─┐
   │ 1. Check December figures against those in worksheet                  │
   │ "tokyo2.wks".                                                         │
   │                                                                       │
   │ 2. Call Dave about estimates for next year.                           │
   │                                                                       │
   │ 3. Translate values into yen.                                         │
   └───────────────────────────────────────────────────────────────────────┘
    F1-help F2-save F3-new file F4-import data F9-expand F10-contract Esc-exit
```

Figure 13-3.   An example of the Notepad used as an organizer for Lotus 1-2-3

keep all of those steps written on a scrap of paper or try to remember them in your head? Instead, you can enter them into a notefile. Then you can press ALT-CTRL or SHIFT-SHIFT to view your list of "to do" items. Pressing ESC removes the file from the screen. As you complete items, you can move them to a section "Done," or you can delete them from the list. If you press CTRL-Q-T, you can add the time and date to a line, each time you complete it.

Writing Without Interrupting the Lotus Position

The function the Notepad serves when used with 1-2-3 is simply to have it on hand to record ideas and information without disturbing the spreadsheet. If you remember a call you have to make, or if you just want to make a note to check the source of some number in your spreadsheet, you can call up the Notepad window, "jot" down the note, and then save the window.

If someone calls and leaves you a phone number, you can call up the Notepad, use F3 to access a new file, type in **phone.dir** to call the telephone directory file, enter the new number, save that file by pressing F2, and then return to your spreadsheet. The next time you want to make a call, you can work directly with the Dialer, using it to dial the number automatically, or at least to look it up. If there is a certain time that you need to make the call, you can call up the Calendar and enter the time and date there.

The Calculator

Although a spreadsheet is a huge calculator of sorts, it sometimes helps to be able to make quick calculations before entering specific numbers into the spreadsheet. SideKick's calculator is handy for this operation, because you can open it, make a calculation, and then paste the result directly into a spreadsheet such as 1-2-3. Use the Calculator commands to enter and manipulate numbers, then when you are ready to paste your result, press P. Choose a Paste key, such as ALT-F1. (Remember: do not assign the uppercase letter "P" as your Paste key.) Then exit the Calculator by pressing ESC or ALT-CTRL, move the cursor to the cell you want to paste the number to, and press the Paste key. Figure 13-4 shows an example of such a number pasted to several cells in a 1-2-3 worksheet.

Turbo Lightning

It doesn't occur to people to worry about spelling in spreadsheets as much as they worry about it in word processing. But a mistake in a spreadsheet can be even more glaring, because it isn't surrounded by so many other words. Turbo Lightning provides one of the few practical ways for you to check spreadsheet spelling, especially where you are entering information here and there in a large spreadsheet, instead of sequentially on line after line. Just load Turbo Lightning into memory and leave it active. A beep sounds if you type a word that Turbo Lightning doesn't recognize.

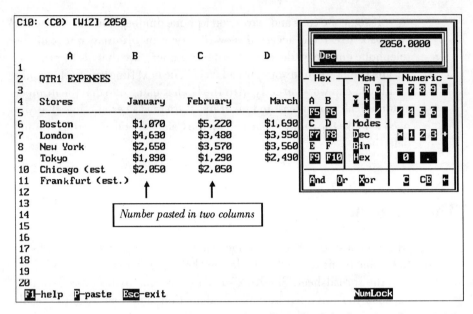

Figure 13-4. An example of pasting numbers from the Calculator into Lotus 1-2-3

SuperKey

SuperKey offers many benefits to Lotus 1-2-3 users. Its simple features of screen blanking (which doesn't work with all versions of 1-2-3 — see Appendix B for further details) and keyboard locking clearly are helpful when dealing with important spreadsheets: you don't want your spreadsheets modified or perhaps even seen by people without the proper authorization. Encryption is also quite applicable to spreadsheet files, which may contain plans and figures that are highly confidential. See Chapter 11 for more details on these SuperKey operations. And of course, there are the SuperKey macros, whose uses are described in the next section.

SuperKey Macros

1-2-3 contains its own macro facility. But that doesn't mean that the SuperKey macros are superfluous. You still can use SuperKey to record, store, and reuse macros for 1-2-3. These macros can be commands, or they simply may be long numbers or titles that you don't want to type in repeatedly. To create your own macros, press ALT-= (this is one of the default Quick Keys), choose and press a macro assign key, and then type the letters, numbers, or commands you want to save in your macro. When you're done recording or typing them in, press ALT- (ALT and the hyphen) to end the macro. You can save this macro to disk by pressing S for the Save command from the Macros menu.

Also, on the SuperKey disk itself is a file called 123.MAC that contains SuperKey macros made just for 1-2-3. These macros let you perform common 1-2-3 operations with fewer keystrokes, in most cases with just a single key combination. (SuperKey also contains files for VisiCalc and SuperCalc 3.) The first step to using the 123.MAC macros is to load them into memory. If you don't care about saving any other macros already in memory, press ALT-/ to call up the SuperKey main menu, and press M to call up the Macros menu. Now press L to load a file of macros, and then type in **123.mac** and press RETURN. The macros then load into RAM, and a Help display appears that lists all of the prerecorded SuperKey macros available in 123.MAC (Figure 13-5). If

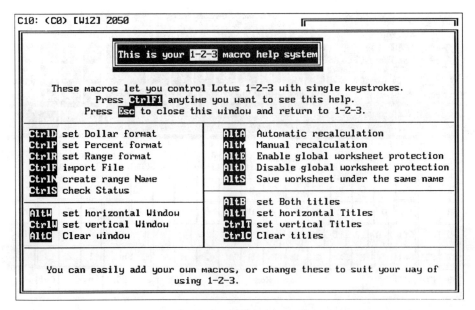

Figure 13-5. The Help display for SuperKey's 123.MAC

you wish, you can recover this Help display at any time during your spreadsheet session by pressing CTRL-F1. (Note: an Auto-Start macro in this file automatically moves the SuperKey command line to the bottom of the screen, so it doesn't obscure your view of some of the 1-2-3 commands.)

If you want to save some macros that you already have in memory, select the SuperKey Merge command by pressing M from the Macros menu instead of pressing the L for "Load" command. Then, the only macros that are deleted are those that use the same assigned keys as any of the new macros.

Keyboard Layout

As explained in Chapter 11, there is a program on the SuperKey disk that allows you to create files of new keyboard layouts. You can use the SuperKey Layout menu to load these files and redefine the keys as you wish. The exact layout you choose most certainly depends on the computer keyboard you have. For instance, your computer may not have

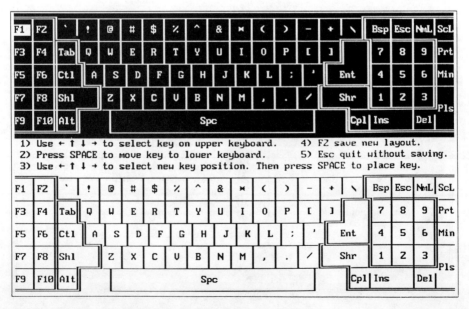

Figure 13-6. The SuperKey Layout program display

a numeric keypad that you feel comfortable with, or it may not have any numeric keypad at all. To aid you in entering numbers into a spreadsheet, you could use SuperKey to change your keyboard.

To start the operation, call up the layout program (Figure 13-6), and choose a section of keys that could emulate a standard, or if you prefer, a customized, keypad. Redefine the keys in that section to the keypad functions. Don't worry if you lose some standard keys in the process, especially if they are just alphabet letter keys; but you should not choose keys that are cursor arrow keys or are fundamental function keys such as ALT, /, and ESC. Then save your changed keyboard as a file, using a file name such as numpad.lay.

When you want to use your new keypad in your spreadsheet, open the SuperKey main menu by pressing ALT-/, press L to call up the Layout menu, and press L again to load a file. Then type in your file name (such as numpad.lay), and press RETURN. Your keyboard now functions with the numeric keypad you defined for it. When you've finished using your keypad, call up the SuperKey main menu, press L to call up the Layout menu, and then press C (for "Clear") to return your keyboard to its original definitions (including whatever macros you had in memory).

14

Using SideKick with WordStar and Other Word Processors

SideKick, SuperKey, and Turbo Lightning can add power to any word processing program. This chapter uses WordStar as an example program, but most of the information provided applies equally to other word processors.

Turbo Lightning

Turbo Lightning is especially easy to use with a word processing program. Load it into memory after SuperKey but before SideKick, and then start WordStar or another word processor. With Turbo Lightning you can check your spelling either as you type or after you finish typing, and you can search for synonyms automatically. WordStar and many other word processors now come equipped with their own spelling checkers, but these rarely offer on-the-fly spell checks, nor do they offer a thesaurus. See Chapter 4 for details on using Turbo Lightning.

Notepad

You may be surprised to hear that the Notepad —a text editor —is a great tool to have on hand when using a word processor, which is also a text editor. After all, isn't that duplicating functions, and doesn't the Notepad offer fewer features than a full-power word processor? Not at all. A second text editor that is available while you are word processing, and can appear in a separate window on top of another document, is useful for many writing or editing tasks. In the case of WordStar, the Notepad even uses WordStar-style commands, making it easy to switch back and forth between the programs. Let's look at a few ways the Notepad can help with word processing.

As an Outline Window

Few word processors have built-in outline programs (along the lines of ThinkTank) that let you collapse text and place it underneath the structure of an outline. It is difficult to create outlines with a standard word processor, because a page full of text can't be viewed at the same time as the outline. This is completely unlike the pen-and-paper environment where pages can be distributed across a desktop. By adding SideKick with its Notepad to your word processing program, you can reproduce at least part of that familiar, and useful, environment.

With SideKick, you can write your outline in the Notepad or read it into the Notepad with the F3 command, and then write the body of the text in the standard word processor. Each time you want to view the outline, press SHIFT-SHIFT or ALT-CTRL to invoke SideKick. When you're ready to return to your main text, press SHIFT-SHIFT or ALT-CTRL again to return to the word processor. You can adjust the position of the window (with the SCROLL LOCK and the cursor arrow keys) and its size (with F9 and F10, and the cursor arrow keys), so that it occupies only a portion of the screen. Figure 14-1 shows an outline in a Notepad window that does not obscure the word processor's display completely. Although you cannot write text into the word processor as long as the Notepad is active, you can compare a page to the Notepad outline.

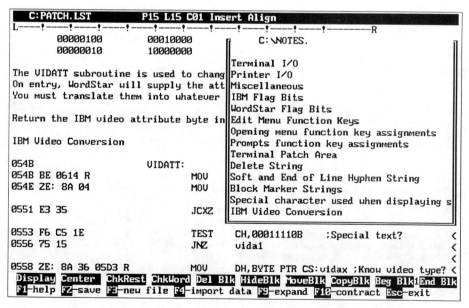

Figure 14-1. Using the Notepad as an outline window with WordStar

Footnotes

Another use for a second text editor is in creating footnotes and similar text-related material. WordStar and many other word processors have special commands for creating lists of footnotes automatically, but if you're working on a quick job and want to make a short list of footnotes, or if your word processor doesn't offer a footnoting facility, you can use the Notepad. To do so, move to the position of your first footnote in the standard word processor file, then open the Notepad window and type in the note for that reference (Figure 14-2). If you size and position the window carefully, you'll be able to see the entire reference as you write the footnote.

Extra Text

If you are cutting text from a document, you may not want to lose the deleted text entirely. To save the text, put it into a notefile, from which

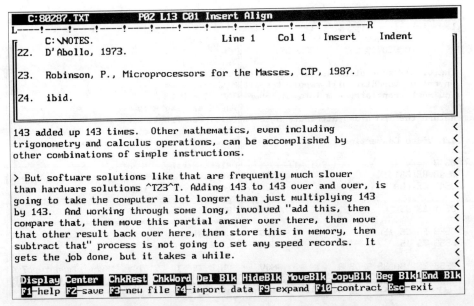

Figure 14-2.   Using the Notepad to create footnotes for a WordStar file

you can select part or all of it to insert elsewhere in the text. You can reinsert text saved in a notefile using either the Notepad's Import command or the SuperKey Cut-and-Paste command.

To use the Import command:

1. Move in the standard word processor file to the text to be deleted, then open the Notepad window on top of the wordprocessor text.

2. Press F4 to import text. The word processor text now reappears on the screen, although the Notepad remains activated.

3. Using the Notepad cursor commands, move the cursor to the top left corner of the "rectangle" that contains the text, and press CTRL-K-B.

4. Then move the cursor to the bottom right corner of the rectangle, and press CTRL-K-K or F8. The Notepad window now reappears on the screen.

5. Using the Notepad cursor commands, move the cursor to the place where you want to store the text —which is often at the end of the notefile —and press CTRL-K-C to copy the text.

6. Press SHIFT-SHIFT or ALT-CTRL to exit the Notepad. Then use the word processor's commands to delete the text from the file. In WordStar, you can mark the block by pressing CTRL-K-B or F7 at the beginning, CTRL-K-K or F8 at the end, and then delete it by pressing CTRL-K-Y. You can also use the line deletion command CTRL-Y as many times as necessary.

To use SuperKey's Cut-and-Paste command:

1. Move the cursor in the standard word processor file to the beginning of the block to be cut.

2. Press ALT-/ and choose a Paste key (such as ALT-F1) by pressing that key (or key combination). You also can initiate a Cut-and-Paste operation by calling up the SuperKey main menu (press ALT-/), then the Macros menu (press M), and finally pressing U. From then on, the process is the same as described in steps 3 to 6.

3. Make sure the cursor is at the top left corner of the "rectangle" of text you want to cut (move it using the cursor arrow keys if necessary), and press B.

4. Then move the cursor to the bottom right corner of the rectangle to be cut, and press RETURN.

5. Now open whatever tool, such as the Notepad, you're using to record the deleted text, and press the assigned Paste key.

6. Return to your word processor (for example, by exiting the Notepad with SHIFT-SHIFT or ALT-CTRL), and use the word processor commands to delete the text, as already described.

In SuperKey, there is also a Cut-and-Paste function you can build into a macro, one that you can execute automatically with a single keystroke. To set up this command, from the Functions menu of the SuperKey main menu, you must be recording a macro. The SuperKey manual describes this command in more detail.

Collecting Information

You can use the Notepad to collect related information from a long text file. As you scroll through the standard word processor file, watch for information on the desired subject. You even might use your word processor's Search command to look for a specific word. When you find such a section, open the Notepad window, and use the F4 Import command, as described in the preceding section, to move the text into the Notepad. Then close the Notepad window, and resume scrolling and searching.

Calculator

While you're working in your word processor, it occasionally may be useful to make some calculation and insert the result into the text. To do so, use SideKick's Calculator: use the Calculator Paste function to move any result directly from its display to that of the word processor.

SuperKey

SuperKey contains a number of features that are useful when working with WordStar or any other word processor. The macros are certainly the most evident of these, but the encryption routines and the keyboard Layout program also are useful.

Macros

When you are working in your word processor, you almost always find that some phrases crop up over and over. Also, you'll discover that you use a small set of commands quite frequently. By recording those phrases and commands as macros in SuperKey, you can simplify your writing work.

Recording Phrases

Imagine that you are writing about a French article on the United States and that the phrase *Les Etats Unis* appears repeatedly in your text. You can insert that phrase by pressing a single key if you have recorded it as a macro. With SuperKey in memory, press ALT = (or work through the Macros menu if you don't want to use this Quick Key approach), and select a macro key. A typical choice is something like CTRL-F6, which probably doesn't overlap with any commands in your other programs. Then type in **Les Etats Unis** and press ALT - (ALT and a hyphen simultaneously). As you type in the phrase you're recording, a notice is displayed at the top of the screen that tells you that a macro is being saved (Figure 14-3).

From then on, each time you press CTRL-F6, the entire phrase *Les Etats Unis* is inserted into your text. If you want to save your macro to disk, along with any other phrases you record under different macro keys (or key combinations), call up the SuperKey main menu (press ALT-/), the Macros menu (press M), and invoke the Save command (S). Give your macro file a name, such as francphl, and press RETURN. The file thus is recorded as FRANCPHL.MAC. Anytime you want to use its macros again, just invoke the Load command (press L) from the Macros menu.

```
KEY: <AltF10> Text- Press <Alt-> to end.
    screen of the software you were using before you "called up" Sidekick
    and then "paste" that data into another application program.  You can
    automatically time and date stamp your notes...and then save them.
    Sidekick allows you to mark a block of text and move it, copy it, delete
    it, write it to another file, or even sort it!!!

    You can also easily activate any Sidekick window from within any  other.

    Here's a quick example of how this works.  At the moment, you're viewing
    the notepad.  Suppose you suddenly needed the  calculator.   Just  press
    <Alt-C>.  Your calculator is ready and at your service.

    Need the calendar? <Alt-L> will bring it right up.  Now,  you  have  the
    notepad, calculator and calendar on-screen at the same time.

    To return to the Notepad, just press <Esc> twice,  and  you'll  see  the
    other two windows vanish.

    If you need a hand at any time, Sidekick has  an  on-line  help  system,
    geared to give  you  information  on  whatever  Sidekick  window  you're
    working within.  Just press function key <F1>.


 F1-help F2-save F3-new file F4-import data F9-expand F10-contract Esc-exit
```

Figure 14-3.   The top line notifies you that a macro recording is in progress

You may want to go beyond creating special macros for special jobs to creating some macros for words and phrases you use consistently in all of your writing. You can merge these macros into a macro file by loading one macro into memory and then invoking the Merge command (press M) from the Macros menu to load the others. Only macros with overlapping assigned keys are in conflict, in which case the previously stored macro is replaced by the newer one.

Recording Commands

You also can record commands as macros. Although you can create special command macros, as described in the preceding section on creating specialized phrase macros, it typically makes more sense to pick out the WordStar (or other word processor) commands you most typically use and record those commands as macros in a general macro file.

For instance, if you often boldface words, you can record the entire command sequence for boldfacing as a single command.

To do so:

1. Press ALT = and an assigned macro key, such as ALT-F10.

2. Press CTRL-A and then CTRL-P CTRL-B.

3. Press CTRL-F and then CTRL-P CTRL-B again.

4. Press ALT - to end the recording.

You now have a boldfacing macro. Place the cursor anywhere on a word in your word processor and then press ALT-F10. The word then appears in boldface. You can create many other macros and record them in a disk file for use later.

Prerecorded Macros

When creating macros, you don't have to start from scratch with no macros, because SuperKey comes with macro files for several word processors. The word processors include macros for Edix, Wordix, WordPerfect, Volkswriter, and WordStar. Figures 14-4 and 14-5 show the menus for the WordPerfect and Volkswriter macros.

WordStar Macros

Figure 14-6 shows the menu for the prerecorded WordStar macros. These macros let you perform file, block and column, and boldfacing and underscoring operations using two-key commands. The block macros can be handy, although the other macros sometimes may interfere with other commands. For instance, CTRL-R, which is the assigned macro key for reading a file, is normally the WordStar command for moving the cursor up one page. If you're accustomed to using the normal definition of this command, this macro may confuse you. The same occurs if you use these macros with the Notepad, because the Notepad uses many of the standard WordStar commands.

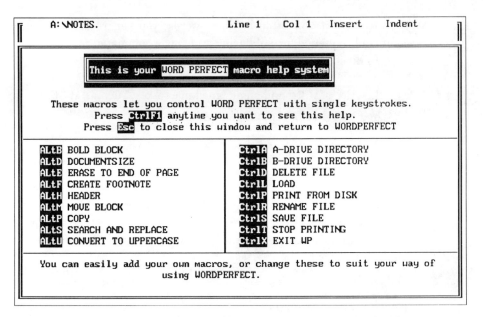

Figure 14-4.   The menu of prerecorded SuperKey macros for WordPerfect

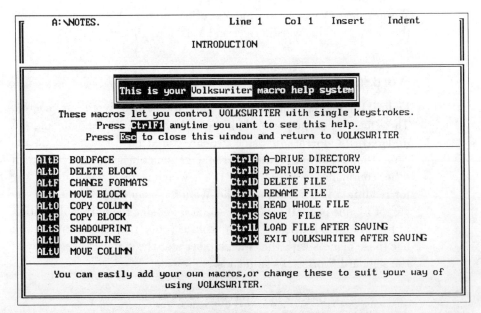

Figure 14-5.   The menu of prerecorded SuperKey macros for Volkswriter

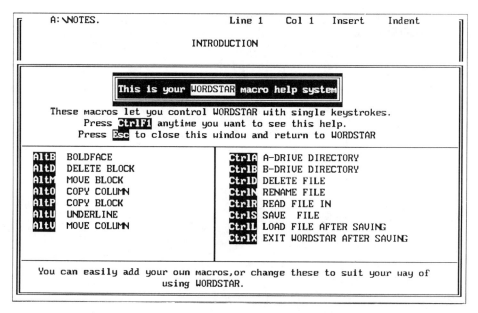

```
     A:\NOTES.                    Line 1    Col 1    Insert     Indent

                            INTRODUCTION


              ┌──────────────────────────────────────────────┐
              │ This is your WORDSTAR macro help system       │
              └──────────────────────────────────────────────┘
         These macros let you control WORDSTAR with single keystrokes.
            Press CtrlF1 anytime you want to see this help.
            Press Esc to close this window and return to WORDSTAR

     AltB   BOLDFACE                  CtrlA A-DRIVE DIRECTORY
     AltD   DELETE BLOCK              CtrlB B-DRIVE DIRECTORY
     AltM   MOVE BLOCK                CtrlD DELETE FILE
     AltO   COPY COLUMN               CtrlN RENAME FILE
     AltP   COPY BLOCK                CtrlR READ FILE IN
     AltU   UNDERLINE                 CtrlS SAVE   FILE
     AltV   MOVE COLUMN               CtrlL LOAD FILE AFTER SAVING
                                      CtrlX EXIT WORDSTAR AFTER SAVING

     You can easily add your own macros,or change these to suit your way of
                            using WORDSTAR.
```

Figure 14-6.   The menu of prerecorded SuperKey macros for WordStar

Altering a Prerecorded Macros Set

If any portion of a macros set doesn't meet your needs, you can modify any or all of the macros and then save them again under a new file name. To do so, just create a new macro using the same assigned macro key, or choose the Edit command from the Macros menu (press E) to edit the previous macro. If you choose to edit the macro, a list of editing commands appears across the top of the display, and the macro itself appears on the next and following lines (Figure 14-7). You cannot delete a single macro at a time, but you can simulate this effect by editing a specific macro to include no commands at all. For example, you may not want the CTRL-B macro from the prerecorded set —which gives a directory of drive B—because you want to maintain the original reformat definition of that key combination.

To edit that macro:

1. Press E to edit from the Macros menu.

2. Press CTRL-B to indicate that you want to edit that macro.

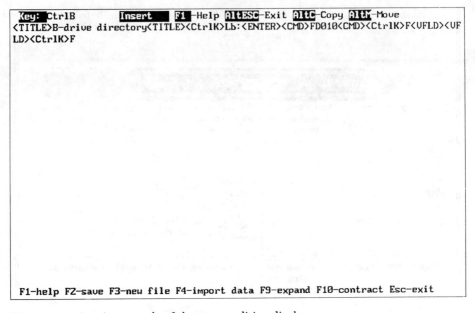

Figure 14-7.   An example of the macro-editing display

3.   Use LEFT ARROW to move the cursor to the second line on the left edge of the display. Then press DEL repeatedly until all of the commands on the line disappear.

4.   Press ALT-ESC to finish editing the macro.

You also can choose to clear the macros from memory, so that they no longer change any of the standard key definitions. As well, you can choose to skip over a macro function for a single instance. All three methods are explained in detail in Chapter 11.

FOREIGN.MAC

Another interesting set of prerecorded macros is the FOREIGN.MAC file. These macros let you use special key combinations to insert foreign-language characters into a word processor document (Figure 14-8). To load these macros into memory, select the Load command (press L) from

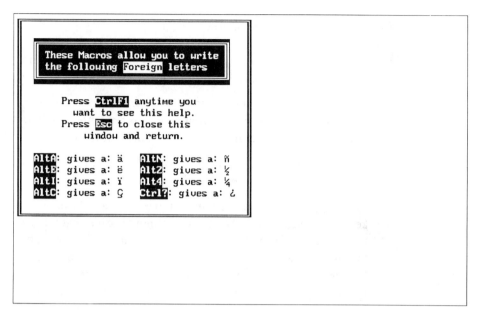

Figure 14-8.   The menu of prerecorded macros for foreign characters

the Macros menu, type in **foreign**, and press RETURN. If you need to view the menu of macros again at any point, just press CTRL-F1.

SuperKey's Layout Program

Keyboards don't place all of the keys right where you want them. For instance, some of the newer keyboards place CTRL at the bottom left corner of the keyboard, instead of in its standard position to the left of the letter "a." This new position may not be too handy for use with WordStar key combinations. But you can use SuperKey's Layout program to change the layout of the keyboard. This program lets you remap the definitions of the keys. For example, many keyboards that place CTRL on the bottom left, place CAPS LOCK in its former position. You can use the Layout program to change CAPS LOCK into another CTRL. If you want, you then can change the bottom-left CTRL into a CAPS LOCK.

To change CAPS LOCK into another CTRL:

1. From the DOS prompt (with the drive and directory for the SuperKey files) type in **layout** and press RETURN.

2. Choose a layout file name and type it in. You may use your name or some other phrase that's easy to remember such as ctrlkey2. After typing in the file name, press RETURN.

3. If your display doesn't show the layout display of Figure 14-9 clearly, press F10. Otherwise, press SPACE BAR.

4. F1 then appears in highlight in the top left corner of the upper keyboard image. Use DOWN ARROW to move the highlight down two spaces, and then use RIGHT ARROW to move the highlight to the right two spaces. CTL (short for CTRL) then appears in highlight, which is the function you want to move. Use this function position even if your actual CTRL key is in some

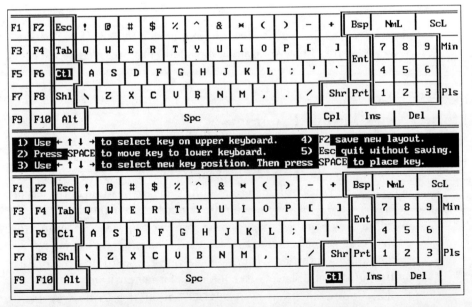

Figure 14-9. The keyboard Layout program definition display

entirely different place on the keyboard. When it is highlighted, press SPACE BAR.

5. The function position you chose on the top keyboard image remains in highlight, and the highlight appears in the equivalent position on the bottom keyboard image. Use the cursor arrow keys to move to the key on which you want to impose the CTRL function. In this case, move 10 positions to the right and two down to CPL (CAPS LOCK). Press SPACE BAR again to place the function.

6. CPL then changes to CTL: your old CAPS LOCK now functions as CTRL, no matter where it is physically on the keyboard.

7. If you want to redefine more keys, use the cursor arrow keys to move the highlight to the upper keyboard image and place it on the function you want to change. Repeat steps 4 to 6.

8. When you're finished redefining keys, press F2 to save the layout file you have created. Otherwise, press ESC to exit the Layout program without saving any of your new key definitions. Using either exiting method, the layout display then disappears.

9. Now, restart your word processing program. Then open the SuperKey main menu by pressing ALT-/. Select the Layout menu by pressing L, and then select Load by pressing L again. Now type in the name of your new layout file and press RETURN. You also may press *key* (*file name* **/LL**) from the main menu.

10. Your CAPS LOCK is now a CTRL. Try it. You can use CAPS LOCK-F to move a word to the right, CAPS LOCK-Y to delete a line, and so on. But CAPS LOCK is only what the top of the key says: each time you press CAPS LOCK, an electrical signal is sent to the computer, which SuperKey ambushes and replaces with a CTRL signal. The computer thus understands any CAPS LOCK as CTRL.

11. When you want to return to your original keyboard definition, choose the Layout menu again and type B (or **key /LC**) for Clear. The original keyboard definitions then resume.

SuperKey's Encryption Routines

You can use SuperKey's encryption facility to encode WordStar files so that no one can read them. If you use the Text mode method of encryption, you can send these files over a modem to another computer. (Note that you must use a telecommunications program other than the Dialer.) Chapter 11 describes how to encrypt and decode files.

15

Using SideKick with dBASE III PLUS and Other Database Managers

The term database manager refers to a broad range of programs, from simple filers to complex relational database managers and even dedicated, specialized data-entry systems. dBASE III PLUS is the most popular database manager for microcomputers. But it is also a language or tool for creating more specific database management applications. In this way, dBASE is as much a programming language as an application program to manipulate databases. Thus, dBASE users also should read Chapter 17 on using SideKick with Turbo Pascal or other programming languages. Some of the hints and suggestions in that chapter apply to dBASE and other database managers.

Although dBASE III PLUS is both popular and powerful, it is specifically made for storing, organizing, and reporting on information. It doesn't have any writing, telecommunications, or macro abilities, and it isn't well suited for moving information between itself and other applications. Because SideKick and SuperKey offer such functions, they can greatly affect the efficiency and completeness of database environments, for both programmers and users. However, dBASE III PLUS comes with a resident program to aid C programming. This program may cause problems when used with SideKick or SuperKey, because it expects to be the only TSR software in memory.

Notepad

There are a number of ways to use the Notepad along with dBASE or any other database manager. The following suggestions are just brief outlines of what may be done. The other chapters in Section II of this book also contain Notepad ideas, some of which can apply to dBASE applications.

Writing About Databases

dBASE III PLUS can generate reports from its stored data, but it doesn't have any kind of text editor. Nor, for that matter, do most database managers. They typically depend on an external word processor for creating any explanatory text that may accompany a report of tables and columns from the database. SideKick's Notepad offers an instantly available word processor for writing memos and papers based on dBASE reports, and you can import those reports into the Notepad for use in your text.

To import dBASE data into Notepad text:

1. Type in the Notepad text first, and then run dBASE; or run dBASE first, and then type in the text in the Notepad.

2. After using either of the preceding methods, open the Notepad on top of a dBASE report, and have the Notepad text ready for importation, by leaving a hole in the text big enough to accommodate the information tables you want to insert from the dBASE report.

3. Press F4 to import the data. The dBASE screen then reappears on top of the Notepad screen.

4. Use the Notepad cursor arrow keys and movement commands to move the cursor to the top left corner of the section to import. Press CTRL-K-B.

5. Then move the cursor to the bottom right corner of the section to import. Press CTRL-K-K.

6. The Notepad display then reappears. Now move the cursor to the top of the hole where you want to place the dBASE information, and then press CTRL-K-C. The information thus is copied into that spot from the dBASE display.

The file then can be printed directly from SideKick (by pressing CTRL-K-P), can be saved to disk, or can be pasted to a larger document in a standard word processor.

To paste the information, including both the Notepad text and the dBASE data, into a standard word processor document:

1. Use the preceding procedure to import data from dBASE into the Notepad.

2. Close the Notepad with a SHIFT-SHIFT or ALT-CTRL command, and then exit dBASE.

3. Start the word processor and read in the appropriate document.

4. Scroll through the document to the place where you want to paste the Notepad contents.

5. Open the Notepad on top of the word processor document by pressing SHIFT-SHIFT or ALT-CTRL. Move to the beginning of the file (or the beginning of the dBASE information if that is all you want to paste), and press CTRL-K-B or F7.

6. Move to the end of the file (or end of the dBASE information if that is all you want to paste), and press CTRL-K-K or F8. The block now is marked.

7. Press CTRL-K-E to begin the Paste Block command.

8. Enter a Paste key assignment, such as ALT-F10, which doesn't interfere with any other command you need to use, and press the keys of that assignment.

9. Answer B to the question about Block or Line mode. If you have any problems with your block pasting, check Chapter 4 for more information on this procedure.

10. Close the Notepad with a SHIFT-SHIFT or ALT-CTRL.

11. Now make sure the cursor is in the appropriate position in the word processor document —at the beginning of the area where you intend to place the Notepad information.

12. Press the assigned Paste key (or key combination). The information then moves into the word processor document.

13. If you want to clear the Paste key, open the Notepad again, and press CTRL-K-E and then DEL.

You also can use SuperKey's Cut-and-Paste function in some similar circumstances.

Writing Alongside Databases

The Notepad is also handy for making notes about topics other than the database, even when most of your memory is occupied by dBASE. You can write a quick Notepad letter without disturbing dBASE: just open the Notepad, write the letter, and save it to disk; you can even print it. As far as dBASE knows, you're just deciding what command to send next.

File Directories

If you are in the middle of a notefile, perhaps merging report text with columns of data, it can be difficult to find out what other files are on your disks. But you can use the Notepad to find out this information at any time. Just save (press F2) the current notefile, and press F3 to call up a new file. When you're asked for a file name, press ***.*** or some other wildcard combination that can give you a complete list of the types of files you are curious about. Be sure to include the correct drive and directory information. After you type in the "file name," press RETURN, which opens a directory window that displays the relevant files on your disk. Figure 15-1 lists the four files (at the top of the window) that correspond to the file name A: *.*. If the file list doesn't fit into a single window, you can leaf through a series of windows by pressing PGDN and PGUP.

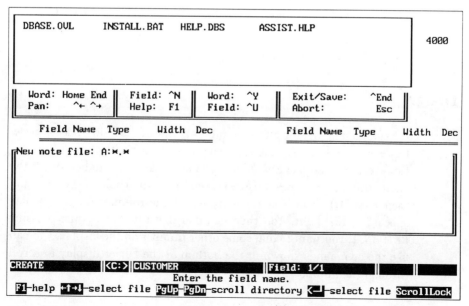

Figure 15-1. An example of a SideKick directory window called up from the Notepad

If you press RETURN at this point, the file that appears in highlight is loaded into the Notepad. But if you don't press RETURN and instead press ESC, you return to your previous notefile, which is undisturbed except for the fact that the cursor has returned to the first line, first column position. You then can press ESC to exit the Notepad and return to your main program.

Calculator

Most database management programs can create *calculated fields*, where inputs from the database can be manipulated mathematically and then reported. But such a situation is different from being able to calculate immediately. SideKick's Calculator lets you make quick, accurate estimates for all sorts of tasks. For instance, if you know that each record has eight fields, of 5, 15, 150, 20, 16, 4, 1, and 200 bytes respectively, and you know approximately how long it takes to search a sample database and that there are just over 1000 records in the database, you can use the Calculator to find out how much disk space and RAM space would be required and about how much time it would take to perform a search. You can also calculate numbers and then insert those numbers directly into the database entry fields.

Dialer

It's common to include phone numbers as one of the fields in a database. However, few database managers can do anything with those numbers. However, you can use SideKick's Dialer to call the number. With the phone number displayed on the screen, open the Dialer (ALT-CTRL and then F5 or D). The first recognizable phone number on the display appears in highlight. You then can dial that number by just pressing RETURN. If you want to dial some other number on the display, you can use the commands shown at the bottom of the Dialer display to scroll through the numbers.

Traveling SideKick

Database application programs and Traveling SideKick have much in common: after all, both the address and engagement files are essentially databases. Traveling SideKick, therefore, is essentially a specialized database manager. SideKick too has some database management aspects, because it can work with the phone directory files (from the address file) and the engagement files (from the Calendar). As mentioned in Chapter 10 on Traveling SideKick, you can convert programs from many sources into Traveling SideKick files. Most database managers, including dBASE III PLUS, can export files in ASCII format, with commas as delimiters (the commas separate the different fields of information).

If you select the ASCII output option from dBASE, you can transform a dBASE file, or the chosen, relevant portions of it, into a Traveling SideKick file. This procedure may be a quick way to build a large, useful phone directory for SideKick.

Turbo Lightning

If you load Turbo Lightning before you enter new data into your database, you can catch misspellings as you type them. Using Turbo Lightning can save you from having to modify records later, records which then already may be in your reports. Chapter 9 contains basic information on starting and working with Turbo Lightning.

SuperKey

Databases are often the life's blood of information for a company, which could survive if word processors, spreadsheets, and telecommunications packages disappeared for a while but would screech to a halt if the database were disabled. Thus, it makes sense to use the SuperKey secrecy and protection features to protect the database. The Screen Off and Keyboard Lock functions are useful for avoiding casual intrusion.

The encryption routines let you put a database file into code, so that no unauthorized user can tell what's in it, even if that person should gain access to a terminal or keyboard. If you use the Text mode of encryption, you even can send the database through a modem (using some other telecommunications program, not the Dialer) to another computer and know that it was safe on the way. In addition, the SuperKey macros can be useful in producing reports automatically and changing the formats of fields.

Macros

dBASE III PLUS does not have a macros facility, so SuperKey's ability to record and save macros can be enormously helpful. You can create macros that automatically produce certain reports, change the formatting of a field, or record/change just about anything else. There is no file of prerecorded dBASE macros on the SuperKey disk, although there is a file of macros for Reflex, a database manager from Borland. Figure 15-2

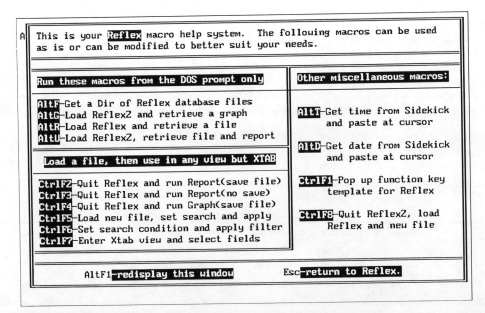

Figure 15-2.   The menu of prerecorded SuperKey macros for Reflex

shows the menu for the Reflex macros. To see how to create, save, and load macros from disk, see Chapter 11 on SuperKey.

Screen Off and On and Keyboard Lock

Perhaps you want to turn the screen off while a dBASE report is displayed, so that no one can see what you are working on. SuperKey can turn off your screen, and it also can lock the keyboard so only the person with the right password can call up your display. Chapter 11 discusses how to perform both of these functions by invoking a single command.

The following example enters both screen off and keyboard lock as a SuperKey macro into your system:

1. Press ALT-/ to call up SuperKey's main menu.

2. Press M to call up the Macros menu, and then press B to begin to record a new macro.

3. Choose a key or key combination to assign to this macro, something like ALT-F10, which hopefully doesn't interfere with any of your other keyboard commands. Press your key or key combination in response to the prompt about an assignment key. A command line then appears at the top of the screen that tells you what operations are available while you create the macro (Figure 15-3).

4. Then press ALT-/ again to call up the SuperKey main menu, so that you can get to the Keyboard Lock and Screen Off functions.

5. Press F to call up the Functions menu, then press K to invoke the Keyboard Lock command.

6. Press ALT-/ and F again, and then press S to invoke the Screen Off command.

Because you're done recording the macro at this point, press ALT - (ALT and a hyphen). The macro is saved under the assigned key. Now when you press the assigned macro key, you are asked for a key word (password) (Figure 15-4). You can type it in once and then again confirm your choice. Now the keyboard is locked and the screen is turned off until you

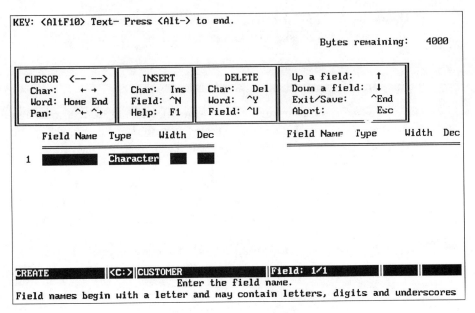

Figure 15-3.   The display when creating or recording a new macro

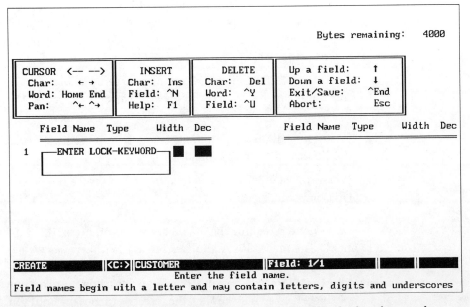

Figure 15-4.   The macro for keyboard lock and screen off asks for a key word
(password)

again type in the key word. As soon as you do so, the keyboard is unlocked and the screen is turned on again.

Encryption

SuperKey can encode and decode files using either the fast Borland method described here or the famous DES method, which is practically unbreakable. Your choice is determined by the SuperKey program you used to load SuperKey into memory (see Chapter 11).

The simplest encoding method is to simply call up the SuperKey main menu, choose the Encryption menu (press E), and then choose encryption by pressing another E. Next, you must enter the name of the database file you wish to encrypt and a key word under which to encode it. Be sure to remember your key word —you need it to decode the file later. Finally, you're asked whether or not you want to use the Text mode. If you choose the Text mode option, your coded file can be sent over a modem line to another computer (using a telecommunications package other than Dialer). If you choose not to use the Text mode, you cover up the original, uncoded file with a coded file. This is the method you'll probably use most with database records.

16

Using SideKick with Crosstalk and Other Communications Programs

Telecommunications programs let your computer talk to other computers over telephone lines or other signal carriers. They handle the computer's modem, which is a piece of hardware that can translate computer signals into phone-line signals. Simple programs just dial the telephone, as does SideKick's Dialer utility. But the Dialer's ability to pick numbers off the screen and keep them in a phone directory file database moves it well beyond the "simple" level into a class of its own. Sophisticated, standard telecom programs offer a variety of commands for capturing and sending data over such lines, and they allow you to communicate freely with anyone else who has a computer.

That's the theory, at least. Actually, most telecom programs lack any sort of editor for preparing or modifying text, and they don't have a complete macro facility for combining a series of operations or communications options into a single command. They expect you to finish all of your editing before you telecommunicate. Some offer the ability to create *logon* scripts, which are saved series of steps for dialing, connecting, downloading information, and then disconnecting from a service. To *download* means to extract information from the system. These scripts, however, cannot be made as flexible as SuperKey's macros, which can be used for everything from creating logon scripts to automating repetitive commands for on-line services.

Thus, the SideKick Notepad and the SuperKey macros can provide features that most telecommunications programs lack, but that most telecommunicators crave. And because Crosstalk has been one of the most popular telecom programs for microcomputers for years, this chapter uses Crosstalk as a model, although the discussions are applicable to almost any other telecom program.

SideKick's Notepad

The Notepad lets you create and receive files and information from most any telecommunications program. The fact that it is always available is especially important, because composing quick replies to *E-mail* (electronic mail) messages is a common task in telecommunicating, and most telecommunications programs and on-line services offer poor editors for such work.

Creating Files to Send: Offline

One way to put the Notepad to work is to use it even before you start your telecommunications program or before you call any bulletin board or service. To do so, first write the letters and create the files that you want to send, then save them to disk. The Notepad files are in ASCII format, and thus can be sent on most any system; many word processors must perform an extra step to turn their files into ASCII that can be sent.

If you have a large number of files to send, you may want to give them all a similar extension, so that later you can locate them more easily with Crosstalk's directory function. Figure 16-1 shows a Crosstalk directory and a list of .LET files.

Creating Files to Send: Online

Although standard word processors can make off-line editing possible, albeit not as quick and easy as can the Notepad, they cannot compete

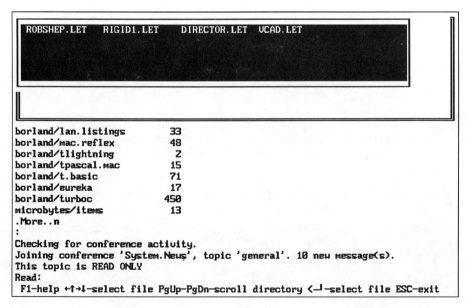

```
 ROBSHEP.LET    RIGID1.LET    DIRECTOR.LET  VCAD.LET




borland/lan.listings      33
borland/mac.reflex        48
borland/tlightning         2
borland/tpascal.mac       15
borland/t.basic           71
borland/eureka            17
borland/turboc           450
microbytes/items          13
.More..n
:
Checking for conference activity.
Joining conference 'System.News', topic 'general'. 10 new message(s).
This topic is READ ONLY
Read:
 F1-help ←↑→↓-select file PgUp-PgDn-scroll directory <┘-select file ESC-exit
```

Figure 16-1.   An example of a Crosstalk directory of Notepad .LET files

with the Notepad at all when it comes to on-line editing. With your telecommunications program running, and even with it connected to another computer over a modem, you can open the Notepad to create or modify letters, memos, and files. Just press F3 from the Notepad to start a new file (choose a file name that hasn't been used yet) or to read in an old file for last-minute inspection and possibly modification. Figure 16-2 shows an example of on-line editing, with the communications program already connected to a remote computer.

Sending Files

Once you have a file, either edited before starting to telecommunicate or during your communication, you can send that file from the Notepad using either of two methods: one method is to save the file to disk by pressing F2 and then using the Crosstalk command (see *filename*) to send a file. The other method is to use a Paste key to send a block directly to an on-line service or bulletin board.

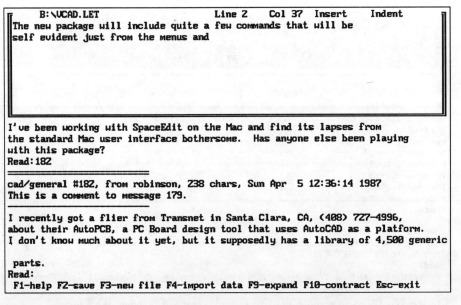

Figure 16-2.   Editing in the Notepad while on-line with Crosstalk

To use a Paste key to send information or a file:

1. Make sure the remote service or bulletin board is connected to your system and that it is ready to receive text. The commands for doing this are different for each on-line system.

2. Open the Notepad and make sure the file is in it. You may have left the file in it while you started your telecom program; or you may have to use F3 to read the entire file into the Notepad, replacing the old file in the Notepad; or you may use CTRL-K-R to read in a file alongside whatever is already in the Notepad.

3. Mark the block you want to send by moving the cursor to the top left corner of the "rectangle" and pressing CTRL-K-B or F7 and then moving the cursor to the bottom right corner of the rectangle and pressing CTRL-K-K or F8.

4. Select the Notepad Paste function by pressing CTRL-K-E.

5. Choose a Paste key such as ALT-F8. Avoid using a key or key combination that already has some other function that you may need to use. Press the Paste key or key combination.

6. Press B for Block mode pasting. In some cases, you must use the Line mode instead, but these instances aren't common. Chapter 4 describes the two modes in more detail.

7. The block of text, which may be anything from a single letter to the entire file, now is assigned to that Paste key. Don't unmark (press CTRL-K-H) that block: the Paste key only pastes what is marked in the Notepad.

8. Close the Notepad window so you can see the display of your telecom program.

9. Press the Paste key, and watch the text move into the telecom program and on to the remote computer. You can see an example of this operation in Figure 16-3.

If you want to send another block, all you have to do is open the Notepad window again, move the cursor to the beginning of that new block, press CTRL-K-B or F7, and then move the cursor to the end of that new block and press CTRL-K-K or F8. The same Paste key you assigned before now pastes

```
menus that I previously thought were "sticky" do in fact have
"root" as an option.   It didn't show in CGA, but did show on
a 640x400 mode.   Hmmm.   Well, at least they're there.

stuart
No more unread messages in this topic
Hit <RETURN> for next active conf/topic.
Read: 182
═══════════════════
cad/general #182, from robinson, 238 chars, Sun Apr  5 12:36:14 1987
This is a comment to message 179.
─────────────────

I recently got a flier from Transnet in Santa Clara, CA, (408) 727-4996,
about their AutoPCB, a PC Board design tool that uses AutoCAD as a platform.
I don't know much about it yet, but it supposedly has a library of 4,500 generic

 parts.
No more unread messages in this topic
Hit <RETURN> for next active conf/topic.
Read: com
Comment to message number 182. Enter text. End with '.<CR>'
The new package will include quite a few commands that will be
self evident just from the menus.   I think it will have an
immediate impact on the market.
 Esc for ATtention, Home to SWitch     ▐   Capture Off   ▐   On: 00:09:00
```

Figure 16-3.   An example of pasting text from the Notepad to Crosstalk

this block: the Paste key always pastes the currently marked block in the Notepad. Now, you exit the Notepad window and press the Paste key to send the new block.

Capturing Text from Crosstalk

Most telecom programs provide some means of capturing two types of incoming information: files and general text. Files are sometimes sent and received using special protocols that treat them as "packets" of information. General text is the information that is displayed on the screen; it consists of both your commands and the remote system's replies, along with whatever messages or short text files the system may send to you.

The Notepad does not become involved in sending or receiving files with special protocols, but it is handy for capturing the general text information that comes in on the display. You can use the Notepad Import function to grab part of or an entire screen display, and then you can save that display to disk.

To grab the information displayed by an on-line service:

1. Open the Notepad window.

2. Press F4. The Notepad window then closes, revealing the Crosstalk display.

3. Use the Notepad cursor arrow keys and cursor commands to move the cursor to the top left corner of the block you want to capture. Then press CTRL-K-B or F7.

4. Move the cursor to the bottom left corner of the section you want to capture. (The command CTRL-F moves one word or, in this case, about one Tab column to the right, and is handy for getting to that corner.) Then press CTRL-K-K or F8 to finish marking the block.

5. The Notepad window now reopens automatically. Move the cursor to where you want the text to be inserted, and press CTRL-K-C. A copy of the text from the Crosstalk display will appear in the Notepad window (Figure 16-4).

```
   B:\HPINFO.                    Line 1    Col 1    Insert    Indent
      Production Planning/PC runs on IBM PCs and compatibles with
 MS-DOS or PC-DOS 2.0 or higher, 512K RAM (640K recommended), a
 hard disk drive, and Lotus 1-2-3 version 2.01 or later.  It also




 between Hewlett-Packard's Materials Management program and Lotus
 1-2-3.
      The program enables you to automatically upload and download
 production data between an IBM PC or compatible or Hewlett-
 Packard 150 Touchscreen microcomputer and the Hewlett-Packard
 3000 minicomputer.  Build-to-stock, build-to-order, and rate-per-
 day Lotus 1-2-3 production-planning templates are included.
      Production Planning/PC runs on IBM PCs and compatibles with
 MS-DOS or PC-DOS 2.0 or higher, 512K RAM (640K recommended), a
 hard disk drive, and Lotus 1-2-3 version 2.01 or later.  It also
 runs on Hewlett-Packard's 150 Touchscreen.  The program runs
 concurrently on the HP 3000 minicomputer, and requires Materials
 Management versions A.07.10 or A.09.03 or higher.  It is not
 .More..
 F1-help F2-save F3-new file F4-import data F9-expand F10-contract Esc-exit
```

Figure 16-4.   An example of importing text from Crosstalk to the Notepad

6. To save the text to disk, press F2.

You can import more text into this same window, or you can open a different file and import text into it.

Keeping a List for Organization

Because you can open the Notepad on top of the active Crosstalk display, you can keep a list of tasks you want to accomplish online in the Notepad. You even can import messages or lists of letters that you know you want to respond to before logging off the service. Just use F9 and F10 to size the Notepad window and SCROLL LOCK and the cursor arrow keys to position the window where it won't obscure the important portion of the screen. Then you can call up the notefile list, check what needs doing, delete what's already been done, and close the Notepad to return to work. You even can use the Sort function to arrange the items by date, title, or some other significant characteristic.

To sort a list of letters to send:

1. Import a list of the letters received, or create such a list in the Notepad, with each item on a separate line and each item only one line long.

2. Mark the beginning of the list with CTRL-K-B or F7 and the end with CTRL-K-K or F8.

3. Press CTRL-K-S to sort the marked block.

4. Answer the question about the first column to sort on by choosing the number of the column you want sorted alphabetically. If this is at the beginning of the line, column 1 is the answer. Then press RETURN. If there is some element deeper in the line, that is in the same column in all of the entries, choose that column number instead.

5. Answer the question about the last column to sort on. If you want to sort on name, and the names begin in the first column and take up at least four columns, choose 4. If you don't care to have everything sorted alphabetically in depth and just want to sort on the first letter of a name, then press RETURN. If you are sorting on identification numbers and the numbers run from column 10 to column 14, choose 14.

6. After choosing the last column for the sort, all of the entries are rearranged on the display, per your sort instructions.

You also can use the Notepad to see what is in a file on disk. For instance, after downloading a long file, you might want to have that file available for quick review while you "converse" online with someone else. Crosstalk doesn't provide an easy way to view a file while you are sending and receiving short messages. Thus, to do so, open the Notepad window, read the file into it, and close the window. Then, you can reopen the window each time you want to scroll through the message and take a look at some portion of it. You can use the Notepad's Search function (CTRL-Q-F) to find a specific part or section of the file.

SuperKey's Macros

The SuperKey macro capability is the prime SuperKey feature used with a telecommunications program. With Crosstalk, for instance, macros can be used to automate and streamline a variety of tasks. Two of the most common uses of macros are for logging on to a system and for commands used on a system.

Logon Scripts

Most personal computer users employ telecommunications programs to permit them to access on-line services. These services are from remote computers running software that transforms them into service machines. Personal computers may be running as bulletin boards: they are ready for outside computers to call in, and then they offer the ability to read messages stored on a disk drive, download information, upload information, and so on. Minicomputers and mainframes may be running software that makes them information services of a more powerful stripe: computers that are ready for many callers to call in at once to exchange messages, read the news or financial reports, research in databases, and even use the larger computer's power for running programs. With both small personal computer billboards and with large on-line services, the sender may call and leave the file at any time; and the receiver may call when it's most convenient to download that same file.

Getting a telecommunications program to connect to a bulletin board or on-line service requires a series of commands: setting up the communications parameters (such as the number of bits and the baud rate), choosing the phone number, dialing that number, waiting for the proper response from the remote system, and then sending the correct password and logon phrases. Although some telecommunications programs, including Crosstalk, let you record these steps on another computer, they don't allow as much flexibility as do the SuperKey macros, which can partition the process into as many steps as you want.

For instance, you might want to use the same password for many different bulletin boards and on-line services (some systems let you choose your own password). To do so, follow these steps to save the password you want as a phrase in a SuperKey macro:

1. Start recording a macro by using the SuperKey command ALT =.

2. Enter the key you want to assign the macro to. Choose a key or key combination that doesn't interfere with some other function you may want to use, for instance ALT-F10.

3. Type in your password phrase. Add a RETURN at the end.

4. Press ALT- (ALT and a hyphen) to indicate that you're done entering the password.

5. Then, whenever a system asks for your password, just press the assigned macro key, such as ALT-F10.

You also can use macros for more extensive commands, such as to set the parameters for communicating with a specific service. In Crosstalk, you must enter two-letter commands followed by the chosen option for that command to set the phone number, baud rate, and so on. SuperKey macros can collect all of these commands into a single command. Remember: your macro commands are software-specific, thus the Crosstalk macro is meaningless outside of Crosstalk.

For example, let's set up a 300-baud, 7-bit, 2-stop-bit, even-parity call to the number (888) 888-8888. SuperKey's macros can perform this chore, but they aren't as easy to use once you have logged on to and off one service and need to change your parameters for another service. The example also illustrates how you can use SuperKey with a program that doesn't have scripts, and it shows you how you can sometimes avoid having to learn the script language for each new telecommunications program by employing SuperKey in its place. Here is the example:

1. Press ALT = to start recording a macro. You also can accomplish this task by calling up the SuperKey main menu, then the Macros menu, and then the Begin option. ALT = is the Quick Key method for bypassing the more explanatory menus.

2. Choose a macro key or key combination, such as ALT-F10. Try to select a macro key or key combination that doesn't interfere with any other command you may want to use. Press the key or keys for that combination. As you record the macro, a command line at the top of the screen tells you which operations you can use and how to end the recording (Figure 16-5).

3. Type in **sp 300** and then press RETURN. This sequence sets the speed.

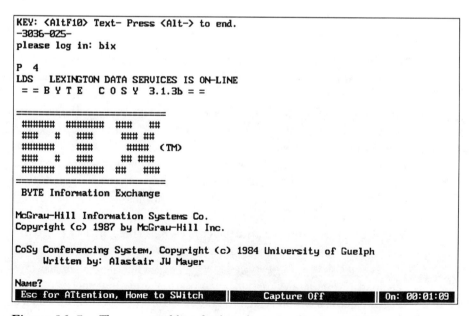

Figure 16-5.   The command line display when recording a macro

4. Type in **da 7**, and then press RETURN. This sequence sets the number of data bits to seven.

5. Type in **pa e**, and press RETURN. This sequence sets the parity to "even."

6. Type in **st 2**, and press RETURN. This sequence sets the number of stop bits to two.

7. Type in **nu (888) 888-8888**, and press RETURN to enter the number to dial.

8. Press ALT- to indicate that you're done recording the macro.

9. Then when you are running Crosstalk and want to insert all of those parameters at once, and enter that phone number, just press the assigned macro key.

You also can create macros for Crosstalk that automatically ask you for a file name and then send that file. Other macros can encrypt a file, send that file, and then log off a system. SuperKey's macros allow for practically infinite possibilities.

On-Line Commands

You also can build macros that don't execute instructions for your own telecommunications program, but instead they execute commands for the remote system. Most bulletin boards and on-line services have their own language of keystrokes and brief (or not so brief) commands for choosing file subject areas, message addresses, and the like. You can record your most frequently used remote system commands in macros and load those into memory whenever you are dealing with a service.

For instance, if your on-line system requires that you type **sk to la** (for "skip to last") to call up the most recent message in some subject area, you may tire of typing in those letters over and over. Thus, you record them as a phrase in a macro, as described in the preceding section, and you can type in the entire phrase with a single keystroke.

If you create a file of special macros, by saving them all to disk, you can load the general Crosstalk macros first and then merge in your special macros when you sign onto the specific service or bulletin board.

By using the SuperKey Merge command to load the specific macros from disk, you don't lose all of the general Crosstalk macros already in memory.

Encryption

The SuperKey Text mode method of encryption lets you encode files in such a way that they can be sent over a modem to most computers. When you choose the Encryption menu (press E) and then the Encryption option (press E), remember to specify Text mode in the third line of that option's menu, as shown in Figure 16-6. The Nontext mode replaces the old file with a new, encoded file that contains all sorts of characters. The Text mode creates a new file, with a new name, that is an encoded version of the old file. The old file itself remains on the disk, and the new file consists entirely of standard, uppercase, alphabetic characters that can

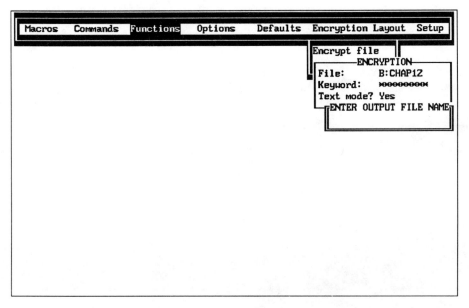

Figure 16-6.   SuperKey's Encryption menu showing the Text mode options

be sent through almost any telecommunications system (although, not the SideKick Dialer). Some systems can send or receive only seven bits of information per character, instead of the full eight bits that are necessary to represent characters beyond the standard alphabet. Thus, some systems can send or receive only files transmitted in the Text mode.

17

Using SideKick with Turbo Pascal and Other Programming Languages

SideKick originally was conceived as a tool for use by the Turbo Pascal programming staff at Borland, so it isn't surprising that it offers a number of features that simplify programming tasks. In addition to the appointment calendar and phone directory utilities, SideKick contains other functions that are tailored more specifically to programming. Many SuperKey features also aid programmers, especially the SuperKey macros. Any of the previously mentioned tools can be used with any programming language, but this chapter uses Turbo Pascal as a model.

ASCII Table

ASCII —the American Standard Code for Information Interchange —is a code that assigns number values to the letters, numerals, punctuation, and other characters used in programming. It is vital to almost all aspects of computer software design. Programmers frequently must refer to an ASCII table to choose control characters, compare values for sorting, and perform a host of other programming tasks. Once SideKick is in memory, you can call up the ASCII Table and look up any ASCII value.

To open the ASCII Table, press SHIFT-SHIFT or ALT-CTRL to call up the SideKick main menu, and then press F6 or ALT-A. The ASCII Table display appears (Figure 17-1). The decimal and hexadecimal ASCII values and the characters to which they are assigned are adjacent columns. As you can see in the figure, Turbo Pascal is running in the background, but you can open the ASCII Table at any time, whether or not you are running Turbo. Only a fraction of the ASCII values fit on one page of the ASCII Table. You can look at the other pages by using the cursor arrow keys and PGUP and PGDN. Chapter 8 discusses the ASCII Table in detail.

Calculator

The SideKick Calculator also suits programmer needs. It can handle standard arithmetic (addition, subtraction, multiplication, and division), and it also can perform logical operations and number conversions, which only special programming calculators could perform in the

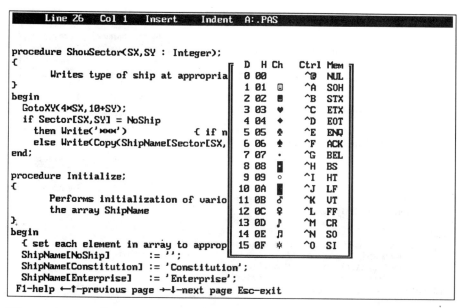

```
  Line 26   Col 1    Insert    Indent   A:.PAS

procedure ShowSector(SX,SY : Integer);
{                                      ┌ D  H Ch   Ctrl Mem ┐
        Writes type of ship at appropria  0 00         ^@  NUL
}                                          1 01  ☐      ^A  SOH
begin                                      2 02  ☐      ^B  STX
  GotoXY(4*SX,10+SY);                      3 03  ♥      ^C  ETX
  if Sector[SX,SY] = NoShip               4 04  ♦      ^D  EOT
    then Write('***')           { if n    5 05  ♣      ^E  ENQ
    else Write(Copy(ShipName[Sector[SX,   6 06  ♠      ^F  ACK
end;                                       7 07  •      ^G  BEL
                                           8 08  ☐      ^H  BS
procedure Initialize;                      9 09  ○      ^I  HT
{                                         10 0A  ☐      ^J  LF
        Performs initialization of vario  11 0B  ♂      ^K  VT
        the array ShipName                12 0C  ♀      ^L  FF
}                                         13 0D  ♪      ^M  CR
begin                                     14 0E  ♫      ^N  SO
  { set each element in array to approp   15 0F  ☼      ^O  SI
  ShipName[NoShip]        := '';
  ShipName[Constitution] := 'Constitution';
  ShipName[Enterprise]   := 'Enterprise';
 F1-help ←↑-previous page →↓-next page Esc-exit
```

Figure 17-1.   The first page of the SideKick ASCII Table, on top of Turbo Pascal

past. Such calculations are performed daily by programmers, particularly those who work with I/O and assembly language patches. The Calculator is described in Chapter 5. You can open the Calculator by starting up SideKick with SHIFT-SHIFT or ALT-CTRL and then selecting the Calculator with F3 or ALT-C. You can open the Calculator at any time, whether or not Turbo Pascal is running, as long as the computer isn't in the middle of a compilation or a disk operation.

Number Conversions

Figure 17-2 shows the Calculator window. At the top is an area — a window within the window — that displays results and entered values. In the bottom left of this display is a phrase that tells what number system the Calculator presently is using. The default is Dec for decimal numbers, which are Base 10 numbers. Most pocket calculators work in Base 10. Because programmers work more frequently in binary and hexadecimal number systems (Base 2 and Base 16), SideKick's Calculator also offers those operating modes You can switch between modes

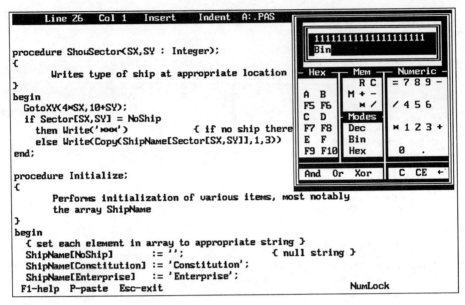

Figure 17-2. The SideKick Calculator, on top of Turbo Pascal

easily by pressing B for binary, H for hexadecimal, or D for decimal. (These modes are shown in a list in the middle of the Calculator window.)

You can enter numbers in any mode, with binary only accepting 1s and 0s, decimal accepting the standard ten numerals (1 through 9 and 0), and hexadecimal accepting the decimal numerals plus A, B, C, D, E, and F. These letters represent the values 10 through 15 in hexadecimal, values that must be represented by a single character to make the arithmetic easy to read. On the left side of the Calculator window is a list of some of the keys you use to enter these letters: F5 for A, F6 for B, and so on.

If a number is in the display when you change the number mode, that number is converted automatically to its equivalent in the new number system. This feature makes conversions, a staple for programmers working with memory addresses and the like, a simple and fast operation.

Binary and Hexadecimal Arithmetic

The four arithmetic functions also can work in and receive results in the current number mode. You can paste arithmetic results directly into a source code file by having that file in an editor beneath the Calculator window and then using the Paste function.

To paste an arithmetic result to a source file:

1. Open a source file in an editor (which could be the Notepad), and then open the Calculator on top of the source file.

2. Calculate to achieve the desired result.

3. Press P to choose the Paste function.

4. Choose a Paste key and press it. A Paste key typically is something like ALT-F10 which hopefully doesn't interfere with any of your other commands. Do not choose P as a Paste key, it complicates matters unnecessarily.

5. Close the Calculator and move the cursor to the point where you want the value to be in the source file.

6. Press the assigned Paste key.

Logical Operations

Programming is not only dependent on binary and hexadecimal numbers, it also uses logical operations such as And, Or, Not, and Xor. SideKick's Calculator automates some of these operations; it lets you enter two values and find the logical result of comparing the two. The bottom left portion of the Calculator window lists the And, Or, and Xor operations, which you perform by pressing A, O, or X. To use these functions, enter a number (in binary, hexadecimal, or decimal), and then press one of the three letters for an operation (A, O, X). Now enter the second number, and press RETURN. The logical result is displayed in the same number base. You also can paste logical operation results directly into a source file in the same manner as you can paste arithmetic results.

Notepad

The Notepad can add power to any programming task. You can use it as a second editor (Turbo Pascal has its own built-in editor) or as the primary editor if your language comes without text-processing abilities. As the primary editor, the Notepad lets you create and modify ASCII files of source code, which can then be compiled or interpreted.

As a Secondary Editor

As a secondary editor, the Notepad lets you organize lists and portions of a program. For example, Figure 17-3 shows an example of the Notepad holding a list of major subroutines. You can open the Notepad to write or browse through such a list, then close it again and return to work in the primary editor. If you squeeze the Notepad window down so that it occupies only part of the screen, you even can write new program

```
    B:\SCALARS.PAS              Line 29   Col 1   Insert     Indent
F}
begin
  GotoXY(4*SX,10+SY);
  if Sector[SX,SY] = NoShip
    then Write('xxx')              { if no ship there }
    else Write(Copy(ShipName[Sector[SX,SY]],1,3))
end;

    then Write('xxx')              { if no ship there }
    else Write(Copy(ShipName[Sector[SX,SY]],1,3))
end;

procedure Initialize;
{
      Performs initialization of various items, most notably
      the array ShipName
}
begin
  { set each element in array to appropriate string }
  ShipName[NoShip]        := '';                  { null string }
  ShipName[Constitution] := 'Constitution';
  ShipName[Enterprise]   := 'Enterprise';
 F1-help F2-save F3-new file F4-import data F9-expand F10-contract Esc-exit
```

Figure 17-3.   SideKick's Notepad as a secondary programming editor

routines, while other sections remain visible for comparison and cross-referencing. Or, you can write new programming sections in the primary editor, using the Notepad to hold the older versions.

The Notepad Sort command lets you sort lists of variables or rules in the Notepad, while the Search command lets you sift through the Notepad's file to find specific variables or line numbers. The Search-and-Replace operation allows you to change, for example, a variable name automatically throughout the source code. For example, if you want to change all occurrences of account1 to accounts-total, you can use the Notepad's Search-and-Replace procedure.

To find and change all occurrences of the variable account1 and change them to accounts-total:

1. Move the cursor to the top of the Notepad file.

2. Press CTRL-Q-A to start the Search-and-Replace operation.

3. Type in **account1** and press RETURN to specify what to search for.

4. Type in **accounts-total** and press RETURN to specify what to use as a replacement variable name.

5. Type in **GN** as options to indicate a global search (of the entire file) and that you don't want to be asked yes or no upon each replacement (N for "no, don't ask"). Then press RETURN.

6. The operation then begins. You can watch it work its way through the file from beginning to end, or you can press any other key to put the display into limbo, while the operation proceeds at a much greater speed. When the operation is complete, the display recovers, and the cursor appears at the end of the file.

As a Logbook

You can use the Notepad to write a log about a program. By pressing CTRL-Q-T each time you are about to make a new entry, you imprint the time and date of the entry on the file. You also can put a .LOG command (use uppercase letters) at the top of the file starting in the first column,

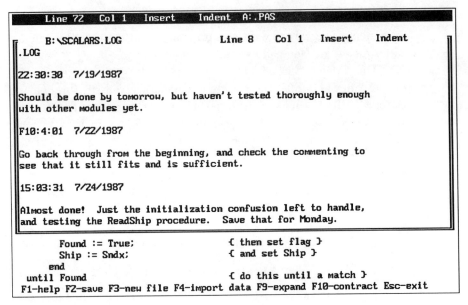

```
┌─────────────────────────────────────────────────────────────┐
│    Line 72   Col 1   Insert      Indent   A:.PAS             │
├─┌────────────────────────────────────────────────────────────┤
│ │     B:\SCALARS.LOG                 Line 8   Col 1   Insert     Indent │
│ │.LOG                                                          │
│ │                                                              │
│ │22:30:30  7/19/1987                                           │
│ │                                                              │
│ │Should be done by tomorrow, but haven't tested thoroughly enough │
│ │with other modules yet.                                       │
│ │                                                              │
│ │F10:4:01  7/22/1987                                           │
│ │                                                              │
│ │Go back through from the beginning, and check the commenting to │
│ │see that it still fits and is sufficient.                     │
│ │                                                              │
│ │15:03:31  7/24/1987                                           │
│ │                                                              │
│ │Almost done!  Just the initialization confusion left to handle, │
│ │and testing the ReadShip procedure.  Save that for Monday.    │
│ └──────────────────────────────────────────────────────────────┘
│        Found := True;                  { then set flag }      │
│        Ship := Sndx;                   { and set Ship }       │
│      end                                                      │
│  until Found                           { do this until a match } │
│ F1-help F2-save F3-new file F4-import data F9-expand F10-contract Esc-exit │
```

Figure 17-4.   Using the Notepad as a logbook with the .LOG command

as shown in Figure 17-4. Then, each time you open the file, the Notepad jumps to the end of the file and inserts the current time and date before you begin work.

In such a logbook, you can include error messages and crash conditions that you want to save for reference. To do so:

1. Open the Notepad on top of the message or crash display.

2. Press F4 to import data. The message or crash display then appears.

3. Use the Notepad cursor arrow keys and cursor movement commands to move the cursor to the top left corner of the block you want to copy to the Notepad. Then press CTRL-K-B or F7.

4. Use the Notepad cursor arrow keys and cursor movement commands to move the cursor to the bottom right corner of the block you want to copy to the Notepad. Then press CTRL-K-K or F8.

5. The Notepad window then reappears. Move the cursor to the place where you want to put the clipping, and then press CTRL-K-C.

Once you have imported such information into the Notepad, you can save it as evidence of what happened, or you can make it into a list of fixes to make and then delete each item in the list as the bug is found and fixed.

SuperKey

The SuperKey macros are the major influence SuperKey can have on Turbo Pascal. The encryption and Layout program features also are useful.

Macros

As discussed in Chapter 11, macros let you combine several or many words or commands into a single keystroke. Using macros lets you avoid repetitive typing and thus avoid mistakes. SuperKey lets you create, edit, and save macros, and even comes with a prerecorded set of macros for Turbo Pascal: TURBO.MAC. There is another file of macros for BA-SICA programming (BASICA is the BASIC language that comes with DOS). Figure 17-5 shows the menu for the Turbo Pascal macros. Figure 17-6 shows the BASICA macro menu. You can use these macros as they are, add other macros to them, or even modify them to suit your own programming style. Some of the macros automatically let you include procedure statements, case statements, and even repeat/until loops in your file. Others let you save a file and then automatically compile that file.

To load the prerecorded macros into memory for use with Turbo Pascal:

1. With Turbo Pascal running (just for your convenience, it can be off when you load the macros), open the SuperKey main menu by pressing ALT-/.

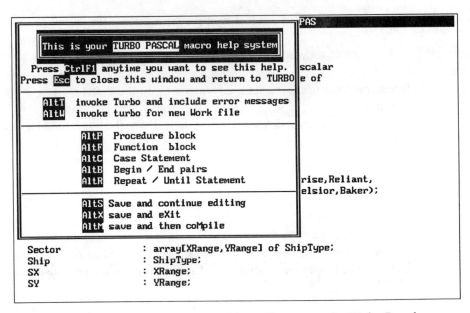

Figure 17-5.   The menu of prerecorded SuperKey macros for Turbo Pascal

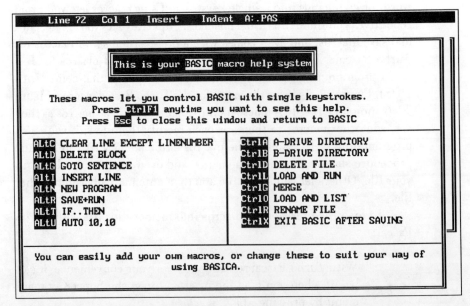

Figure 17-6.   The menu of prerecorded SuperKey macros for BASICA

2.   Choose the Macros menu by pressing M.

3.   Choose Merge if you already have some other macros in memory that you still want to be able to use: press M again. If you don't care about saving any macros in memory, choose Load by pressing L.

4.   Type in **turbo**, and then press RETURN to specify the Turbo macros.

5.   A menu for the Turbo Pascal macros appears. If you need to see this menu again at any point, just press CTRL-F1.

If you modify the Turbo Pascal macros, you may want to save them to a new file using the Save option from the Macros menu, before you turn off your computer.

Encryption

If you want to protect your source code or your object code from unauthorized perusal, you can use SuperKey's encryption routine. This routine changes the file into a coded block that cannot be read without your chosen key word (password). If you choose to use the Text mode method of encryption, you even can send the file over most telecommunications systems, without fear that it may be violated or corrupted. (You cannot use Dialer as your telecommunications system.) For instance, say you have finished an important routine and have included comments that clearly explain what you have done. If you want to ship your program to someone for comment, you can encrypt it and put it up on a bulletin board for that person to *download* (extract from the system). You can call that person and give him or her the key word. Note that the other person must have a copy of SuperKey to be able to decode the file.

A

Patches to Fix or Enhance SideKick and SuperKey

This appendix contains patches that you can use to fix certain problems in SideKick and SuperKey or to change the function of the programs. A patch is a small piece of program code that replaces a similar piece of code in the SideKick or SuperKey main file. The new code changes old functions or causes new functions to appear.

DEBUG's Place

To use a patch, you need a utility program that comes with DOS called DEBUG.COM. This program is made for *debugging* other programs. It has its own commands and syntax, which you can learn from a book on DOS, for selecting a portion of another program and then inspecting or changing the program code in that portion.

Getting Help

To use DEBUG with the patches in this appendix, you don't have to learn any of DEBUG's special commands; just mimic the commands as they are written here. Be sure to check the version number of your SideKick or SuperKey program before you try patching. Different versions sometimes require different patches. If you have any trouble, write or call Borland's technical support. They are also a source of news for any new patches for newer versions or for newer features of the programs.

Choosing a Patch

You don't have to use any of these patches, nor do you have to use all of them at once. Rather, you can pick and choose from among them for the ones you want to use. Select only the patches that fit the version and copy-protection status of your program. Most of the patches come in sets and you only have to use the set that applies to your program. For instance, if you always use the full SideKick — SK.COM — you don't need to bother patching the limited forms such as SKN.COM and SKM.COM.

Starting and Using DEBUG

Before using any of these patches, you have to call up DEBUG and start it running. Find DEBUG on your DOS disk (use the command **dir debug. com** on the various DOS disks until it turns up) and copy it to the drive and directory that contains your SideKick or SuperKey files. For a typical floppy-disk based system, this means using the command **copy debug.com a:**. For a hard-disk system, the typical command is **copy debug.com c: \sk**, although this depends on what you named your SideKick and SuperKey directories. (You only need to patch the version of SideKick or SuperKey that you plan to use. Some patches list a different sequence of commands for each version of SideKick (SK.COM, SKC.COM, and so on) or SuperKey (KEY.COM and KEYDES.COM).) *Note: make sure you have a backup copy of your SideKick and SuperKey files before attempting this procedure, because a mistake could destroy your program.*

Now start DEBUG, as described in the instructions, and type in the commands exactly as they are printed on the following pages. End each line by pressing RETURN. Also, where you see the word Return, press RETURN, don't type out the word R-e-t-u-r-n.

It doesn't matter if you type in all uppercase or lowercase letters: also, the DEBUG prompt is a hyphen, it is not the standard disk letter with a $>$ sign. If you run into trouble, type q and press RETURN to quit DEBUG, then try the program again or call Borland.

SideKick Patches

AT & T 40-Column Mode

The following patch allows SideKick to restore the AT&T video screen mode properly when using the modes that SideKick currently supports: text, 640 x 200 or 320 x 200 color graphics, and Hercules monochrome graphics. It corrects the problem of the screen going into the 40-column mode and/or the graphics mode after exiting from SideKick. This patch is for SideKick version 1.56A.

If your copy of SideKick is not copy protected, beginning at the A$>$ prompt (C$>$ if you are using a hard-disk system), type in the entries in

the first column. You then should see the corresponding result shown in
the second column on your screen. The x's represent a value in memory.
These values do not have any effect on the patch.

Type	This Appears
debug SK.COM	-
a 1380	xxxx:1380
jmp 1394	xxxx:1382
	-
w	writing xxxx bytes
q	DOS prompt
debug SKN.COM	-
a 135E	xxxx:135E
jmp 1372	xxxx:1360
	-
w	writing xxxx bytes
q	DOS prompt
debug SKC.COM	-
a 126A	xxxx:126A
jmp 127E	xxxx:126C
	-
w	writing xxxx bytes
q	DOS prompt
debug SKM.COM	-
a 121D	xxxx:121D
jmp 1231	xxxx:121F
	-
w	writing xxxx bytes
q	DOS prompt

If your version of SideKick is copy protected, beginning at the A>
prompt (C> if you are using a hard-disk system), type in the entries in
the first column. You should then see on your screen the corresponding
result shown in the second column.

Type	This Appears
debug SK.COM	-
a 1396	xxxx:1396
jmp 13AA	xxxx:1398
	-
w	writing xxxx bytes
q	DOS prompt
debug SKN.COM	-
a 1374	xxxx:1374
jmp 1388	xxxx:1376
	-
w	writing xxxx bytes
q	DOS prompt
debug SKC.COM	-
a 1280	xxxx:1280
jmp 1294	xxxx:1282
	-
w	writing xxxx bytes
q	DOS prompt
debug SKM.COM	-
a 1233	xxxx:1233
jmp 1247	xxxx:1235
	-
w	writing xxxx bytes
q	DOS prompt

For Loading TSR Programs
After SideKick

Some application programs redirect INT 9, and so have complete control of the keyboard. Since SideKick uses INT 9, it has a retrapping routine to recapture INT 9 when it needs control of the keyboard and then to pass INT 9 back to the other program. This feature helps make SideKick as compatible as possible with programs that take over the keyboard, such as XYwrite, SmartCom, and the Leading Edge word processor.

However, retrapping INT 9 prevents other TSR programs from functioning when they are loaded after SideKick. Although it is not a good idea to load a TSR program after SideKick if it is not necessary, this patch can stop the retrapping operation and allow TSR programs that are loaded after SideKick to work. It does have the side effect, though, of making SideKick incompatible with XYwrite, SmartCom, the Leading Edge word processor, and other programs that redirect INT 9.

The file created by this DEBUG process is called SKP.COM. You can save SKP.COM and use it as your SideKick when you need to load TSR programs after SideKick (invoking it by typing in **skp** instead of **sk**), or you can rename it SK.COM and use it just as you would use the SideKick SK.COM version. This patch is for SideKick version 1.56A.

Type	This Appears
debug SK.COM	-
a91D	xxxx:091D
jmp 93D	-
n SKP.COM	-
w	writing xxxx bytes
q	DOS prompt

This patch is for SideKick version 1.52.

Type	This Appears
debug SK.COM	-

Type	This Appears
a904	xxxx:0904
jmp 91C	-
n SKP.COM	-
w	writing xxxx bytes
q	DOS prompt

To Stop Notepad from Making .BAK Files

Normally, when you use a Notepad command to save the current file to disk (either F2 or CTRL-K-D), SideKick renames the older disk version of the file as *filename*.BAK. SideKick also saves the older version in the Notepad window under the old filename without an extension. If you want to save disk space by not creating these backup files, you can use the following patch. This patch is for SideKick version 1.52A.

Type	This Appears
debug SK.COM	-
e59BD	xxxx:59BD 42.
2E	-
e5AA4	xxxx:5AA4 42.
2E	-
w	writing xxxx bytes
q	DOS prompt
debug SKN.COM	-
e5BF2	xxxx:5BF2 42.
2E	-
e5CD9	xxxx: 5CD9 42.
2E	-
w	writing xxxx bytes
q	DOS prompt

This patch is for SideKick version 1.56A.

Type	This Appears
debug SK.COM	-
e5B1A	xxxx:5B1A 42.
2E	-
e5C01	xxxx:5C01 42.
2E	-
w	writing xxxx bytes
q	DOS prompt
debug SKN.COM	-
e5D4A	xxxx:5D4A 42.
2E	-
e5E36	xxxx:5E36 42.
2E	-
w	writing xxxx bytes
q	DOS prompt

To Make Notepad Default to Graphics Mode

The Notepad normally opens in Text mode (the default mode), in which it can display only standard ASCII characters. Using CTRL-Q-G, you can change the Notepad to Graphics mode, which can display standard ASCII characters and extended ASCII characters (with foreign characters and graphics symbols), for your computing session. But if you always want to work in Graphics mode, or at least want to have Graphics mode as the default, you can use the following patch. Then to change to Text mode, you can use CTRL-Q-G, even though the status line GRAPH message stays lit. This patch is for SideKick version 1.56A. If your version of SideKick is not copy protected, beginning at the A> prompt (C> if you are using a hard-disk system), type in the entries in the first column. You then should see on your screen the corresponding result shown in the second column.

Type	**This Appears**
debug SK.COM	-
e 3A0F	xxxx:3A0F 80.
C6 06 F1 22 FF 90 90	-
w	writing xxxx bytes
q	DOS prompt

If your version of SideKick is copy protected, beginning at the A> prompt (C> if you are using a hard-disk system), type in the entries in the first column. You then should see on your screen the corresponding result shown in the second column.

Type	**This Appears**
debug SK.COM	-
e 3CF9	xxxx:3CF9 80.
C6 06 F6 26 FF 90 90	-
w	writing xxxx bytes
q	DOS prompt

SideKick Calculator
Fix for ATs

As explained in detail in Chapter 5, when SideKick's Calculator is running on the IBM AT and compatibles (based on the 80286 processor chip), it sometimes formulates an incorrect product in certain multiplications. This patch fixes the Calculator so it does not make that rare mistake. This patch is for SideKick version 1.5xx. For this patch, it doesn't matter whether your copy of SideKick is copy protected or not copy protected.

Type	This Appears
debug SK.COM	-
R	(A table is displayed. Record the value following the CX, i.e., CX = nnnn)
S100 nnnn 3C 63 76 02 FE C8 (where nnnn is value of CX from above)	aaaa:zzzz
Ezzzz (where zzzz is from step above)	aaaa:zzzz 3C.
SPACE BAR 4 times	FE.
B SPACE BAR	C8.
63	-
w	writing nnnn bytes
q	DOS prompt

SuperKey Patching

There are two versions of SuperKey on each disk: KEY.COM and KEYDES.COM. These versions differ only in what encryption method they use, as described in Chapter 11. You only need to patch the one you use.

Changing the Standard Date Format for SuperKey

This patch lets you change the output format of SuperKey's Date function. There are several versions of the patch, depending on what new date format you want to use.

MM/DD/YYYY to DD/MM/YYYY   This patch is for SuperKey version 1.03A. If you are using the KEY.COM version of SuperKey, beginning at the A> (C>if you are using a hard-disk system), type in the entries in the first column. You then should see the corresponding result shown in the second column on your screen.

Type	This Appears
debug KEY.COM	-
e 59EB	xxxx:59EB 8A.
88 D0	-
e 59F8	xxxx:59F8 8A.
88 F0	-
w	writing xxxx bytes
q	DOS prompt

If you are using the KEYDES.COM version of SuperKey, beginning at the A> (C>if you are using a hard-disk system), type in the entries in the first column. You then should see the corresponding result shown in the second column on your screen.

Type	This Appears
debug KEYDES.COM	-
e 660B	xxxx:660B 8A.
88 D0	-
e 6618	xxxx:6618 8A.
88 F0	-
w	writing xxxx bytes
q	DOS prompt

MM/DD/YYYY to YYYY/MM/DD   This patch is for Super-Key version 1.03A. If you are using the KEY.COM version of SuperKey, beginning at the A> (C>if you are using a hard-disk system), type in the entries in the first column. You then should see the corresponding result shown in the second column on your screen.

Type	This Appears
debug KEY.COM	-
e 59E3	xxxx:59E3 02.
04	-
e 59E9	xxxx:59E9 33.
58 90 90 90	-
e 59EA	xxxx:59EA 02.
04	-
e 59F6	xxxx:59F6 33.
B1 02 88 F0	-
e 59FD	xxxx:59FD 83.
47 47 B0 2F AA 88 D0	-
e 5A05	xxxx:5A05 04.
02	-
e 5A0C	xxx:5A0C 04.
02	-
w	writing xxxx bytes
q	DOS prompt

If you are using the KEYDES.COM version of SuperKey, beginning at the A> (C> if you are using a hard-disk system), type in the entries in the first column. You then should see the corresponding result shown in the second column on your screen.

Type	This Appears
debug KEYDES.COM	-
e 6603	xxxx:6603 02.
04	-
e 6609	xxxx: 6609 33.
58 90 90 0	-
e 6612	xxxx:6612 02.
04	-
e 6616	xxxx:6616 33.
B1 02 88 F0	-

Type	This Appears
e 661D	xxxx:661D 83.
47 47 B0 2F AA 88 D0	-
e 6625	xxxx:6625 04.
02	-
e 662C	xxxx:662C 04.
02	-
w	writing xxxx bytes
q	DOS prompt

MM/DD/YYYY to YYYY/MM/DD   This patch is for Super-Key version 1.11A. If you are using the KEY.COM version of SuperKey, beginning at the A> (C>if you are using a hard-disk system), type in the entries in the first column. You then should see the corresponding result shown in the second column on your screen.

Type	This Appears
debug KEY.COM	-
e 5DFE	xxxx:5DFE 02.
04	-
e 5E04	xxxx:5E04 33.
58 90 90 90	-
e 5E0D	xxxx:5E0D 02.
04	-
e 5E11	xxxx:5E11 33.
B1 02 88 F0	-
e 5E18	xxxx:5E18 83.
47 47 B0 2F AA 88 D0	-
e 5E20	xxxx:5E20 04.
02	-
e 5E27	xxxx:5E27 04.
02	-
w	writing xxxx bytes
q	DOS prompt

If you are using the KEYDES.COM version of SuperKey, beginning at the A> (C>if you are using a hard-disk system), type in the entries in the first column. You then should see the corresponding result shown in the second column on your screen.

Type	This Appears
debug KEYDES.COM	-
e 6A 1E	xxxx: 6A 1E 02.
04	-
e 6A 24	xxxx: 6A 24 33.
58 90 90 90	-
e 6A 2D	xxxx: 6A 2D 02.
04	-
e 6A 31	xxxx: 6A 31 33.
B1 02 88 F0	-
e 6A 38	xxxx: 6A 38 83.
47 47 B0 2F AA 88 D0	-
e 6A 40	xxxx: 6A 40 04.
02	-
e 6A 47	xxxx: 6A 47 04.
02	-
w	writing xxxx bytes
q	DOS prompt

MM/DD/YYYY to DD/MM/YYYY   This patch is for Super-Key version 1.11A. If you are using the KEY.COM version of SuperKey, beginning at the A> (C>if you are using a hard-disk system), type in the entries in the first column. You then should see the corresponding result shown in the second column on your screen.

Type	This Appears
debug KEY.COM	-
e 5E06	xxxx: 5E06 8A.
88 D0	-
e 5E13	xxxx: 5E13 8A.
88 F0	-
w	writing xxxx bytes
q	DOS prompt

If you are using the KEYDES.COM version of SuperKey, beginning at the A> (C> if you are using a hard-disk system), type in the entries in the first column. You then should see the corresponding result shown in the second column on your screen.

Type	This Appears
debug KEYDES.COM	-
e 6A26	xxxx:6A26 8A.
88 D0	-
e 6A33	xxxx:6A33 8A.
88 F0	-
w	writing xxxx bytes
q	DOS prompt

B

Incompatibility Problems and Solutions

SideKick works smoothly with almost all software that runs on the IBM PC and its compatibles, but a few programs require special handling when working with SideKick. A few programs do not work well with SideKick at all and probably shouldn't be used. This appendix discusses these special programs and how to handle them.

One general rule that aids your compatibility is that during installation, you must set SideKick to blank the screen over graphics when SideKick is running on top of a graphics display. Otherwise, it temporarily changes the display mode to the Text mode, thus disrupting the partially hidden display. When you exit SideKick, the Graphics mode returns, and the display that was temporarily disrupted reappears.

Also, if you are having difficulty getting the Paste function to work properly with one of these special programs, sometimes all you must do is set a higher Paste delay factor. Try this, as explained in Chapter 4, before giving up on a program.

Lotus 1-2-3

As mentioned in the SideKick user's manual, Lotus 1-2-3 expects a data disk to be loaded into drive B. If you try to open SideKick on top of Lotus 1-2-3 and you don't have a disk in drive B, SideKick may "chirp" its computerized soundmaker four times. This chirping indicates that the error condition —no disk in drive B —has been discovered by Lotus and was reported to you by SideKick. To use Lotus 1-2-3 in this situation, either ignore the chirping or put a disk into drive B.

Lotus Symphony

Lotus Symphony has the same default data disk drive problem that does Lotus 1-2-3. To use Lotus Symphony in this situation, try the same fixes listed in the section on Lotus 1-2-3.

Microsoft Windows

The Microsoft Windows environment is based on graphics and not on characters. SideKick doesn't work inside of this program at all. There are special environments that SideKick does work inside of such as Microsoft's Desqview.

You still can use SideKick with Windows. To do so, SideKick should be loaded prior to Windows. It can be invoked over Windows, but not within a window.

Microsoft Word

Microsoft Word normally works in the Graphics mode. If you want to cut text from the Microsoft word screen to the SideKick Notepad, you must open Microsoft Word with the command **word/c**, instead of the command **word**. This instruction makes the program work in the Text mode instead of in the Graphics mode.

Smartcom

The Smartcom telecommunications program is the source of more on-line complaints from SideKick users than from any other. Smartcom's keyboard routines conflict with those of SideKick, and the two don't work well together at all. If you must use them together, remember to exit the SideKick Notepad Window with the same command you used to enter that window, such as SHIFT-SHIFT or ALT-CTRL. *Don't* change the command you use (entering with SHIFT-SHIFT and exiting with ALT-CTRL, for instance) or exit by pressing ESC. Sometimes following this sequence can help you avoid trouble, but not always.

XYWrite

The XYWrite word processor, like Smartcom, fights with SideKick over keyboard rights. The result is sometimes a mess, which you can try to avoid by following the same suggestions listed in the section on Smartcom.

TSR Programs

There are many, many other TSR programs for the IBM PC and its compatibles. They range from printer drivers to outline processors and more. Chapter 2 discusses what you can do to try to assure that other TSR programs work alongside SideKick and SuperKey. Always remember, load SuperKey first, then Turbo Lightning, and SideKick last for the best chances of compatibility.

Trademarks

AT®	International Business Machines Corporation
Crosstalk®	Microstuf, Inc.
dBASE® III PLUS™	Ashton-Tate
DOS™	International Business Machines Corporation
Epson®	Seiko Epson Corporation
FX-80™	Epson America, Inc.
Hayes®	Hayes Microcomputer Products
Hercules®	Hercules Computer Technology
IBM®	International Business Machines Corporation
Lotus®	Lotus Development Corporation
1-2-3®	Lotus Development Corporation
PCjr™	International Business Machines Corporation

Preview I/O™	AST Research, Inc.
Maxwell™	1200 VP modem Racal-Vadic
Random House®	Random House, Inc.
SideKick®: The Desktop Organizer	Borland International, Inc.
Smartcom®	Hayes Microcomputer Products
SuperKey®	Borland International, Inc.
Traveling SideKick®	Borland International, Inc.
Turbo Pascal®	Borland International, Inc.
U.S. Robotics®	U.S. Robotics
Ven-Tel®	Ven-Tel, Inc.
WordStar®	MicroPro International Corporation
XT™	International Business Machines Corporation

Index

A

Activation commands, 44
Address database (Traveling SideKick), 6
Address files, using with SideKick, 241
Addresses
    changing, 235
    entering in Traveling SideKick, 232
    finding, 234
    removing, 235
    Traveling SideKick, 228
ALT-CTRL, 33
Appointment
    calendar, setup, 216
    files, 162-164
Appointments database (Traveling SideKick), 6
Arithmetic, four-function, 139
Arrow keys, 34, 54, 88-89
ASCII characters, 75
    extended, 43
    standard and extended, 198
ASCII table, 32, 197-208
    anatomy of, 202
    definition of, 5
    moving the window, 202
    opening, 199
    using with programming languages, 356
AT&T 40 column mode, patching, 369
Auto-indent, 76
Auto-proof mode (Turbo Lightning), 122
AUTOEXEC.BAT, 30, 293

B

Backing up
    SideKick files, 20-23
    SuperKey files, 259
    Traveling SideKick, 223
BAK file extension, 64
BAK files, patch for eliminating, 373
Batch files, 30, 290-293
Binary arithmetic, 359
Binary mode, Calculator, 143
Binder (Traveling SideKick), 6
BIX, 27
Blank lines, adding, 82
Block markers, 92
Block mode, 96
Block operations, 92
Blocks
    copying, 95
    deleting, 87, 94
    marking, 93
    moving, 95
    pasting, 95-100
    pasting multiple, 98
    pasting repeatedly, 98
    printing, 95
    reading, 93
    sorting, 103
    writing, 67, 94
Bootable disks, formatting, 22

Borland
  calling, 27
  writing to, 26
BYTE Magazine, 27

C

Calculated fields, database, 334
Calculator, 32, 133-152
  choosing the, 135
  definition of, 4
  patch for fixing with IBM PC AT, 375
  using SuperKey with, 148
  using with databases, 334
  using with programming
    languages, 356-360
  using with spreadsheets, 307
  using with the IBM PC AT, 151
  using with word processors, 318
Calculator Memory Commands, 147
Calendar, 32, 153-172
  definition of, 4
  deleting sections of, 167
  monthly anatomy of, 156
  opening, 154
Calendars, engagement, 246
Case sensitivity in search operations, 111
Characters
  ASCII, 204
  special, 43
Codes, encryption, 274
Colors, setting, 43
COM ports, 178
Command stack
  DOS, 266-268
  SuperKey, 8, 295-297
Commands
  ASCII table, 204
  Calculator, 137-138
  changing Notepad, 72
  cursor, 88-92
  Daily Schedule, 165
  on-line (communications program), 352
  phone directory, 184
  recording as macros, 320
  setup, 213
  WordStar-style, 80

Communications programs, using SideKick
  with, 341-354
Compuserve, 27
CONFIG.SYS, 293
Contract mode, 55
Control characters
  ASCII, 199
  print, 116,118
CONVERT, 229-232
Copy protection, 20
Copying blocks, 95
Crosstalk
  sending files with, 344
  using SideKick with, 341-354
Cursor commands, WordStar-style, 90-92
Cursor keys, 34, 54
Cursor, moving the, 88-92
Customizing installation, 40
Cut and paste
  Notepad, 67
  SuperKey, 8, 270

D

Daily Calendar (Traveling SideKick), 246
Daily Schedule
  commands, 165
  window, 160-162
Data encryption (SuperKey), 9
Data, importing, 100-102
Database managers, using SideKick
  with, 329-340
Databases (Traveling SideKick), 6
Date and time stamping, 77
Date clock, DOS, 158
Date format
  patch for SuperKey, 376
  Traveling SideKick, 254
Date limits, Calendar, 158
dBASE III PLUS, using SideKick with, 329-340
DEBUG, using to patch SideKick and
  SuperKey, 368-369
Deleting information in Calendar, 166
Deleting
  macros (SuperKey), 284
  text, 87

Dialer, 32, 173-196
    definition of, 4
    opening, 180
    using with databases, 334
Dictionary
    adding to the Turbo Lightning, 126
    Turbo Lightning, 10
Directories
    creating, 29
    viewing, 64
Directory, DOS, 159
Disk drives, 19
Disks
    bootable, 22
    formatting, 22
Display, clearing Calculator, 142
Document-level margins, 57
DOS, 3, 17, 289-300
    using SuperKey command stack with,
        295-297

E

Editing
    commands, Notepad, 79-132
    macros, 284
    modes, 74-77
EDLIN, 290
Encryption
    SuperKey, 274
    using with communications programs, 353
    using with databases, 339
    using with programming
        languages, 363-365
    using with word processors, 328
Engagement calendars, 246
    using with SideKick, 251
Engagements, 242-252
    changing, 246
    entering, 243
    finding, 244
    removing, 246
Environment
    editing the, 123
    setting the Turbo Lightning, 122

Epson FX-80 printer control characters, 118
ESC, 33, 64
Extended ASCII, 205

F

Fast replace, 115
File names, 64
    SuperKey, 276
Files
    address (Traveling SideKick), 228-236
    address and engagements, 253
    appointment, 162-164
    AUTOEXEC, 30, 293
    automatically loaded, 61
    batch, 30, 290-293
    choosing and loading Notepad, 60
    CONFIG.SYS, 293
    converting with Traveling SideKick, 229
    DOS, 290-295
    editing Notepad, 81
    encrypting, 275
    engagement (Traveling SideKick), 242-252
    keyboard layout, 272
    loading new Notepad, 63
    loading Traveling SideKick, 227
    LOG, 77
    macro, 283
    merging macro, 283
    Notefile size of, 69
    Notes, 49
    online, 343
    phone directory, 190
    printing, 116
    printing DOS, 294
    README, 23
    saving, 66
    sending by modem, 344
    SideKick, 24
    size of Notefile, 40
Find
    limits on, 108
    options for, 110-116
    repeating, 108
Find and replace, 105-116

Finding telephone numbers, 192
Fixes (SideKick and SuperKey), 367-381
Floppy disks
    backing up to, 21
    loading SideKick from, 28
Footnotes, using Notepad for, 316
FOREIGN.MAC, 324
Formatting backup disks, 22
Four-function arithmetic, 139
Full-screen check, 125

G

Graphics, setting, 42
Graphics characters, 43
Graphics mode, 75
    making Notepad default to, 374

H

Hard copy, 67
Hard disks
    backing up using, 21, 23
    loading SideKick from, 29
Hayes-compatible modem, 175
Help, 16, 36, 82
Hexadecimal arithmetic, 359
Hexadecimal mode, Calculator, 143

I

IBM PC AT
    patch for fixing Calculator with, 375
    using Calculator with, 151
Importing data, Notepad, 100-102, 317
Incompatibility problems and
    solutions, 383-386
Indent, 76
Insert mode, 76, 83
Installation menu, Dialer, 176
Installation program, changing Notepad, 67
Installation, customized, 40
Interrupting a find, 107

K

KEY.COM, 275
Key words, 277

Keyboard layout
    changing with SuperKey, 271
    using with spreadsheets, 310
Keyboard lock and unlock (SuperKey), 9, 268
    using with databases, 337
Keyboard macro programs, 7
Keyboard type-ahead buffer (SuperKey), 265
Keys, redefining, 299

L

Layout files, keyboard, 273
Layout program, 300, 325. *See also* Keyboard
   layout
    using with word processors, 325
Lightning Setup, 128
Limited SideKicks, 37
Line mode, 96
Lines, deleting, 87
Loading SideKick, 12-45
LOG file, 77
Logical operations, Calculator, 145-146, 359
Logon scripts, using SuperKey for, 349
Lotus 1-2-3
    incompatibility problems with, 384
    using Notepad with, 302-307
    using SideKick with, 301-312
    using SuperKey with, 308-311

M

Macros (SuperKey), 8, 258, 279-287
    foreign language, 324
    prerecorded, 285
    using with communications
      programs, 349-353
    using with databases, 335-339
    using with DOS, 297-300
    using with programming
      languages, 363-365
    using with spreadsheets, 310
    using with word processors, 319-328
    WordStar, 321
Main menu
    SideKick, 14, 31
    Turbo Lightning, 120

Make directory command (mkdir), 29
Margins
    changing Notefile, 71
    changing Notepad window, 56
Markers, block, 92
Memory
    loading SuperKey in, 261
    required, 18
Memory, Calculator, 145
Menu commands (Traveling SideKick), 226
Menus, utility, 16
Microsoft Windows, incompatibility problems
    with, 385
Microsoft Word, incompatibility problems
    with, 385
Modems, 19
    Hayes compatible, 175
    types of, 175
    using with Dialer, 174
Moving
    blocks, 95
    windows, 53-60
MS-DOS. *See* DOS
Multiple utilities, loading, 35
Multiple windows, 51
Multitasking, 2-4

N

New File option, 65
Notefile section, Setup, 215
Notefile size, 40, 69
Notepad, 32
    commands, changing, 72
    definition of, 4
    editing commands, 79-132
    opening and exiting, 81
    opening and setting up, 47-78
    patch for default graphics mode, 374
    using with communications
        programs, 342-349
    using with databases, 330-334
    using with programming
        languages, 360-363
    using with spreadsheets, 302-307

Notepad, *continued*
    using with SuperKey, 270
    using with word processors, 314-318
NOTES, 25
Notes file, 49
Number conversions, using Calculator for, 357
Numbers
    entering in Calculator, 139
    pasting, 149

O

On-line services, 27
Operating systems, 3
Outlining, using Notepad for, 314
Overflow warning, Calculator, 140
Overwrite mode, 76, 86

P

Paragraph-level margins, 58
Paragraphs, reformatting, 84
Parentheses, using in Calculator, 141
Passwords (SuperKey), 277
Paste delay factor, 99
    setting, 215
Paste key, 96
    deleting, 100
Paste limitations, 98
Pasting
    blocks, 95-100
    numbers from Calculator, 149
    repeated, 98
Patch, Calculator, 151
Patches (SideKick and SuperKey), 367-381
Path command, 29
PC-DOS, 3. *See also* DOS
Peripherals, suggested, 17
PHONE.DIR, 25
Phone directory, 173-196
    anatomy of, 188
    commands for, 184
    creating or modifying, 190
    currently displayed, 185
    loading a new, 186
    setup, 216
    using other programs with, 191
    window, 183

Playback delay, 271
Port, modem, 178
Print control characters, 116, 118
Printers, 19
  using with Traveling SideKick,
    236-239, 253
Printing, 67
  address files, 236
  blocks, 95
  DOS files, 294
  files, 116
  schedules, Calendar, 170
Programming languages, using
  SideKick, 355-365
Pull-down menus (Turbo Lightning), 121
Pulse dialing, 176

Q

Quick keys (SuperKey), 286

R

RAM-resident, 6
README, 24, 25
  SuperKey, 261
  Traveling SideKick, 223
README.COM, 25
Reformatting text, 84
Registering SideKick, 25
Removing SideKick, 39
Replace, find and, 105-116
Replacement, limits on, 113
Restoring text, 88

S

Saving files, 66
  in Traveling SideKick, 254
Saving
  macros (SuperKey), 282
  window sizes and positions, 59
Schedule window, 160-162
Screen blanking (SuperKey), 9
Screen off and on (SuperKey), 268
  using with databases, 337
Screen protect (SuperKey), 9, 269

Screen types, 42
SCROLL LOCK, 34, 53
Search string not found, 108
Searching operations, 105-116
Searching telephone numbers, 192
Setup option, 45
Setup utility, 209-218
Setup window, 62
  anatomy of, 213
  moving, 212
  opening, 210
  Phone Directory, 188
Setup (Traveling SideKick), 252
SHIFT-SHIFT, 33
SK.COM, 12, 24, 37
  patching, 368
SK.HLP, 24, 29
SKC.COM, 24, 38
SKINST, using with Dialer, 175
SKINST.COM, 24, 67-74
SKINST.MSG, 25
SKM.COM, 24, 38
SKN.COM, 24, 37
Smartcom, incompatibility problems with, 385
Sorting
  address files, 237
  blocks, 103
Special characters, Dialer, 178
Spreadsheets, using SideKick with, 301-312
Starting SideKick, 12-45
SuperKey, 7-9, 257-288
  activating, 264
  hardware requirements, 258
  installing, 259
  patches for, 376-381
  removing from memory, 262
  using with communications
    programs, 349-353
  using with databases, 335-339
  using with programming
    languages, 363-365
  using with spreadsheets, 308-311
  using with word processors, 319-328
Symphony, incompatibility problems with, 384
System requirements, 17-19

T

Tabs, 89
Tape, keeping a, 148
Technical support, 27
Telecommunications program, 174. *See also* Communications
Telephone and modem, hooking up, 179
Telephone Directory. *See* Phone directory
Telephone numbers, 177
    dialing from other programs, 181
    finding, 192
Telephone support, 27
Terminate and Stay Resident, 6-9. *See also* TSR
Text
    adding, 83
    capturing from Crosstalk, 346
    deleting, 87
    find and replace, 105-116
    importing with Notepad, 317
    macros, 279
    mode, 75
    mode (SuperKey), 277
    processor, 48
    reformatting, 84
    saving from word processors, 316
    undeleting, 88
Thesaurus (Turbo Lightning), 10, 127
Time and date stamping, 77
Tone dialing, 176
Traveling SideKick, 5, 221-256
    installing, 224
    setup, 252
    starting, 225
    using Calendar with, 171
    using Dialer with, 194
    using with databases, 335
TSKINST, 224
TSR programs, 6-9
    controlling, 39
    incompatibility problems with, 386
    patch for loading after SideKick, 372
Turbo Lightning, 9-10, 117-131
    hardware requirements, 119
    installing, 119

Turbo Lightning, *continued*
    options, 129
    setup, 128
    using with databases, 335
    using with spreadsheets, 307
    using with word processors, 314
Turbo Pascal, using SideKick with, 355-365

U

Undeleting, 88
User groups, 26
Utilities, selecting, 14, 32
Utility windows, 32

V

Versions of SideKick, 28

W

Wildcards
    using, 65
    searching using, 109-110
Windows
    ASCII table, 201
    Calculator, 136
    Calendar, 155
    command stack, 266
    Dialer, 180
    directory, 333
    moving and resizing, 53-60
    multiple, 51
    phone directory, 183
    saving size and position of, 59
    setup, 211
    utility, 32
Word processors, 48
    using SideKick with, 313-328
Word-check (Turbo Lightning), 124
Words, deleting, 87
Wordstar, 51
    using SideKick with, 313-328
WordStar-style commands, 80

X

XYWrite, incompatibility problems with, 385

The manuscript for this book was prepared and submitted to Osborne/McGraw-Hill in electronic form.

The acquisitions editor for this project was Nancy Carlston. The technical reviewer was Rebecca Meyers. Lyn Cordell was the project editor.

Cover art is by Bay Graphics Design Associates. Cover supplier is Phoenix Color Corporation. This book was printed and bound by R.R. Donnelley and Sons Company, Crawfordsville, Indiana.

Other related Osborne/McGraw-Hill titles include:

Advanced Turbo C®

by Herbert Schildt

Ready for power programming with Turbo C®? You'll find the expertise you need in *Advanced Turbo C®*, the Borland/Osborne book with the inside edge. In this instruction guide and lasting reference, Herb Schildt, the author of five acclaimed books on C, takes you the final step on the way to Turbo C mastery. Each stand-alone chapter presents a complete discussion of a Turbo C programming topic so you can pinpoint the information you need immediately. *Advanced Turbo C®* thoroughly covers sorting and searching; stacks, queues, linked lists, and binary trees; operating system interfacing; statistics; encryption and compressed data formats; random numbers and simulations; and expression parsers. In addition, you'll learn about converting Turbo Pascal® to Turbo C and using Turbo C graphics. *Advanced Turbo C®* shows you how to put the amazing compilation speed of Turbo C into action on your programs.

$22.95p
0-07-881280-1, 325 pp., 7⅜ x 9¼

The Borland-Osborne/McGraw-Hill Programming Series

Turbo Pascal® Programmer's Library

by Kris Jamsa and Steven Nameroff

You can take full advantage of Borland's famous Turbo Pascal® with this outstanding collection of programming routines. Now revised to cover Borland's new Turbo Pascal Numerical Methods Toolbox™, the *Turbo Pascal® Programmer's Library* includes a whole new collection of routines for mathematical calculations. You'll also find new date and time routines. Kris Jamsa, author of *DOS: The Complete Reference* and *The C Library*, and Steven Nameroff give experienced Turbo Pascal users a varied library that includes utility routines for Pascal macros as well as routines for string and array manipulation, records, pointers, and pipes. You'll find I/O routines and a discussion of sorting that covers bubble, shell, and quick-sort algorithms. And there's even more ... routines for the Turbo Toolbox® and the Turbo Graphix Toolbox® packages. It's all here to help you become the most effective Turbo Pascal programmer you can be.

$21.95p
0-07-881286-0, 625 pp., 7⅜ x 9¼

The Borland-Osborne/McGraw-Hill Programming Series

Advanced Turbo Prolog™ Version 1.1

by Herbert Schildt

Herb Schildt now applies his expertise to Borland's remarkable Turbo Prolog™ language development system, specifically designed for fifth-generation language programming and the creation of artificial intelligence on your IBM® PC. *Advanced Turbo Prolog™* has been extensively revised to include Turbo Prolog version 1.1. The new Turbo Prolog Toolbox™, which offers more than 80 tools and 8,000 lines of source code, is also described in detail. Schildt focuses on helping you progress from intermediate to advanced techniques by considering typical AI problems and their solutions. Numerous sample programs and graphics are used throughout the text to sharpen your skills and enhance your understanding of the central issues involved in AI. Expert systems, problem solving, natural language processing, vision and pattern recognition, robotics, and logic are some of the applications that Schildt explains as he leads you to Turbo Prolog mastery.

$21.95p
0-07-881285-2, 350 pp., 7⅜ x 9¼

The Borland-Osborne/McGraw-Hill Programming Series

Using Turbo C®

by Herbert Schildt

Here's the official book on Borland's tremendous new C compiler. *Using Turbo C®* is for all C programmers, from beginners to seasoned pros. Master programmer Herb Schildt devotes the first part of the book to helping you get started in Turbo C. If you've been programming in Turbo Pascal® or another language, this orientation will lead you right into Turbo C fundamentals. Schildt's emphasis on good programming structure will start you out designing programs for greater efficiency. With these basics, you'll move on to more advanced concepts such as pointers and dynamic allocation, compiler directives, unions, bitfields, and enumerations, and you'll learn about Turbo C graphics. When you've finished *Using Turbo C®*, you'll be writing full-fledged programs that get professional results.

$19.95p
0-07-881279-8, 350 pp., 7⅜ x 9¼

The Borland-Osborne/McGraw-Hill Programming Series

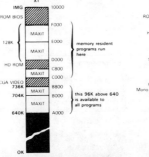

SideKick and SuperKey Command Card

SIDEKICK

General

Loading SideKick into memory: **sk**

Opening the main menu: SHIFT-SHIFT or ALT-CTRL

Getting help: F1

Selecting (opening) a utility:
- Notepad: N, ALT-N, or F2
- Calculator: C, ALT-C, or F3
- Calendar: L, ALT-L, or F4
- Dialer: D, ALT-D, or F5
- ASCII Table: A, ALT-A, or F6
- Setup Window: S, ALT-S, or F7

Closing (exiting) a utility: ESC, SHIFT-SHIFT, or ALT-CTRL

NOTEPAD

Save a file: F2 or CTRL-K-D

Load a new file: F3

Read a file from disk: CTRL-K-R

Import data: F4

Stop an operation: CTRL-U then ESC

Block commands:

Mark block beginning: CTRL-K-B or F7

Mark block end: CTRL-K-K or F8

Write a block to disk: CTRL-K-W

Print a block: CTRL-K-P (if used without a marked block, prints the entire file)

Sort a block: CTRL-K-S

Delete a block: CTRL-K-Y

Paste a block: CTRL-K-E

Editing:

Toggle between Insert and Overwrite modes: INS or CTRL-V

Toggle between Text and Graphics modes: CTRL-Q-G

Reformat a paragraph: CTRL-B

Deletions:

Delete a line: CTRL-Y

Delete a word: CTRL-T

Delete a character under the cursor: CTRL-G

NOTEPAD (*continued*)

Cursor movements:

Move a line down in the notefile: CTRL-X or DOWN ARROW

Move a line up in the notefile: CTRL-E or UP ARROW

Move a character left in the notefile: CTRL-S or LEFT ARROW

Move a character right in the notefile: CTRL-D or RIGHT ARROW

Move a word right in the notefile: CTRL-F or CTRL-RIGHT ARROW

Move a word left in the notefile: CTRL-A or CTRL-LEFT ARROW

Move a page up in the notefile: CTRL-R or PGUP

Move a page down in the notefile: CTRL-C or PGDN

Move to notefile beginning: CTRL-Q-R

Move to notefile end: CTRL-Q-C

Move notefile a line up in the window: CTRL-Z

Move notefile a line down in the window: CTRL-W

Search

Search for a string: CTRL-Q-F

Search and replace a string: CTRL-Q-A

Calculator

Change numeric modes: D for decimal
H for hexadecimal
B for binary

Clear all values: C

Clear latest entry: E

Calculate: = or RETURN

Paste value: P

Enter memory mode: M
- Put a number into memory: M
- Recall a number from memory: R
- Clear memory: C
- Operate with a number in memory: +, /, *, or −

Logical operations:
- AND two values: A
- OR two values: O
- XOR two values: X

Calendar

Change month: RIGHT ARROW and LEFT ARROW
Change year: UP ARROW and DOWN ARROW
Change date: Type in date and press RETURN

Inspect single-date schedule: Return
Entering schedule information (from single-date schedule window):

1. Select time: UP ARROW, DOWN ARROW, PGUP, or PGDN
2. Enter information: Type in the information.
3. Save information: RETURN

Delete single-time schedule information:

1. Select time: UP ARROW, DOWN ARROW, PGUP, or PGDN
2. Use BACKSPACE to delete all characters
3. RETURN

Block operations on schedule information:

Print a block: F2
Choose a new schedule file: F3
Print an entire schedule: F4
Delete a block: F5

Dialer

Dial a number on screen: Open Dialer and press RETURN
Scroll through a directory: UP ARROW and DOWN ARROW
Dial a highlight number from a directory: RETURN
Choose a new directory: F3
Search through initials in a directory: F5
Search through an entire directory: F6
Stop a search: F7

ASCII Table

Scroll through pages: UP ARROW, DOWN ARROW, LEFT ARROW, or RIGHT ARROW

Setup window

Selecting a line for changes: UP ARROW and DOWN ARROW
Entering changes: Type in the changes and press RETURN
Save the new file setup: F2
Save the new window setup (sizes and positions): F3
Save the new file and window setup: F4

SUPERKEY

Loading SuperKey into memory: **key**
Opening the main menu: ALT-/
Closing (exiting) any SuperKey menu: ESC

Macros:

Recording a macro: ALT =
Loading a macro: ALT-/, M, L, *macro file name*, and press RETURN
Clearing a macro: ALT-/, M, and C
Merging a macro file into present macros: ALT-/, M, M, *macro file name*, and press RETURN
Saving present macros to disk: ALT-/, M, S, *macro file name*, and press RETURN
Edit a macro: ALT-/, M, and E
Skip a macro to make use of normal key function:

Encryption:

Encrypting a file: ALT-/, E, and E
Decoding a file: ALT-/, E, and D

Keyboard layout:

Creating a new keyboard layout: **layout** from the DOS prompt and press RETURN
Loading a new keyboard layout: ALT-/, L, L, *file name*, and press RETURN
Clearing the keyboard layout: ALT-/, L, and C
Cut and paste: ALT-/, M, and U